# ESSAYS ON
# Ancient and
# Modern Judaism

# Arnaldo Momigliano

# ESSAYS ON
# Ancient and
# Modern Judaism

6-1-95

*Edited and with an Introduction by*
Silvia Berti
*Translated by*
Maura Masella-Gayley

The University of Chicago Press
*Chicago and London*

Arnaldo Momigliano (1908–1987) was professor of history at the University of London and at the Scuola Normale Superiore in Pisa. He was also the Alexander White Visiting Professor at the University of Chicago.

The University of Chicago Press, Chicago 60637
The University of Chicago Press, Ltd., London
© 1994 by The University of Chicago
All rights reserved. Published 1994
Printed in the United States of America
03 02 01 00 99 98 97 96 95 94    1 2 3 4 5
ISBN: 0-226-53381-6 (cloth)

First published as *Pagine ebraiche*, © 1987 Giulio Einaudi editore s.p.a., Torino

Library of Congress Cataloging-in-Publication Data

Momigliano, Arnaldo.
    [Pagine ebraiche. English]
    Essays on ancient and modern Judaism / Arnaldo Momigliano ; edited and with an introduction by Silvia Berti ; translated by Maura Masella-Gayley.
        p.    cm.
    Includes bibliographical references and index.
    1. Judaism—Historiography.   2. Jewish scholars.   I. Berti, Silvia.   II. Title.
    BM160.M6613   1994
    296′.09—dc20                                                93-37253
                                                                    CIP

⊗ The paper used in this publication meets the minimum requirements of the American National Standard for Information Sciences—Permanence of Paper for Printed Library Materials, ANSI Z39.48-1984.

# Contents

# CONTENTS

# Introduction

## I

When faced with important works, we often experience an immediate cultural identification with the most macroscopic aspects of those works. This experience is often hasty and superficial, and may cause us to neglect other aspects that are not as evident and thought out.

To a certain extent, this is what has happened with the work of Arnaldo Momigliano. Among the masters of historical studies in this century, Momigliano has studied with unparalleled erudition and subtlety the key problems of the history of the ancient world and the relationship between different cultures of the civilization of Hellenism and of the Roman Empire. We shall not find a scholar for whom Momigliano's contributions do not confirm his role in contemporary culture, nor is there a historian, whatever his or her chronological and disciplinary range, who is not indebted to the peculiar curiosity and openness of Momigliano's historiographical thought. Yet a basic theme, important enough perhaps to represent the line of a hypothetical intellectual biography, has remained as if concealed or at least out of focus: Momigliano's meditation on the history and culture of Judaism. This is not surprising if one considers the scarce sensibility of Italian intellectuals in regard to Judaism. It is not that Momigliano's works on Jewish subjects are not famous; rather, Judaism is considered, in general, as one among his many objects of interest.

This book of essays on Judaism, collected from among the most significant in the wide range of Momigliano's production, should show how central the subject of Judaism is to Momigliano, from his early essay on Flavius Josephus to the most recent ones on the Sibylline Books and on his friend Moses Finley.

The first part of this book, devoted entirely to ancient Judaism, examines the relationship between Hellenism and Judaism with a focus on the figure of Flavius Josephus, including a salient moment of Maccabean history, the problem of Jewish apocalyptics, and the ties between pagan culture, Judaism, and historiography. All readers of this book, including those who are not experts in ancient history, will be aware of a deeply personal intellectual motivation. This impression is enhanced when we come to the second part of the book. The essay on the Jews of Italy, heartfelt and rich with details, pursues the historic events of various Italian Jewish communities through the intimate evocation of Piedmontese Jewish life and family traditions; see, for example, the pages on Felice Momigliano. Faithful to the historicist need to research the origins of a personal historical problem—possibly the only sure Crocean trait of his personality—Momigliano deftly profiles the intellectual biography of men born at the end of the nineteenth century, men who like himself are deeply tied to their Jewish roots and have devoted their lives of research and questioning to the study of the classical world. The essay on the founder of Jewish "classical scholarship" Jacob Bernays (the son of an eminent rabbi from Hamburg), later a teacher at the Jüdisch-Theologisches Seminar in Breslau, provides a remarkable example. The essay on Bernays is followed by a series of portraits of an ideal family: Eduard Fraenkel, the great philologist and scholar of Latin poetry; Gertrud Bing (also from Hamburg), director of the Warburg Institute and guardian of that rich tradition; the Russian Elias Bickerman, the master of Hellenistic Judaism; and Moses Finley, the historian of Greek democracy and of the economic structures of the ancient world, to whom Momigliano devotes an essay that draws from psychoanalysis and historiography as he attempts to explain the interest in slavery as the reemergence of a repressed Jewish past. The essays on Scholem, Benjamin, and Strauss complete the range of Momigliano's subtle meditation on Judaism, which unfolds as an exegetic rather than a declarative process, questioning rather than providing answers.

Momigliano's intellectual itinerary was in every sense an uncommon one. It may be of some use to try to understand how the ethical experience of Judaism, inherited by birth and education, soon became for Momigliano a conscious and beloved duty, a cause of pride for belonging to a great intellectual tradition, a rich source for the questioning of the past, to the point of becoming, perhaps, the most authentic inspiration of his work.

## II

Family memories often emerge in Momigliano's writings. These memories evoke an atmosphere of reserved and intense domestic feelings, a tenacious love for learning and for the intimate joys of the holidays. This is the world described in the writings of Primo Levi and Augusto Segre, the world so dear to Paolo De Benedetti, which has been reconstructed by Stuart Hughes.[1]

Momigliano spent his childhood in Caraglio, a small town very close to Cuneo. He was born in 1908 into an old family of Piedmontese Jews whose austerity combined traditional religious culture and innovatory ferments rich in philosophical, literary, and political inspiration. Among the brothers of his grandfather Donato (who died very young) was Marco Momigliano, who, in 1866, as grand rabbi, reorganized the Jewish community of Bologna.[2] The strongest personality in the family, however, belonged to his grandfather's other brother, Amadio. A Talmudist who was especially in touch with Kabbalistic culture (he also exchanged letters with Elia Benamozegh), Amadio took charge of Arnaldo's early education. From 1914 to 1924 they lived in the same home; these were little Arnaldo's most formative years. Late in life, Amadio would read the *Zohar* in the evenings.[3] He taught Arnaldo Hebrew and developed a complete grammar for him. For Arnaldo's eighth birthday Amadio transcribed Rashi's medieval commentary on Genesis. Like many Jewish children, Momigliano knew by heart the proverbs of Solomon and the *Pirke Avot*, the maxims of the fathers; at age eleven, he had already read the books of the Old Testament. Momigliano's Jewish education continued to take place entirely within the family, which included other rabbis, such as Dario Disegni, who later became director of the Rabbinic College of Turin.

Although Momigliano studied privately in Cuneo, a great part of his traditional education took place within the walls of his home at Caraglio: Momigliano never went to school. But he did not waste time at home. At eleven he had read Renan and was growing up in an intellectual climate where there was great awareness that the merging of Greek culture with Judaism and the development of Christianity were decisive events for our civilization. The interest in Christianity, represented by Arturo Carlo Jemolo, a fine historian of Jansenism (Arnaldo's cousin on his mother's side of the family), was thus an integral part of

1. I am referring primarily to P. Levi, *Il sistema periodico*, Turin, 1975; A. Segre, *Memorie di vita ebraica: Casale Monferrato—Roma—Gerusalemme, 1918–1960*, Rome, 1979; P. De Benedetti, "Gli ebrei di Asti ed il loro rito," *Il Platano* 2 (1977): 17–28, and other writings; H. Stuart Hughes, *Prisoners of Hope: The Silver Age of the Italian Jews 1924–1974*, Cambridge, 1983.

2. See the recent book by Marco Momigliano, *Autobiografia di un Rabbino italiano*, with a note by A. Cavaglion, Palermo, 1986.

3. The *Zohar* is the classical text of the Kabbalah, which Scholem ascribes to Moses ben Shem Tov de León (c. 1270–90).

family culture.[4] There was also Attilio Momigliano, the famous literary critic, who was quite close to Croce and who carried out a fine study of Manzoni as a Catholic writer. We cannot appreciate fully how important the presence and teaching of Felice Momigliano must have been for young Arnaldo. Felice was a socialist, a scholar of Mazzini, Renan, and prophetism. Felice's vision, which combined all of these elements, was of a sort of Jewish modernism or reformed Judaism (indeed a brave point of view for those times in Italy) combined with a strong national conscience and inspired by the same ethical imperative. The fact that Felice would read and comment on the non-Orthodox Spinoza to Arnaldo when he was twelve is significant in relation to both men. Thus, between Amadio and Felice Momigliano Arnaldo was assimilating a form of religion that implied above all faithfulness to the tradition of the fathers; at the same time, he was developing a lay point of view and learning to think in historical terms.

## III

Momigliano became acquainted with the work of Benedetto Croce while a university student. As a pupil of De Sanctis and Rostagni, he developed an interest in history and Greco-Roman culture. After writing a dissertation on Thucydides under the guidance of and in complete agreement with De Sanctis (1929), Momigliano began working on the Maccabees. Beginning in the early 1930s, the study of Hellenistic Judaism provided Momigliano with a very personal basis for wider research prospects.

Even Momigliano's familiarity with Droysen, constant and fundamental through the years, must be seen in this perspective. We can provide only a brief account of his meditation, in connection with the point that interests us here. Momigliano had remarked about Droysen's article "Alexander the Great" that the Prussian historian's doctoral thesis had contained the idea that "Christianity was closer to Greekness than to Judaism,"[5] a historical viewpoint that Droysen elaborated in the first two volumes of his work on Hellenism. Although for Droysen Hellenism represented the cultural condition out of which

4. A. C. Jemolo, *Il giansenismo italiano prima della Rivoluzione*, Bari, 1928. In addition to better-known works, Jemolo has left us some delicate memoirs of Jewish Piedmontese life in *Anni di prova*, Vicenza, 1969.
5. A. Momigliano, "Per il centenario dell''Alessandro Magno' di J. G. Droysen: un contributo," in *Contributo alla storia degli studi classici*, Rome, 1955, p. 266. For a more detailed discussion of Droysen's thesis, see "Genesi e funzione attuale del concetto di Ellenismo," in ibid., pp. 165–93.

Christianity would emerge, he stressed the coming together of Greek and Oriental elements without considering the Jews.[6] Now, if Momigliano was able to point out the absence of Judaism in Droysen's meditation (an absence he later interpreted as a willful omission), the reason is that Judaism was both what moved him and what he was seeking. As Momigliano wrote in 1969 with reference to his writings from the period 1933–35, "above all, Hellenism meant to me the period when the Jews were confronted with Greek civilization." Once this seed was sown, it bore fruit in most of his later historiographical production. Thus, we should not be surprised that Momigliano was grateful to Droysen, whom he chose as "a viaticum, on taking his leave from a Jewish home in a Piedmontese village."[7]

Momigliano's decision to study the Maccabean question—resulting in his first important work—reveals the level of maturity of his meditation on Judaism: it was thanks to the insurrection of the Hasmoneans, led by Judas Maccabean, that the Jews of Judaea, Jews, who refused to undergo Hellenization and to abandon the faith of the fathers, became independent.[8] The Temple was reconsecrated. As Momigliano wrote much later, "a new devotion to the law (whether written or oral), an increasingly scrupulous regulation of religious duties" helped to restrain the influence of foreign civilization on Judaism. "Hellenism no longer represented a mortal danger."[9] Here we are reminded of Momigliano's remarks in a completely different context, the Weberian interpretation of Judaism as a religion for pariahs:

> If the word "pariah" indicates a people who accept their position as inferiors in an alien social system, . . . the Jews were not pariahs. The Jews went on giving laws to themselves and

6. Momigliano, "J. G. Droysen between Greeks and Jews," in *Quinto contributo alla storia degli studi classici e del mondo antico*, Rome, 1975, 1:109–26. Although this essay was not included in this book because it does not pertain to the Jewish tradition of classical studies, it contains certain pages (pp. 222–28) that the reader may want to bear in mind.

7. Momigliano, review of B. Bravo *Philologie, Histoire, Philosophie de l'Histoire, Étude sur J. G. Droysen, historien de l'Antiquité*, Varsovie, 1968, in *Quinto contributo*, 2:902.

8. See Momigliano, *Prime linee di storia della tradizione Maccabaica*, Rome, 1930. (Anastatic reprint of the second edition, Amsterdam, 1968). Some interesting observations on religious policy toward Jews can be found in Momigliano's next book, *L'opera dell'imperatore Claudio*, Florence, 1932, pp. 61–77.

9. Momigliano, *Alien Wisdom: The Limits of Hellenization*, Cambridge and London, 1975, p. 114. Momigliano has returned to the Maccabees in recent essays. In addition to the essay published in this book, see "The Date of the First Book of Maccabees," in *Sesto contributo alla storia degli studi classici e del mondo antico*, Rome, 1980, 2:561–66.

treated their pact with God as their own legal title to the future recovery of their own land in a messianic age. Their morality encompassed rebellion against injustice and martyrdom—attitudes one does not normally associate with pariahs (p. 176).

It is interesting to consider Momigliano's study of Hellenized Jews such as Jason of Cyrene, the source of 2 Maccabees, and, above all, Flavius Josephus. In 1931, while meditating on the *Against Apion,* Momigliano stressed the Hellenic modes of Flavius's adherence to Judaism (Moses as the legislator rather than the prophet). Almost forty years later, he returned to the subject in his introduction to the Italian translation of Pierre Vidal-Naquet's *Du bon usage de la trahison.* There he defined Flavius's form of Judaism as "flat, not false or trivial but rhetorical and generic" (p. 77). Josephus's longing that Judaism express itself in symbiosis with the Greco-Roman civilization, a longing that distanced him both from the apocalyptic currents and from rabbinic Judaism, raised a modern question, and at the same time led to the questioning of the Hellenistic world when the problem of this symbiosis could be studied at a crucial point. At the age of twenty-three, in the above-mentioned essay that was published in *La Rassegna Mensile di Israele,* Momigliano wrote, "The greatest concern of Judaism today is its function in modern civilization: whether this function exists and, admitting that it does, how can we define it" (pp. 58–59). This issue, which the Holocaust has rendered more dramatic and inevitable, is always present in Momigliano's work.

It is not surprising that a historian like Momigliano, one who from his early youth was so sensitive to the Jewish cause and to defining the peculiarities of Greek historiography, should have become interested in Flavius Josephus, a historian of the Jews for the Romans, who wrote in Greek. But while Jews quickly neglected Josephus's works, they were assimilated by Christian culture. Even more significant—perhaps because of the triumph of Pharisaic legalism, which emphasized the Law and the repetition, through memory, of great biblical events—until the nineteenth century, Jews completely lost interest in historiography as an autonomous field of inquiry, except for minor historical episodes. In his most recent work, Momigliano claims that in the apocalyptic literature kept under control by the rabbis it is possible to discern a discourse on history where, in accordance with the messianic idea, the past and the future come together. More specifically, Momigliano has indicated that both Christians and Jews—who share an eschatological faith in the end of the world—were able to transmit their historical conception to the pagans using Sibylline Oracles of pagan origin. The fact that apocalyptics cannot be found outside the Jewish or the Christian tradition perhaps can be explained in terms of the difficulty the Jews had in thinking the continuity of history after the destruction of the Temple of Jerusalem and of the difficulty the Christians had in considering themselves the heirs of the Roman Empire: "Sibylline oracles thus provided the possibility of interpreting political and religious events from a Jewish or Christian point of view at a time when neither Jews nor Christians were capable of writing history" (p. 107). Finally, future research will decide the extent to which the study of this prophetic literature will be able to enrich our understanding of the relationship between Judaism and historiography.

If Jews survived after the Maccabean revolt because of their obstinate unity and religious faith while some important Hellenized Jews disappeared from the memory of their own people, one might be tempted to think that Momigliano claims that Judaism has evolved internally, regardless of external factors. This is far from the truth. Between Wellhausen and Meyer, Momigliano did not hesitate to choose Meyer. He was, of course, very well acquainted with and indeed treasured Wellhausen's work on the Sadducees and the Pharisees and on Greco-Roman Judaea.[10] But he was not persuaded by Wellhausen's criterion of research, which tended to isolate Jewish history and to interpret it along immanent lines of development. Eduard Meyer is one of the great historians with whom Momigliano has not ceased to converse.[11] He began reading Meyer at the university when he was studying under the guidance of De Sanctis, at a time when *Ursprung und Anfänge des Christentums* (1921–23) was a recent, controversial work. Also important for Momigliano were Meyer's *Entstehung des Judentums* (1896) and *Die Israeliten und ihre Nachbarstämme* (1906). Momigliano's view of history and his study of Judaism were deeply marked by Meyer's vision of classical antiquity, which stressed mutual influences among Greece and Rome, Persia and Judaea, Mesopotamia and Egypt.[12] A book of unique interpretive novelty and of almost virtuosistic doctrine like

10. See Momigliano, "Religious History without Frontiers: J. Wellhausen, U. Wilamowitz and E. Schwartz," *History and Theory* suppl. 21, 4 (1982), later in an Italian translation in *Tra storia e storicismo*, pp. 169–78.

11. See Momigliano, "Premesse per una discussione su Eduard Meyer," in *Settimo contributo alla storia degli studi classici e del mondo antico*, Rome, 1984, pp. 215–31.

12. Momigliano pays homage to the teachings of Meyer in a review *Christianity, Judaism and Other Greco-Roman Cults: Studies for Morton Smith at Sixty*, ed. J. Neusner, Leiden, 1975: "I must end by admitting to the expectation that in a not very distant day ancient historians and theologians will make a pilgrimage to the tomb of Eduard Meyer whom nowadays nobody quotes any longer. He remains after all the only historian of this century who succeeded in producing (*inter alia*) a diptych, however crude, of pre-rabbinic Judaism and New Testament Christianity" (in *Sesto contributo*, 2:778).

Momigliano's *Alien Wisdom* can be understood better against this distant background. Momigliano's interest in Persia in relation to other civilizations, especially to the forms of political and religious organization and the historiography of postexilic Judaism is also typical in this sense.[13] If, as concerns the development of Judaism, "Philo did not prevail" as Momigliano claims, nor did other forms of denaturalizing Hellenization, the rabbinic Judaism, which did triumph, became indebted to Greek penetration, for example, in adopting the concept of *paideia* within the Jewish ideal of a life devoted to learning and disciplined by intellectual rigors. From this point of view, Momigliano's thesis blends with that of Elias Bickerman, the Russian Jew who was his master and colleague in Hellenistic Roman studies. But there was an overall rejection of Hellenization: "The choice was represented by the Torah" (p. 24).

Hence Jews and Latins, despite the linguistic and cultural isolationism of the Greeks, created the basis for the *collegium trilingue* that is the essence of our civilization. But this Hellenistic basis (and this appears to be Momigliano's ideal conclusion to the problem) was achieved only through Christianity: "the fusion of Greek, Latin and Jewish tradition is Christian. The Jews (and the Arabs) continued to face Greek thought in isolation. They were never deeply concerned with Latin ways of living or thinking."[14]

All of this is the result of recent work. As we have seen, however, a strong thread pulls together Momigliano's studies on ancient Judaism, beginning with the early essay on Flavius Josephus. By that time, Bickerman's work had already become important for Momigliano. In the 1930s the two men were already exchanging letters (Bickerman wrote a review of Momigliano in *Monatsschrift für Geschichte und Wissenschaft des Judentums* in 1934). This exchange became more intense in 1937–38 (*Der Gott der Makkabäer* is from 1937) and continued after the war. Bickerman's typical subtlety in the study of history as well as his historiographic consciousness also influenced Momigliano. Other important influences on Momigliano were the eminent philologist Felix Jacoby and Arthur Darby Nock, the historian of ancient religions. Momigliano had the opportunity of getting acquainted with both of them only later on, during the hard years of the war and his exile in England.

13. See Momigliano's essay, "Fattori orientali della storiografia ebraica post-esilica e della storiografia greca," in *Terzo contributo alla storia degli studi classici e del mondo antico*, Rome, 1966, 2:807–18.
14. Momigliano, "The Fault of the Greeks," in *Sesto contributo*, p. 518.

## IV

In 1938 Momigliano, like all Italian Jews, had to face the horror of racial persecution and fled to Oxford. Eleven members of his family, among them his parents, were killed in Nazi concentration camps. We can easily suppose that for a man like Momigliano, who had been educated in a double Italian Jewish tradition, the radical change brought about by Fascism, which led to the elimination of one-fourth of the Italian Jewish population, must have caused unbearable pain. During those difficult years, he probably had the opportunity to rethink our *question juive* as well as what he had written on Italian Jews and the formation of the unitary process of the Risorgimento. In a 1933 review of a book by Cecil Roth, Momigliano noted that the history of the Jews of Italy was essentially "the history of the forming of their national conscience" (p. 225). The development of this conscience went hand in hand with the participation by many Jews in the wars of the Risorgimento, as Momigliano recalls (see chap. 12 below). These remarks aroused the interest and the assent of Antonio Gramsci. Gramsci noted, perhaps with excessive optimism, that the absence of anti-Semitism in our country could be explained with the overcoming of "Catholic cosmopolitanism" by a new anti-Catholic lay spirit inspired by the Risorgimento, which was bound to favor a gradual "nationalization"—to repeat Gramsci's words—of the Jews (p. 229). This important statement no doubt accounts for the peculiarity of the Italian situation.

These remarks, however, call for a few other considerations. It is certainly true that Italian Jews identify themselves substantially with Italian social and cultural life, a fact that explains, in part, the (relatively) small presence of anti-Semitism in Italy. For example, in Italy names like Ottolenghi or Volterra are not considered differently from names like Laurenti or Franceschini. This is, of course, a highly positive fact. But there is a negative side as well, namely, the almost complete foreignness of the non-Jewish world to the specificity of the culture and traditions of the sons of Israel, an attitude that can be described as a form of imperturbable ignorance, which can lead to unconscious anti-Semitism. Under the pretext of a false concept of equality, Jews often are asked to renounce values and customs that many cannot give up without losing their identity. This attitude helps to explain how even a man of the intellectual status of Benedetto Croce, a man deeply sympathetic to the Jews at the time of the racial campaign, urged them "to eliminate those elements of distinction and division in which Jews have persisted for centuries, and which as they have provided a pretext for persecution in the past, it is to be feared that they will provide a

pretext for persecution in the future" (p. 139). This embarassing statement, written in 1947 (!), is similar to previous remarks by Croce,[15] remarks that should be read in the context of his famous "Perché non
possiamo non dirci cristiani."[16] Momigliano later commented on these
words with bitter pride, "Only a complete lack of contact with Jewish
culture can explain the fact that not even Benedetto Croce managed to
understand that Italian Jews have the right (which subjectively can be a
duty) to remain Jewish" (p. 139). It is perhaps for this reason that
Momigliano declined the offer the Neapolitan philosopher made him
that same year to take over the direction of the Italian Institute for Historical Studies, a position that Federico Chabod filled immediately (a
position predisposed for Adolfo Omodeo, who had died prematurely).

During the war, English universities were teeming with Jewish refugees, who were primarily of German origin. Saxl and Bing transferred
the Warburg Institute from Hamburg to London with the firm intention
of preserving it as a fundamental expression of German Jewish culture.
Momigliano's contact with these people led him to devote himself
more closely to ancient history and to the great tradition of German
classical philology, with which he was already very familiar and of
which that group represented the *tradition vivante*. This world, to
which he was already very well accustomed, assumed the more familiar aspect of the *Deutsschjudentum*. As is generally recognized, Jews
made a decisive contribution to the blossoming of classical studies in
Germany.[17] The presence of Jewish scholars was especially important
for the study of Latin culture and the history of Rome; we will mention
only a few names here: Ludwig Traube, Friedrich Leo, Eduard Norden,

---

15. See the significant example, "La storicità e la perpetuità della ideologia massonica"
(1919), in *L'Italia dal 1914 al 1918. Pagine sulla guerra*, Bari, 1950, pp. 259–60. In this text
Croce claims that because of their "innate messianism" Jews "are usually intellectualists
and devoid of a sense of history"; this explains why they are present in great numbers in
the Masonry. Croce also claims:

> I would never become an anti-Semite, although I admit the reality of a "Semitic
> question"; I believe this is a question that concerns the Israelites themselves; it
> is up to them to solve the issue by keeping abreast with the higher culture and
> the higher thought achieved by classical-Christian-European civilization, and
> by developing a historical mind after centuries away from our history.

Similar statements can be found in "La questione ebraica nel mondo," in *Pagine sparse*,
Bari, 1960, 2:525–27, and in "Contro i nazionalismi di qualsiasi sorta," in *Nuove pagine
sparse*, Bari, 1966, 1:345–46.

16. B. Croce, *Discorsi di varia filosofia*, Bari, 1945, 1:11–23.

17. On this subject, see "Jews in Classical Scholarship," which Momigliano wrote for
the *Encyclopaedia Judaica*, in *Sesto contributo*, 2:583–87.

Eduard Fraenkel. It is hard to say why. Possibly because Theodor Mommsen proved more inclined than others to welcome Jewish students, or possibly because the study of Greek history was marked by a strong nationalistic character in which the Greeks came close to playing the role of the Germans' predecessors (in a line that goes from Jaeger, Pohlenz, to the extreme position of Berve). Felix Jacoby, the unrivaled philologist and interpreter of Greek historiography, was a brilliant exception. Momigliano, who had reviewed Jacoby's *opus magnum* in the period following his graduation,[18] taught at Oxford together with Jacoby and shared with him the bitterness of emigration. Everyone who has heard Momigliano speak of Jacoby or Norden remembers the austere intellectual admiration that the memory of the two masters had for Momigliano; we cannot but regret that he has not sketched their profiles. Fortunately, other profiles compensate us for this lack. Of that variegated world of émigrés (which Momigliano continued to frequent in the persons of Leo Strauss, Herbert Bloch, and Ernst Kantorowicz) Momigliano knows every aspect. He is capable of reconstructing that world through subtle analytical remarks and affection into concise biographical sketches. This is the case of Eduard Fraenkel—a disciple of Leo, Wilamowitz, and Gundolf, and a scholar of Plautus, Horace, and Virgil—whom Momigliano has portrayed in his learned candor and in his quest for truth: "He studied the classics as his forebears had studied the Torah" (p. 216). It is also the case of Gertrud Bing, proud and free in her aristocratic, Hamburgian interpretation of Judaism.

This culture is deeply present in Momigliano, the understanding of which derives from a deep sense of belonging, and the acknowledgment of a debt to a tradition of study and life. While Momigliano's most immediate adherence is to Russian Jewish culture, more genuine and less subject to exterior compromises, his relationship to German Jewish culture could be said to be the opposite of Scholem's. Unlike Scholem, who rejected his German background after having regained his Jewish identity, Momigliano, through his intimacy with the German Jewish world, established the basis for his future study of German "classical scholarship," to which he has devoted memorable contributions in recent years. Momigliano's essays on Usener, Wellhausen, Wilamowitz, Schwartz, Mommsen, and Weber, so typical of his historiographic style, have an important precedent: the Jew Jacob Bernays. Momigliano's sensitivity to the master-disciple relationship, to the

---

18. See Momigliano's review of F. Jacoby, *Die Fragmente der griechischen Historiker* (Berlin, 1923) in *Bollettino di Filologica Classica* 36 (1929–30): 198–99.

intellectual genealogy of a generation and its changes, so strong in his writings, owe a great deal to the Jewish way of understanding teaching as the transmission of a tradition.

Stronger than the sense of participating in a *Kultur*, however, the need to find in the historiography of the past the origin of a personal historical problem has prevailed in Momigliano. The figure of Bernays is in this sense emblematic for many reasons. Bernays was the first great scholar whose research combined Judaism and the classical world to the mutual advantage of both. Unlike Momigliano, however, who from this point of view is closer to Bickerman in stressing the common points between Jews and Greeks, Bernays did not think much of Jewish Hellenistic literature in which rejoicing in the Law was too weak.[19] Other analogies come to mind as well. Not unlike Bernays who, with a study on Scaliger, had gained an enviable command of classical erudition between the sixteenth and the eighteenth centuries, which later became an integral part of his new historical method, Momigliano detected in the antiquarian evaluation of the original document, the meticulous method of discerning the true from the forged, an indispensable element of his reflections on the historical method,[20] to which he was later to return in various ways. Nor can Bernays's and Momigliano's common interest in Gibbon be viewed as an external coincidence. As Momigliano wrote in a later essay, "it is not surprising to find that the first great Jewish classical scholar of the nineteenth century, Jacob Bernays, was also the first to plan a book on Gibbon as a historian free from Christian preconceptions."[21] Momigliano's study of Gibbon, proposed in 1936, followed the same approach.[22] Momigliano is the first to have introduced the English historian to Italian culture with full historiographic awareness. Giorgio Falco had in fact previously attempted such a study, but by a fundamental misunderstanding believed he could ascribe to Gibbon a Catholic, providentialistic interpretation of the Middle Ages (this may have had something to do with Falco's conversion from Judaism to Catholi-

19. Bernays's answer to the question "What is Jewish faith?" has always been rigorously and absolutely "Halakah," normative, an orthodoxy that comes close "to the point of neurosis," as Scholem writes in "Jews and Germans," in *On Jews and Judaism in Crisis*, New York, 1976, p. 85.

20. See the fundamental essay "Ancient History and the Antiquarian," in *Contributo*, pp. 67–106.

21. Momigliano, "After Gibbon's *Decline and Fall*," in *Sesto contributo*, p. 269.

22. Momigliano, "La formazione della moderna storiografia sull'Impero romano," in *Contributo*, pp. 107–64, now in *Sui fondamenti della storia antica*, pp. 89–152.

cism).[23] The anti-Semitic campaign triggered by Treitschke in 1880 takes us back to events that bring Momigliano and Bernays together in spite of the difference in time and historical circumstances. At that time, Theodor Mommsen, the great liberal historian and an intimate friend of Bernays, sided with the Jews (among whom he had many friends) but urged them to convert. This is what Croce did many years later. Instead of conversion, however, Croce had recommended a complete assimilation of Jews in "the higher culture" achieved by "the classical-Christian-European civilization."[24] Such was (and is) the loneliness of the Jews, not only vis-à-vis their persecutors but often vis-à-vis their defenders as well.

In paraphrasing what the author of these essays has written about Maimonides in "Hermeneutics and Classical Political Thought in Leo Strauss" (p. 188), I would say that the example of Bernays was not external for Momigliano.

## V

One of the most penetrating essays in this collection, characterized by a very personal interpretation in line with its object, is the note on Leo Strauss. That Momigliano should sooner or later become interested in Leo Strauss was to be expected, and for a good reason. Strauss combines in his typical elevated vision the two worlds that are always present in Momigliano—Judaism and classical culture. Strauss's hermeneutics transfuse the analytical skill worthy of a Talmudist into the study of Plato, Xenophon, and Aristophanes, and adds speculative clarity to the exegesis of Maimonides and medieval Jewish philosophy. The problem that motivated this difficult choice in Strauss was the relation between faith and reason. As Momigliano writes, the author of *Religionskritik Spinozas* (1930) wanted to be a "philosopher *in* Judaism" (p. 189). He succeeded in living and thinking in the groove of this impossibility, making this his strength. The tension between faith and reason is released and achieves its highest result in the exercise of interpretation (for example, Maimonides' *Guide of the Perplexed*) and in the art of the commentary, possibly the most characteristic element of Jewish culture, even if at times it indulges in a sort of *pilpul*, minute Talmudic sophistics.

23. G. Falco, *La polemica sul Medio Evo*, Biblioteca della Società Storica Subalpina, Turin, 1933.
24. See note 15.

The point where Momigliano no longer follows Strauss (and would not follow Lev Šestov) is the point where the dichotomy reappears in the contraposition between *Jerusalem and Athens* (1967). It is even more difficult to agree (certainly for myself and, if I am not mistaken, for Momigliano as well) with the Straussian thesis of the superiority of the ancients over the moderns, a thesis that opposes the objectivity of the law of nature to the subjective natural rights of the moderns in a pointed criticism of modern liberalism and individualism. The ancient ideal of the good society that exists by necessity and is thus valid for everyone ends up being structured, in Strauss, into a kind of ontology of morals. A similar vision, which turns morals into something absolute and reduces it to "isness" (is ethics possible at all except in terms of "ought to be"?), ends up rendering morals entirely ineffective. This cannot but weaken Strauss's criticism, although it is very productive in other ways, bringing Weber close to historicism, in his evaluation of the intrinsic poverty of a position that does without morals or value judgments. Thus Strauss puts his readers in the difficult but healthy position of constantly having to make distinctions and avoiding immediate answers.

When it comes to criticizing historicism, however, Momigliano is again quite close to Strauss. It is certain that the "memorable encounters" (p. 188) between the two masters at the University of Chicago have left a lasting mark in the mind of the Piedmontese historian. In his essay "Historicism Revisited," Momigliano places his work as a historian in a perspective that manages to combine (possibly a unique case in our contemporary historiography) a detachment from idealistic historicism and a firm reference to theoretical and ethical presuppositions. Momigliano's approach is hardly thinkable without Strauss's teaching, without those pages in Strauss's "Natural Right and History" (1953) that deal with Weberian valuelessness in particular. Momigliano writes:

> Either we possess a religious or moral belief independent of history, which allows us to pronounce judgment on historical events, or we must give up moral judging. Just because history teaches us how many moral codes mankind has had, we cannot derive moral judgment from history. Even the notion of transforming history by studying history implies a metahistorical faith.[25]

25. Momigliano, "Historicism Revisited," in *Sesto contributo*, p. 28.

A few Straussian elements are indirectly present in the telling pages Momigliano devotes to the greatest historian of Judaism of the twentieth century, Gershom Scholem. Having experienced in his youth the revival of certain forms of German romanticism, where the esoteric theme and the connection between myth and language were particularly relevant, Momigliano easily recognizes these elements in both Strauss and Scholem.[26] Those were the years in which the influence of Stefan George was growing. Scholem had read George with a passion during the period of his early experience with Talmudic studies.[27] As we can see from *Persecution and the Art of Writing* (1952), Strauss theorized esotericism and interiorized the model of the esoteric philosopher, at times not without some irritating complacency. Scholem, on the other hand, by devoting his life to the study of symbolism in the Kabbalah and to various developments in Jewish messianism, in one form or another, made esotericism his object. But the method he used as a historian in the study of this universe was marked by a philological rigor, which owes the *Wissenschaft des Judentums* a great deal more than he has ever been willing to admit.

It is revealing, however, that at a conference held in 1963, during a meeting between Jews and Protestants, Strauss claimed when referring to Scholem's *Zur Kabbala und ihrer Symbolik*, "the most profound truth cannot be written and not even said."[28] Strauss and Scholem have other points in common. The common tie to German culture (which Scholem never entirely acknowledged) and a debt to the tradition of the *Wissenschaft*, which led to radically different results in the writings of the two men, may represent a nonexternal observation post. Scholem met Strauss for the first time in 1927 and was immediately impressed;[29] this experience was probably mutual. For several years, their writings had

26. In a passing observation in his memorable essay on Usener, Momigliano has hinted at the possibility that Scholem was somehow indebted to Usener for his interpretive vision of Kabbalistic language ("Hermann Usener," in *Tra storia e storicismo*, p. 174). Scholem's essay, "Der Name Gottes und die Sprachtheorie der Kabbala" (1970), which he wrote fifty years after his initial project on the subject, appears to me to confirm this observation. Scholem's essay may be found in *Judaica*, Frankfurt am Main, 1973, 37–71.

27. Scholem, "Von Berlin nach Jerusalem," in *Jugenderinnerungen*, Frankfurt am Main, 1977, p. 68.

28. Strauss, "Perspectives on the Good Society," in *Liberalism Ancient and Modern*, New York, 1968, p. 272.

29. In a 1932 letter, Benjamin wrote to Scholem, "I . . . am glad to hear you take an interest in Leo Strauss, who always made an excellent impression on me, too." See *The Correspondence of Walter Benjamin and Gershom Scholem, 1932–1940*, ed. G. Scholem, New York, 1989, p. 24. See also Scholem's note to the letter.

been appearing side by side in Buber's review *Der Jude*. Before long they began to criticize the Buberian vision of "Erlebnis" in Judaism (Scholem in particular disagreed with Buber's interpretation of Hasidism). Although Strauss and Scholem both admired the strength of Rosenzweig's thought, they had similar reasons for disliking him. Strauss considered *Der Stern der Erlösung* a philosophical system more than a Jewish book. He noted maliciously that the biblical Judaism that was supposed to inspire it "was not identical with the Judaism of the age prior to Moses Mendelssohn."[30] Scholem, on the other hand, who, as Momigliano remembers (pp. 192–93), had a violent clash with Rosenzweig, could not stand "the way he saw Judaism as a kind of pietistic Protestant church," even less "the Jewish-German synthesis he wanted to create."[31]

Scholem's obsessive insistence on the condition of Jews in German society is perhaps what ultimately explains the meaning of his life and work. Since his early youth, Scholem had been rebelling against the illusion, so deeply rooted in his family, of a Jewish-German dialogue. In his opinion, this dialogue had already produced for Jews a blind and senseless assimilation and a subsequent loss of Jewish identity. Strauss's view of the Jewish question in Germany was not altogether different: "political dependence was also spiritual dependence. This was the core of the predicament of German Jewry."[32] But these remarks, which probably have something to do with the genesis of Strauss's theoretical distrust of liberal democracy, were conceived and written many years after the Holocaust. "The German-Jewish problem was never solved. It was annihilated by the annihilation of the German Jews."[33] It is no small feat for Scholem to have understood this in the early 1920s. While mitigated by an inevitable respect, Scholem's condemnation of the *Deutschjudentum* also involved the *Wissenschaft* in the "attempt to reduce Judaism to a purely spiritual, ideal phenomenon," which left aside "those features which were not relevant if viewed from the perspective of such spiritualization."[34] For Scholem,

30. Strauss, "Preface to Spinoza's Critique of Religion," in *Liberalism Ancient and Modern*, p. 237. Momigliano also considered Rosenzweig's attempt to reconcile Judaism and Hagelianism artificial.

31. Scholem, "With Gershom Scholem: An Interview," in *On Jews and Judaism in Crisis: Selected Essays*, ed. W. J. Dannhauser, New York, 1976, p. 20.

32. Strauss, "Preface to Spinoza's Critique of Religion," p. 227.

33. Ibid.

34. Scholem, "The Science of Judaism—Then and Now," in *The Messianic Idea in Judaism*, New York, 1971, p. 305.

Jewish awareness, the study of Hebrew, and becoming a scholar of the long-forgotten mystical tradition were but one decision, even if developed over a great number of years. His intellectual problem was "to arrive at an understanding of what kept Judaism alive."[35]

For Scholem, the answer was obviously not orthodoxy. He was deeply convinced that without a mystical basis, Halakah would not have had the strength to survive in the long run. Scholem's originality lies in his having paved a new way, rich in historiographical results, that provided an alternative to both assimilation and orthodoxy. As Momigliano did not fail to point out, "that point is where his Zionist and his Kabbalistic pursuits intersect" (p. 196). For Scholem, this solution is present as a complete synthesis. In his view, only Zionism, in a fundamentally individualistic and hardly transmissible sense, made it possible to recover the whole Jewish inheritance and bring about a rebirth of Judaism. Like the hero Sabbatai Zevi, the protagonist of his masterpiece, Scholem hands down to us problems that are radical and difficult to solve.[36]

These lines are only a quick introductory note. Anyone wishing to undertake an intellectual biography of Momigliano will have to examine, with the competence of a classical scholar, Momigliano's contribution to the understanding of Judaism from within his ever growing vision of the ancient world and his historiographic meditation. The attempt also will have to be made to define his position in the context of the revival of Jewish studies of recent years. The great number of published works devoted to the most diverse aspects of Judaism is truly remarkable: the Kabbalah and the interpretation of the Talmud, Hasidism and Zionism, the Bible as literary form and expression, and Marranism. This is certainly one of the most interesting trends in current historiography, even if the importance of the phenomenon appears to have gone unnoticed in Italy. As Yosef Hayim Yerushalmi has recently stated, the relationship between Jews and their past has always been regulated by memory, not by history. Every year Jews relive through memory key episodes of their history (for example, in the Pesach feast).[37] Today, the need to remember by the writing of history is clearly connected with the Holocaust and with the moral imperative shared by those who feel that what Nazi barbarism wanted to erase forever

35. Scholem, "With Gershom Scholem: An Interview," p. 20.

36. Scholem, *Sabbatai Sevi: The Mystical Messiah 1626–1676*, Princeton, N.J., 1973. On the theological problems of Sabbatai Zevi's conversion, see the Scholem's fundamental essay "Redemption through Sin," in *The Messianic Idea in Judaism*, pp. 78–141.

37. Y. H. Yerushalmi, *Zakhor: Jewish History and Jewish Memory*, Seattle and London, 1982.

should be known and preserved. For the time being, it is difficult to say more.

We can see how these two perspectives come together as we confront Momigliano's work. For Momigliano, the ancient obligation of remembrance is effortlessly translated into the gravity of historical thought as a form of religious life. The "Religion der Vernunft" in which Hermann Cohen believed becomes for Momigliano a "Religion der Geschichte," invariably inspired by the sources of Judaism. Momigliano's stylistic expression in writing history is also revealing. As Scholem wrote of Benjamin, "in the least the most is revealed."[38] This is true of Momigliano was well. Momigliano's choice of the essay, his preference for fragmentary forms of narration instead of the often deceptive general histories, reveals how his accurate, analytical mind, typical of the Jewish culture of the commentary, is capable of dealing with a problem that bears within itself the marks of the universal.

Rabbi Gamaliel's famous maxim says, "Get yourself a master." To the readers who will retain, in the long run, the light-bearing awareness of these writings, I would like to suggest that name of Arnaldo Momigliano.

SILVIA BERTI

*Milan, July 1987*

While the proofs of this book were being corrected, we learned of the death of Arnaldo Momigliano. We are seized by a deep sadness and discomfort. Momigliano will no longer be here to encourage pupils and friends with his extraordinary and affectionate learning, his attentive openness. We shall miss the irony, the levity, and the gravity of his conversation, his noble obsession with truth. Confronted with the greatness of his work, we cannot help but think how much we have lost. Our saddest thought goes to the young, and to those who never had the chance to meet him.

S. B.

38. Scholem, "Walter Benjamin," in *Walter Benjamin und sein Engel: Vierzehn Aufsätze und kleine Beiträge*, ed. R. Tiedeman, Frankfurt am Main, 1983, pp. 13–14.

# Preface

This book arose from the personal initiative of Silvia Berti and I do not wish to interfere with her choice or judgment, however deep my gratitude to her.

I will add just a few lines of personal information. I was born in Caraglio (Cuneo) in September 1908. There I lived with my family and received a private education, studying in part with professors from Cuneo during the time of my gymnasium and lyceum before attending the University of Turin in 1925. Among the Jews of my generation, I was one of the few who received a strictly Orthodox education. Amadio Momigliano (1844–1924), my grandfather Donato's brother, had adopted my father, Salomone Riccardo, after the death of my grandfather. To myself and my sisters, "Uncle Amadio" was, of course, our paternal grandfather, and it is as such that I shall speak of him here. Amadio was a modest businessman and landowner, and he remained active as such until the time of his death. He was a man of great piety who also had a strong civic sense. Amadio was exceptional for his hospitality, his great interest and competence in Hebrew and Aramaic texts beginning with the Bible, as well as for his interest in European social movements. At the age of eighty, the rabbis of Italy (among whom was Dario Disegni, who had married one of my father's sisters) awarded him a rabbinic diploma *honoris causa*, which he accepted with pleasure but without saying a word.

Amadio was a special person. Through his constant study and respect for the *Zohar*, the medieval mystical text, Amadio had become a reader and friend of Elia Benamozegh, the mystic rabbi of Leghorn. He spent the evenings of his last years reading the *Zohar* in Aramaic, but he never would talk about or discuss it, not even, I believe, with the rabbis who came to visit him. I don't know whether he had ever discussed the *Zohar* previously with his beloved brother Marco, the famous rabbi of Bologna. The world that was closest to him was not one of praxis but of theory. He never communicated this, however, either to my father or to me, his beloved nephew. Later in life I tried to find out if there had been a tradition of Kabbalistic studies in the family or among close relatives, but there appears have been none.

Our religion was all in the family. We would go to Cuneo (where we kept an apartment for these events) only for Rosh Hashanah and for Yom Kippur. This is why I cannot separate my domestic feelings from the everyday religious ceremonies that our family celebrated, and from the Sabbath, when everything changed. We would often spend Saturday afternoons at "Paniale," a half-rustic, half-urban dwelling surrounded by fields and chestnut groves, which we had bought after measuring the distance an Orthodox Jew was permitted to walk away from home on the Sabbath. My real experience with Judaism consists in an intense, austere, domestic piety: children who are blessed by their fathers on Friday nights; mothers who embrace their husbands and children.

Our orthodoxy was met with great tolerance by the surrounding world. For several years when we were children, my sisters and I attended a school run by nuns. We were regularly absent on Saturdays and during the official Jewish holidays, and we did not pray with the other children. We still remember Mother Gabriella Testa as the ideal "teacher."

Our four cousins, who had been born out of a mixed marriage of another of father's sisters, were as dear to us as any. Above all, the atmosphere for discussion in such an Orthodox home was very free. I shall mention the socialist Riccardo Momigliano (who was a congressman and later became a senator), who had little sympathy for Judaism, and Felice, Amadio's nephew and my father's first cousin, who was a professor at the Magistero of Rome and died a suicide in 1924. Felice was deeply Jewish, but he combined Mazzinianism, idealist socialism, and above all the ethical teaching of Jesus separated by redemptive notes. A frequent visitor in our home over long periods of time until 1922, Felice became my second teacher. It was from Felice that I learned about prophetism, Mazzini, and socialism as well as the rudiments of Latin and Greek. One may be tempted to smile at the idea of finding me thinking (at the age of eight to ten) about the Deus-Natura of Spinoza as an alternative to the God of the prophets, but there is no reason to smile at the fact that my father, in the last letter I received from him from Switzerland in 1942 (shortly before he was killed by the Nazis, together with my mother), recommended that I seek comfort in the prophets and in Spinoza. From Attilio Momigliano, a more distant relative, I learned the love for poetry and later became friends with him in every sense.

Around 1928, when Amadio Momigliano was already dead, the intellectual ideas of Arturo Carlo Jemolo penetrated the family circle. Arturo Carlo Jemolo was the author of a book on Jansenism in Italy in the eighteenth century, which my father had given me for my twentieth birthday. He was a Sicilian Catholic on his father's side, but he had a grandmother Momigliano on his mother's side (whom he later converted to Christianity). Until the time of his death, he remained a devoted and open friend in religious matters; it is from him that I learned much of what I know about Italian Catholicism.

At Caraglio our Judaism was respected. Although he was not actively engaged in politics, "'l cavaier amadiu" had ties with all the local mutual societies and charities; "'l cavaier Riccardo" was major of Caraglio between 1917 and the end of the war. For us, Mazzini represented the link between Judaism and the Italian Risorgimento; our patriotism was never questioned.

Except, of course, for my mother, to whom I was very close, I was less influenced by my mother's family—a family of industrialists from Turin. Over time I began to appreciate men like my grandfather's brother Camillo Levi, the eminent organic chemist of the Politecnico of Milan, and my cousins, like the brothers Eugenio Elia and Beppo Levi, both mathematicians. The former died as a volunteer in World War I while the latter returned to Italy, after an exile in Argentina during World War II, and became a colleague at the Accademia dei Lincei. I do not intend to speak here of the Fascist period. My most important thought from those unfortunate years concern non-Jewish friends, like Carlo Dionisotti and Guido Calogero, from whom I never separated. I shall also mention Jewish and non-Jewish friends who died for the freedom of Italy in the Resistenza: one name, that of Leone Ginzburg, is enough. This book is dedicated to Primo Levi and Giampiera Arrigoni, who represent all of my friends.

Regardless of what will be written on the period in which Fascists and Nazis collaborated in sending millions of Jews to concentration camps (my father and mother were among the victims), I shall repeat that the great slaughter would never have taken place in Italy, France, and Germany (not to say more) had there not been a centuries-old indifference on the part of the peoples of these countries toward their Jewish fellow citizens. This indifference was the ultimate result of the hostility of the churches, which viewed "conversion" as the only solution to the Jewish problem.

I solemnly repeat that Jews have a right to their religion, the first monotheistic and ethical religion in history, the religion of the prophets of Israel. To this day, our morality depends on it. Anyone in Italy, France, Germany, or elsewhere who prevents Jews from exercising their religion is guilty of implicit or explicit barbarism.

ARNALDO MOMIGLIANO

*The University of Chicago Hospital*
*July 1987*

# Part One

# 1

# Biblical Studies and Classical Studies: Simple Reflections upon Historical Method

Principles of historical research need not be different from criteria of common sense. And common sense teaches that outsiders must not tell insiders what they should do. I shall therefore not discuss directly what biblical scholars are doing. They are the insiders.

What I can perhaps do usefully is to emphasize as briefly as possible three closely interrelated points of my experience as a classical scholar who is on speaking terms with biblical scholars: (1) our common experience in historical research; (2) the serious problems we all have to face because of the current devaluation of the notion of evidence and of the corresponding overappreciation of rhetoric and ideology as instruments for the analysis of the literary sources; (3) what seems to me the most fruitful field of collaboration between classical and biblical scholars.

Let me admit from the start that I am rather impervious to any claim that sacred history poses problems which are not those of profane history. As a man trained from early days to read the Bible in Hebrew, Livy in Latin, and Herodotus in Greek, I have never found the task of interpreting the Bible any more or any less complex than that of interpreting Livy or Herodotus. Livy is of course less self-assured about the truth of what he tells us about Romulus than the Pentateuch is about Abraham. But the basic elements of a sacred history are in Livy as much as in the Pentateuch. It so happens that the Romans entrusted their priests with the task of registering events; and in one way or another the priestly code of Rome contributed to the later annals written by senators or by professional writers. It is unnecessary to add at this eleventh hour that

An address to the section on method at the centennial conference of the Society of Biblical Literature, Dallas, November 6, 1980. Originally published in English in *Annali della Scuola Normale Superiore di Pisa*, 3d series, vol. 11 (1981), no. 1, pp. 25–32. Reprinted by permission of Giulio Einaudi editore s.p.a.

the problems about understanding the texts, guessing their sources, and determining the truth of their information are basically the same in Roman as in Hebrew history. The similarity extends to the means and methods of supplementing and checking our literary sources by archaeology, epigraphy, numismatics, and what not. Whether biblical or classical historians, we have also learned that archaeology and epigraphy cannot take the place of the living tradition of a nation as transmitted by its literary texts. At the same time we have been cured of early delusions that the reliability of historical traditions can be easily demonstrated by the spade of the archaeologists. A nice example was provided two years ago by the discovery, by now famous, of an archaic Latin inscription in the town of Satricum. What is now known as the *Lapis Satricanus* is a simple dedication to Mars (Mamars) by the companions (*sodales*) of Publius Valerius. This is the text, on two lines with something missing at the beginning:

*ei steterai Popliosio Valesiosio*
*suodales Mamartei*

The date of the inscription is unlikely to be earlier than 530 B.C. or later than 480 B.C. Roman tradition tells us of a Roman consul Publius Valerius Poplicola for the first year of the Republic (traditionally 509 B.C.); but the reality of this consul had been doubted, for good and for bad reasons. Are we now to regard the Publius Valerius who appeared in Satricum as identical with the Roman consul of 509 B.C.? And can we claim this identification as a vindication of traditionalism? Biblical scholars are used to such problems.

On the other hand, we have learned that archaeology allows us to pose problems which the literary tradition does not even suggest. When we catalogue the furniture of the tombs of eighth-century B.C. Latium, we are by implication asking questions about the material culture of Iron-Age Latium, its relations to Etruria, to Greece, etc., which are simply outside the literary tradition. But of course there is a difference between asking intelligent questions and producing plausible answers. We have to learn to live with a disproportion between the intelligent questions we can ask and the plausible answers we can give. This is the only consolation I can offer to my biblical colleagues who have not yet found a plausible answer to their intelligent questions about Genesis, chapter 14, and who do not delude themselves that the Ebla tablets are going to oblige in this respect. The most dangerous type of researcher in any historical field is the man who, because he is

---

1. P. Stibbe, *Lapis Satricanus*, Accademia Olandese, Rome, 1980.

intelligent enough to ask a good question, believes that he is good enough to give a satisfactory answer.

If I said there is no basic difference between writing biblical history and writing any other history, it is because I wanted to introduce what to my mind is the really serious problem about writing any history today. There is a widespread tendency both inside and outside the historical profession to treat historiography as another genre of fiction. The reduction of historiography to fiction takes various forms and is justified with varying degrees of intellectual sophistication. It is sometimes presented in the simple form of reducing any literary product (including historiography) to the expression of ideological points of view; that is, of explicit or concealed class interests. It is also offered, with greater sophistication, as an analysis of historical works in terms of rhetorical postures; and, finally, it is elaborated by combining ideological and rhetorical analysis with the purpose of proving that any historical account is characterized by a rhetorical posture which in its turn indicates a social and political bias. The conclusion is in all cases the same: there is no way of distinguishing between fiction and historiography.

I shall not speak about the specific forms this rhetorical analysis takes in biblical studies. At present, the most eminent representative in this country of the combination of the rhetorical with the ideological approach in order to dissolve historiography into fiction is my friend Hayden White. He is a dominating influence in the two periodicals *History and Theory* and *New Literary History* and, remarkably enough, has found strong support in Peter Munz's recent book *The Shape of Time: A New Look at the Philosophy of History*, published in 1977. This support is particularly remarkable because Peter Munz by origin and formation represents German historicism filtered through English analytical philosophy. Needless to say, Hayden White's main work is *Metahistory* (1973). His volume *Tropics of Discourse: Essays in Cultural Criticism* collects important papers which are partly earlier and partly later than *Metahistory*. Among his most recent papers I note his discussion of Droysen's *Historik* in *History and Theory*, 1980, no. 1, and the essay on *Literary and Social Action* in *New Literary History*, Winter 1980, no. 2.

In his earlier work Hayden White emphasized the rhetorical postures of the historians. Going back to Giambattista Vico, he tried to reduce all historiography to four basic attitudes, expressed or perhaps rather symbolized by the rhetorical figures of metaphor, metonymy, synecdoche, and irony. Metaphor, according to White, prevailed in the sixteenth and seventeenth centuries, metonymy in the eighteenth century, synecdoche in the early nineteenth century, irony in the late nineteenth century, followed up by the present-day irony about irony. The book on *Metahistory,* however, proved that these chronological distinctions had little importance for White, as he showed there that all four rhetorical modes were vital and competitive in the nineteenth century when Ranke stood for synecdoche, Michelet for metaphor, Tocqueville for metonymy, and Burckhardt for irony. Nor is it clear that these figures of speech really represent different political and social attitudes, for three conservatives like Ranke, Tocqueville, and Burckhardt wrote in different rhetorical keys.

More recently White gave me the impression of attributing less importance to rhetorical categories. He has been treating literature (including historiography) as a commodity which comes into the market with the peculiarity of being able to speak about the conditions of its own production. He has also stated that in the nineteenth century historiographies of whatever kind served to defend the status quo, which may cause some surprise in regard to Karl Marx.

Now, all this may be right or wrong but is irrelevant to the fundamental fact about history—that it must be based on evidence as a *conditio sine qua non,* whereas other forms of literature are not compelled to be so based, though of course nothing prevents a novel or an epic poem from being pedantically founded upon authentic archival documents. One is almost embarrassed to have to say that any statement a historian makes must be supported by evidence which, according to ordinary criteria of human judgment, is adequate to prove the reality of the statement itself. This has three consequences. First, historians must be prepared to admit in any given case that they are unable to reach safe conclusions because the evidence is insufficient; like judges, historians must be ready to say "not proven." Second, the methods used to ascertain the value of the evidence must continually be scrutinized and perfected, because they are essential to historical research. Third, the historians themselves must be judged according to their ability to establish facts. The form of exposition they choose for their presentation of the facts is a secondary consideration. I have of course nothing to object in principle to the present multiplication in methods of rhetorical analysis of historical texts. You may have as much rhetorical analysis as you consider necessary, provided it leads to the establishment of the truth—or to the admission that truth is regretfully out of reach in a given case. But it must be clear once and for all that Judges and Acts, Herodotus and Tacitus, are historical texts to be examined

2. I have discussed the historiographic theory of H. White and P. Munz at length in *Comparative Criticism: A Year Book* 3 (1981): 259–68.

with the purpose of recovering the truth of the past. Hence the interesting conclusion that the notion of forgery has a different meaning in historiography than it has in other branches of literature or of art. A creative writer or artist perpetrates a forgery every time he intends to mislead his public about the date and authorship of his own work. But only a historian can be guilty of forging evidence or of knowingly using forged evidence in order to support his own historical discourse. One is never simple-minded enough about the condemnation of forgeries. Pious frauds are frauds, for which one must show no piety—and no pity.

I shall only add that I have purposely confined my remarks to rhetorical analysis and refrained from any generalization about form-criticism, of which rhetorical analysis is only a variety. I am very conscious that, at least in men like Hermann Gunkel, form-criticism has been a powerful instrument for historical understanding, not a sign of helplessness before realities.

To conclude, I will ask myself where a classical scholar can help biblical scholars most usefully. My answer would be that, in the field of political, social, and religious history, differences are more important than similarities—and therefore knowledge of Greco-Roman history can be useful only for differential comparison. Hence the failure in the attempt to import the Greek notion of amphictyony into the far more complex history of the Hebrew tribes.

But Jewish historiography developed at least from the fifth century B.C. in conditions shared by Greek historiography. Both had constantly to refer to the reality of the Persian Empire. More specifically, there are questions of dependence of later Jewish historiography on Greek historiography which have seldom been formulated with the necessary clarity. I shall give two examples. The idea of the succession of the universal empires is to be found first in Greek historians from Herodotus to Dionysius of Halicarnassus, passing through Ctesias, Polybius, and that strange Roman disciple of the Greeks, Aemilius Sura, probably an elder contemporary of Polybius. It is a notion dependent on the basic Greek discovery of political history. Outside Greek historical thought, the idea of a succession of empires appears first in the Book of Daniel, chapter 2, if we date this chapter, as I believe we must, about 250 B.C. I must state explicitly that no theory of universal succession of empires is to be found in the Book of Tobit, chapter 14, whatever may be its date.

The idea of the succession of reigns with different degrees of perfection is of course familiar to Iranian thought, but only with reference to the Iranian State. On the other hand, the Babylonians of the Hellenistic age registered in their chronicles (or so-called prophetic chronicles) the succession of rulers of different nationality in Babylonia. Neither in Iran nor in Babylonia have we so far discovered the notion of a succession of universal empires, as Daniel knew it. The only proper comparison is with the Greeks. Daniel has much in common with Iranian and Babylonian texts, but not about the succession of universal empires. We must therefore ask the question whether the author or, rather, authors of Daniel—beginning with the author of chapter 2—got the idea from the Greco-Macedonians who ruled the East after Alexander. Personally, I answer this question in the affirmative. Until evidence to the contrary is provided, I take it that about 250 B.C. a Jew, either in Mesopotamia or in Palestine, got hold of the Greek idea of succession of universal empires and transformed it.

I am less positive about another question of this kind. In Herodotus book 7, part 2, the military scene is dominated by the defense of the pass of the Thermopylae. The ideological scene is dominated by the conversation between Xerxes and the Spartan Demaratus, who explains to Xerxes why the Greeks, and especially the Spartans, will not yield to the Persians: they do not obey individual men, but the Law. In the Book of Judith, before Judith herself appears on the scene, our interest is concentrated, on the military side, on the Jewish Thermopylae, the mysterious place Bethulia, while the ideological background is filled by the conversation between Holophernes and Achior, who is not a Jew, but unpredictably (because he is an Ammonite) will become one. Achior explains to Holophernes that the Jews will not yield so long as they obey their Law.

When Judith appears, she presents herself to the Assyrians as the person who can reveal the secret path through the mountains, exactly as the traitor Epialtes does in Herodotus.

The structure of the second part of Herodotus 7 and of the first section of the Book of Judith is articulated on the same sequence of an ideological dialogue and of a peculiar military situation. We must ask ourselves whether the author of the original Hebrew Judith knew Herodotus directly or indirectly. Here, as I have said, I am less sure about my answer, but my inclination to give again a positive answer is reinforced by another, better-known, coincidence between the Book of Judith and a Greek historical text. It has long been recognized that the five days the thirsty Jews besieged in Bethulia give themselves before surrendering have their exact counterpart in the five days the thirsty Greeks besieged by the Persians in Lindos give themselves before surrendering: the Greek story is contained in the Chronicle of Lindos, a compilation from previous sources written in 99 B.C.

Whatever his date, the author of the original Hebrew text of Judith seems to have been acquainted with stories reported by Greek historians about the wars of the Greeks against Persia. If there was anything which conceivably could interest the Jews, it was what the Greek historians thought about oriental empires and especially about Persia. Daniel and Judith may perhaps be defined as texts which in Hellenistic times and under Greek influence tried to present an image of the Jews as subjects of the previous universal empires: this image was of course very relevant to what the Jews could do or could hope for under the Greco-Macedonian universal empire.

Notwithstanding the example provided by Eduard Meyer, classical historians have been slow in understanding what Persia meant to the other nations. But we are now beginning to make some progress. This is my favorite field for exchange of information between classical and biblical historians.

# 2

# Jews and Greeks

## I

Greek and Hebrew texts as well as archaeological evidence show that at least from the tenth century B.C. (not to mention the Micenean Age) Greeks went to Palestine as sailors, merchants, and mercenaries. It appears that King David employed Cretan mercenaries. In Samaria, Greek pottery is dated prior to the destruction of the city in 722. At Tall Sukas, south of Latakia in western Syria, a Greek settlement (including a temple) appears to have survived with a few interruptions for over a century, until the year 500 B.C. or thereabouts. In Ashkelon, Greek pottery appears at the end of the seventh century when the city probably was controlled by Egypt. When Egyptian armies penetrated Palestine in the seventh and sixth centuries B.C., they were made up in part of Greek mercenaries. It has even been suggested that a sort of fortress from the end of the seventh century (Mesad Hashavyahu), north of Ashdod, was occupied by Greek mercenaries of a king of Judah. When Jews returned from the Babylonian exile in the fifth century, trade with the Greeks was reestablished. Ashdod, the Philistine capital, has revealed a considerable quantity of Attic pottery from the end of the sixth century and the beginning of the fifth. In the fourth century, some Greeks were living in Acre and the oldest coins from Judaea are imitations of Athenian coins. Since Jews shared with the Greeks the reputation for being good mercenary soldiers, there were other opportunities for them to become acquainted with the Greeks in the armies of Babylonian, Egyptian, and Persian rulers.

Yet there is no sign that before Alexander the Great the Greeks knew the Jews by name or possessed information as to their political and religious peculiarities. Herodotus went to Tyrus, not to Jerusalem. For Herodotus as well as for both his Greek contemporaries and forebears, the Phoenicians were a recognizable entity to whom one owed, among other things, the discovery of the alphabet. The existence of Jews appears to have remained concealed under the notion of Palestine (Herodotus 2.104; 7.89). Jewish writers from the Hellenistic and Roman period did their best to discover indirect hints to Jews in classical Greek texts, but were themselves surprised at the poverty of their results.

Judging from the Bible, Jews from the time before Alexander knew somewhat more about the Greeks, but not very much. They would designate the Greeks by a specific word (which was commonly used throughout the Near East), *Yawan*, that is to say, Ionia. They also had a special word for the inhabitants of Cyprus, *Kittim* (from the city of Kition). The name does not appear to have been limited to the Phoenician part of Cyprus. In the table of nations in Genesis 10, Kittim is a son of Yawan. In the prophecy of Balaam (Numbers 24:24) the Kittim coming from the sea make war unsuccessfully with the Assyrians, a confrontation perhaps echoing the battles between Greeks and Assyrians from the end of the eighth and the seventh century B.C. In the Hellenistic period the term Kittim came to designate the Greeks in general, the Seleucids in particular, and even the Romans. Further, Ezekiel and Joel—in texts bearing different dates (sixth or fifth century B.C. or even later)—know the Greeks (Yawan) as slave merchants who buy the children of Judah and Jerusalem. There is a quick flash of a higher world when Yawan is mentioned in the last chapter of Isaiah (end of the sixth century B.C.) as a nation whose glory God will proclaim. There is no evidence that Jews knew of Sparta or Athens before Alexander the Great penetrated Palestine in 332 B.C.

## II

Under the Persians, Judaea was a semiautonomous province of the fifth satrapy ("beyond the river," that is, beyond the Euphrates looking at it from Persia), which spread out for a thousand square miles and had its center in the city temple of Jerusalem. The high priest and the council that ruled the country under the authority of the Persian governor had to deal with the powerful Jewish community they had left behind in Mesopotamia, with the hostility of the Samaritans, and with the powerful Jewish sheiks of Ammanitis, the Tobiads. The quality of Persian rule was never questioned in the Hebrew tradition. Biblical legends related to Persian rule (in the Books of Esther, Judith, and Daniel) are so unreal that they defy any explanation, but they are consistently favorable toward Media and Persia. In the Book of Daniel, King Darius deprives himself of food and sleep when he is forced to throw his Jewish servants into a lion's den. Although Jerusalem and Jericho rebelled and were punished by the Persians around 350 B.C., late classical sources (Solinus 35.4; Geronymus, *Chronica*, 2.113, ed. Schoene) appear to suggest that Jews forgot these events. Under Persian rule, Jews in fact had created the theocracy that was bound, later, to remain their ideal point of reference. Nehemiah, the leading mind (around 450 B.C.), created a new social order by abolishing debts, improving the conditions of the Levites, opening Jerusalem to Jewish immigrants, and reducing the influence of his enemies, the Tobiads. Further, by prohibiting marriage with non-Jews, Nehemiah strengthened religious uniformity (he probably dealt a blow to landed aristocracy) in a manner that proved acceptable to many but that perhaps was indirectly criticized in the Book of Ruth. In this new society, the worship of Yahweh excluded all other worships. The study of the Holy Law became a sign of social distinction outside of the priestly class, and piety was no longer confined to the ceremonies of the temple. The figure of the scribe—the predecessor of the rabbi—and the building of the synagogue became the typical traits of this association of learning, private worship, and exclusivism in postexilic Judaism. Although the Greek word "synagogue" does not have this meaning before the first century B.C. (its synonym "proseuche," however, appears in texts from the third century B.C.), the institution of the synagogue certainly dates from before the dispersion of Jews throughout the Mediterranean (the so-called Diaspora), which began at the end of the fourth century B.C. In Judaea, the new tendency of the laymen toward learning and religious instruction contributed vigorously to preserving Hebrew as the main literary and liturgical language; Aramaic was not only the primary spoken language in Judaea but was used in the Bible as well (Esdras, Daniel)

Exclusivism never prevented the unconscious or surreptitious assimilation of foreign ideas. In the Persian period, contacts between Persian magi and Jews of lowly condition took place even at a personal level, as is demonstrated by an Aramaic papyrus from Elephantine in Egypt (E. G. Kraeling, *Brooklyn Museum Aramaic Papyri*, 1953, p. 175). Hasmodeus, the bad demon of the Book of Tobias is clearly of Iranian origin, although Tobias appears to have been written in Mesopotamia in the Hellenistic period by a Jewish devotee. It is possible that the deep dualism present in the so-called Manual of Discipline, one of the Dead Sea Scrolls (second century B.C.?), owes something to Zoroastrian influence. The word "raz," used for mystery in Daniel and elsewhere, is Iranian. Although Iranian influence on Judaism and on primitive Christianity no doubt has been exaggerated by the school of

Reitzenstein, it is not negligible although difficult to date. It can be traced back to the Persian rule over Palestine, or it can be seen as concomitant to the prestige of the magi, which was widely spread in the Hellenistic world.

## III

During the 120 years following the death of Alexander, during which the Ptolemies of Egypt dominated Palestine, the Jewish society that had formed under Persian rule appears to have been able to adjust to the new situation without causing revolutionary turmoil. Ptolemaic administration interfered to a much greater degree, and was considerably more demanding than Persian rule. Tax collectors were everywhere, and tax collection provided the Tobiads with an excellent opportunity to reestablish their power in Jerusalem. Greek armies often crossed the country. Priests from the upper classes and the lower landed nobility fared much better than the Levites and the lower classes. Many Jews were deported as slaves; others became soldiers or military colonists of Hellenistic kings (especially, of course, of the Ptolemies). Voluntary emigration became attractive, and kept serious social conflicts under control. Jews became one of the most important ethnic groups in Alexandria, although they were not granted the full rights of Alexandrine citizenship. They spread throughout Egypt and formed considerable communities along the whole of the Mediterranean and the Black Sea. In Asia Minor their settlement was favored by the Seleucids. By 150 B.C. Rome must have already been inhabited by Jews. The Diaspora was above all an urban phenomenon involving a variety of professions, but in Egypt (where the Diaspora is better known to us) we also find peasants.

A Greek education became desirable in Judaea as well, both for its intrinsic merits and for its usefulness in daily contacts with the rulers. The Tobiads were the first to have Greek preceptors. Centers of Greek language developed around the tiny territory of Judaea, thanks to the colonization and assimilation of the local upper classes. The Greek gymnasium began casting its shadow over the Jewish school (yeshiva) connected with the synagogue. Outside Judaea, Jews from Mesopotamia preserved an Aramaic dialect as their primary spoken language; in other areas, Jews adopted Greek as their tongue. Because of special study and recent emigration, it was possible for some Jews to maintain some knowledge of Hebrew and Aramaic religious literature from Judaea and Mesopotamia, but the great majority of the people were incapable of saying the simplest prayers in their original language. It seems that not even Philo the philosopher was capable of understanding Hebrew. The nephew of the Ecclesiastic (Jesus Ben Sira) emphasized pointlessly the difference between the Hebrew original and the Greek translations of the holy texts (prologue to Ecclesiasticus). It is not surprising that certain rabbis believed that the Jews had deserved the exodus under Moses because they had remained loyal to their language in captivity. It is possible that occasional Greek translators of important passages from the Bible were used in the synagogue of Greek-speaking Jews, just as Aramaic translators were necessary to communicate with the uneducated in Judaea and Mesopotamia. Not later than the third century B.C., a written translation of at least part of the Bible became available in Egypt. A legend that gained favor in the second century B.C., and that was to inspire the Letter of Aristeas, ascribed the translation of the Pentateuch to seventy or seventy-two Palestinian Jews who had been charged with the task by the high priest at the invitation of King Ptolemy II. We do not know of any other Greek or Hellenistic government that became involved with the translation of the Pentateuch (while at least one case is known in Rome, the translation from foreign languages became more frequent). The legend used to explain the translation of the Septuagint (LXX) does not appear to have a factual basis; it may be compared to a later statement by Philo according to which God himself approved the translation (*Moses* 2.36). In the course of two centuries, the whole Bible became available in Greek; the last book to have been translated was possibly Esther, around 77 B.C. This was not the only translation available in Greek—we know of at least three others, by Aquilas, Simmacus, and Theodosius—but it remained the most famous. The Jews from Alexandria were pround of it, at least until it was adopted by the Christians, and they celebrated the achievement with a yearly feast, the motivations for which must have been unparalleled in the Hellenistic world. A translation on this scale also must have been unique: traditions that speak of long Zoroastrian texts translated into Greek must be taken with a grain of salt.

We can assume that the emigration from Judaea and the change of language must have favored apostasy. Of the "fall" of Dositeus, an individual from the third century B.C., known from a papyrus, mention is made in 3 Maccabees 1:3. But apostasy appears to have been rare and more than compensated for by proselytism. In the first century A.D., even a dynasty from Adiabene in northern Mesopotamia was converted to Judaism. Nor did any dramatic decline in piety take place. Pilgrimages to Jerusalem gave life to religious ties and, at least for a diligent minority, to some linguistic competence in liturgical Hebrew. Yearly pecuniary offers were sent to the Temple. The habit of living together in what became Jewish quarters favored the preservation of ancestral ways of life and beliefs. Jews adjusted to Greek customs. The "first Greek Jew" is typically a slave from the beginning of the third century B.C. who was seeking help in regaining freedom by sojourning in the oracle-temple of Anfiarao in Beothia (*Suppl. Epigr. Graecum* 5.293). Both in the Diaspora and in Judaea, Jews very often assumed or received Greek names. One of the high priests from the beginning of the second century B.C. was called Menelaus, and one of the most popular rabbis was called Antigonus (of Socho). Jews would often receive two names: one in Hebrew for dealings within the community and one in Greek for dealings with the outside world (and perhaps for domestic life). It seems Jews adopted the custom of a double name from the Phoenicians.

The gymnasium and the theater attracted Jews: Philo was a frequenter of theaters and, interestingly, we find that in Miletus, at least in Roman times, special seats were assigned to Jews in the theater. We possess ample fragments of a tragedy of Exodus by a Jew called Ezekiel handed down to us by Clement of Alexandria and Eusebius of Caesarea. The tragedy cannot be dated later than the first century B.C. as it is already mentioned by Alexander Polyhistor, a contemporary of Pompeius. It is clearly influenced by Euripides, but it ingeniously exploits the expedient of a dream in order to present the figure of Moses according to Hebrew postbiblical notions. Jews also wrote epic poems about Jewish history. The "Greek of the synagogue" must have occasionally caused people to laugh if Cleomedes, a vulgarizer of the cosmology of Posidonius (first century A.D.?), discredits the arguments of Epicurus by comparing them to what is heard within and around the synagogues. Yet, the evidence we possess of Greek written by Jews demonstrates a knowledge of Greek rhetoric, not to mention Greek syntax.

## IV

In Judaea and elsewhere, Greek culture had two aspects: on the one hand, it defied different ways of life; on the other, it encouraged a dialogue and mutual understanding with other traditions. The most obvious limit to Greek curiosity was linguistic: Greeks were rarely willing to make the effort to learn a foreign language. They also maintained this attitude vis-à-vis the Romans when they switched from being the conquerors to a conquered people. There is no indication that a Greek ever managed to have a command of Hebrew or of any other Oriental language in order to study the sacred books of the Orient in the original. Even when books were available in translation, as is the case with the Bible, they did not circulate outside the circle of believers. Most of the indirect hints to biblical passages that modern scholars believe they recognize in Hellenistic authors are obviously imaginary: all that remains is a probable allusion to Deuteronomy 29:1 in Hecataeus of Abdera (which implies a knowledge of Jews more than of the biblical text) and a rather uncertain hint to the creation story in Genesis in the treatise on the nature of the world attributed to the Pythagorean Ocellus Lucanus (second or first century B.C.). The first sure quotation of a biblical passage, the reference to Genesis 1 contained in *On the Sublime* ascribed to Cassius Longinus, is not prior to the first century A.D. The Talmud vaguely mentions that the cynic Enomaus of Gadara, a friend of Rabbi Meir (beginning of the second century), knew the Bible. This list continues with the allusions we also find in Galen and in the Neoplatonic Numenius of Apamea (end of the second century), but these belong to the very different world of religious controversy that accompanied the spread of Christianity. The quotation from *On the Sublime* is a sure exception, given that it attaches literary value to the Bible, that is, to something non-Greek. But the author of *On the Sublime* reveals that he is very well acquainted with the ideas of the rhetorician Caecilius of Calactes (beginning of the first century A.D.), who was a Jew. It is therefore possible that Caecilius provided the quotation. Before more people began to read the Old Testament, thanks to the spread of Christianity, the Bible remained essentially a Jewish book.

It would be interesting to know whether anyone became a proselyte of Judaism simply because of having read the Bible. Although Juvenal presupposes the knowledge of the Pentateuch when he portrays a Jewish proselyte, we are not sure of what a proselyte was required to know. We have very little information concerning the instruction of proselytes, not to speak of those "sympathizers" who did not intend to embrace Judaism completely and were known as the "God fearing" (Lat., *metuentes*): the information about the initiation of Christian catachumeni to the Bible is also scarce. The general impression one receives from our documentation is that whatever the level of the understanding that Gentiles have of the Jews, they did not acquire such knowledge from reading the Bible. Proselytism was initially due to the attraction exerted by a certain way of life, by a specific set of ceremonies and religious taboos, and, among the most cultivated people, by a specific notion of God and creation as is demonstrated by the Jews' complete refusal of pagan cults. Proselytes could become sufficiently competent in the study of the Bible to the point of translating it into Greek, as Aquilas did in the time of Hadrian. Proselytes or the sons of proselytes could, in fact, become respectable rabbis, as is the case with

Rabbi Meir, to whom the legend attributes a descendency from the emperor Nero (Babylonian Talmud, *Gittin* 56a). This reveals the deep sense of involvement to which conversion to Judaism, once perfected, could lead. Greek writers who speak of Jews and Judaism draw their knowledge from personal observations and conjectures, or from what they have heard. The most we can expect from these writers is a presentation of Judaism that conforms to the categories of Greek ethnography. Plato and his followers had prepared the Greeks to appreciate Oriental wisdom. When Jews were discovered at the end of the fourth century B.C., they appeared, of course, as a new variety of Brahmins or magi. Theophrastus, a pupil of Aristotle, considered them the first nation to have abolished human sacrifice (it is possible that he got indirect news of the story of Isaac)—a people who contemplates the stars, invokes them in their prayers, and fasts frequently. Another Peripatetic philosopher, Clearcus of Soli, in a dialogue on *Sleep*, represents his master Aristotle as speaking of a meeting (probably fictitious) with a Jew "who was Greek not only for his language but in his soul as well." This Jew no doubt had something very interesting to say about sleep, about the behavior of the human soul during sleep, but the indirect quotation ends too soon and does not satisfy our curiosity. According to Clearcus, Aristotle considered the Jews the descendants of the Indian philosophers called Kalanoi. The comparison between Jews and Indian philosophers is also mentioned by Megasthenes, the great authority in the field of Indian things (beginning of the third century B.C.). The Jews' reputation as philosophers is also presupposed by Hermippus (end of the third century B.C.) when he claims that Pythagoras had been a disciple of Jewish thinkers. Posidonius (around 60 B.C.) is perhaps the last to emphasize the philosophical importance of the teaching of Moses as a religious and political leader. In this period, the interpretation had lost the function it supposedly had when it first was introduced two and a half centuries earlier; it was now being used to illustrate a contrast with the current situation.

In the climate of idealization at the end of the fourth century B.C., Hecataeus of Abdera had to elaborate a more complex picture when he decided to introduce Jews in his description of Egyptian history and society. Jews were once again a force to be reckoned with under Ptolemy I in Egypt. Their national legend focused on Joseph's ascent to power in Egypt and on the ensuing exodus of the descendants of Jacob from the country. We ignore whether Egyptians before Hecataeus had already reacted to these traditions; we also ignore whether it was their idea to associate the exodus with the banishing of the Hyksos. Hecataeus knows of the exodus, and he presents it as the banishment of foreigners from Egypt. He displays sympathy for the foreigners, among whom he includes Danaos and Cadmus: the Jews led by Moses settled in Palestine while Danaos and Cadmus went on and settled in Greece. By founding the Temple of Jerusalem, promulgating laws, dividing up the land in equal parts and making it inalienable, Moses belonged to the great tradition of philosopher-leaders. The experience of the exodus provided a justification for the harsh and misanthropic aspects of his legislation. Hecataeus himself admitted that his picture of Judaea no longer corresponded to contemporary reality. What remained vital was the projection into the past of the friction that the settlement of Jews in Alexandria and in other areas under the aegis of Macedonian conquerors had created between Jews and Egyptians.

Flavius Josephus devotes large sections of his *Against Apion* to uncovering the hostile version of Exodus that the Egyptian priest Manetho supposedly has written in his history of Egypt in Greek from around 270 B.C. In Manetho's story, the identification of Jews with the Hyksos is rendered more unpleasant by a further identification of Jews with lepers. No other ancient source ascribes such things to Manetho, and we find various internal difficulties in Josephus's account. We should ask ourselves whether Josephus made use of an interpolated text by Manetho, just as Manetho and other Jewish apologists made use of an interpolated text by Hecataeus of Abdera. It is certain, however, that there existed hostile versions of the Exodus from Egyptian sources. As long as Jews got along sufficiently with the Greek population of Alexandria and enjoyed the support of the Ptolemies, Egyptian hostility did not matter very much. The trouble for Egyptian Jews came from finding themselves too involved in the factions that were tearing apart the Macedonian monarchy in Egypt in the second and first century B.C.

## V

The documentation we possess appears to indicate that, until at least 50 A.D., the Jews of Egypt maintained prestige, acquired prosperity, and developed peculiar intellectual features. In the third century B.C., a Jewish historian, Demetrius, prepared for Greek readers one of those accounts which it was believed that non-Greeks should give the Greeks concerning their past. Later, in the second century (?) B.C., Artapanus wrote a biography of Moses where Moses appears as the teacher of Orpheus and legislator of the Egyptians before becoming the leader of the exodus. Moses supposedly introduced the cult of animals to the advantage of the Egyptians. In the rivalrly between the king of Egypt and Moses, Moses prevailed because he enjoyed the favor of the Egyptian and Ethiopian masses. Also in the second century B.C., the Letter of Aristeas made known not only the legend that Ptolemy Philadelphus had organized the translation of the Septuagint but also portrayed the king in friendly disputes with the Jewish wise men. If the "novel" of *Joseph and Aseneth* (a text difficult to date) belongs to this period, it paradigmaticaly idealizes the love between the biblical parvenu Joseph and Aseneth, the daughter of the priest of Heliopolis, who becomes a Jewish proselyte. Around 160 B.C. Aristobulus applied the allegorical method of the Greeks to the interpretation of the Bible and dedicated an explanation of the Pentateuch to Ptolemy VI (2 Maccabees thus presents Aristobulus as the teacher of Ptolemy VI). Aristobulus believed that Pythagoras, Plato, and other "ancient" poets—such as Homer, Hesiod, Orpheus, and Aratus—had acquired knowledge from the Pentateuch, in a pre-Alexandrine version of course. The existence of a version of these texts that precedes the Septuagint is implied also by the Letter of Aristeas, where we find that the historian Theopompus (fourth century B.C.) became insane when he tried to use it. From the fragments we possess of Aristobulus, we learn that forged or modified verses by Greek poets circulated to show that their authors had a knowledge of Judaism. Thus, it is possible that other examples of similarly forged verses were produced in Egypt (for example, a moral poem by Phocylides).

Uncertainties regarding the origin and the chronology of Hellenistic Hebrew texts prevent us from tracing the development of the thought that led to the philosophy of Philo in the first half of the first century A.D. Philo himself vaguely acknowledges his predecessors. There supposedly were innumerable opportunities in the synagogues and in Jewish schools in Alexandria for reinterpreting Judaism in terms of Greek philosophy. An obvious candidate as a predecessor of Philo is the unknown author of the Wisdom of Solomon, which addresses the kings of the earth and invites them to heed Wisdom, the intermediary between God and man. But the book is not necessarily the product of a single author, and the final line, where the author attacks the Egyptians, might be too much for an Egyptian Jew. We can say that, in general, there is no reason to consider those philosophical observations that culminate with Philo as the expression of Egyptian Jews alone.

# VI

Jerusalem, not Alexandria, was the city where the future of Judaism was at stake.

Until just before the persecution by Antiochus IV (170 B.C.) Hellenism appears to have created many fewer problems in Judaea than among the Jews of Egypt. Yet if we confine ourselves to the interpretation of the two texts that probably belong to the period of the peaceful penetration of Greek culture in Judaea—Ecclesiastes or *Kohelet* (end of the third century B.C.) and Ecclesiasticus by Jesus Ben Sira (beginning of the second century B.C., the first Hebrew text to possess a sure author)—we discover very strong reactions to Hellenism, for the Greeks are never mentioned. Ecclesiastes has no doubts concerning the almightiness of God, who is the God of the Fathers. However, the text shows that it has lost the sense of history, or rather the sense of a direction of the events that characterizes all other biblical texts, including Job. It wanders in a labyrinth of reflections and interpretations to which it is far too easy to apply the label of Epicureanism or skepticism. If the obscure term "Kohelet" means "speaker, man who speaks in an assembly," it can be taken as a hint about those speakers who walked the streets of the Hellenistic world. The man who wrote the word *Kohelet*, and who appears to have known him personally, describes him as a wise man "who taught wisdom to the people, pondering, exploring, and formulating many maxims" (12:9) But unlike a Greek philosopher, Kohelet did not teach the ways to a better and different life, because man "is incapable of discovering the meaning of the work of God, which takes place under the sun."

Ben Sira, who had meditated on Ecclesiastes, reacted to all the temptations of the alien world by joining the school of the wise men of the Jewish tradition from Enoch to the high priest Simon, who had died shortly before. It is possible that Ben Sira's praise of the Fathers was influenced formally by Hellenistic biography; it certainly reminds us of the Roman elogies and book 6 of the *Aeneid*, but Ben Sira does not know these texts. The intention of this elogy is a clear rejection of Hellenic wisdom. The central figure is Aaron, the high priest; his advice is directed at a harmonious cooperation between the temple and the synagogue. A few years after Ben Sira had written his work, King Antiochus IV, with the help of higher-ranking Jewish priests, including the Tobiads, and a considerable part of the Jewish upper classes from Jerusalem, transformed the city temple into a Greek polis with naked youth in the gymnasium as its prominent feature. Ben Sira's admonitions had not been in vain. Through a series of measures the cult of Yahweh was Hellenized and transformed into that of Zeus Olympus; the Sabbath and circumcision were prohibited, and the books of the Torah were burned.

The change from Ptolemaic rule to Seleucidic rule was a major event for the crisis in Judaea. The Ptolemis never pursued Hellenization systematically; in fact, they were happy to employ Jews in the administration of Egypt. The Seleucids, on the other hand, always relied (rather unsuccessfully) on urban settlements of a Greek type, and on the loyalty of Greeks to hold together their enormous multinational state. After a disastrous peace with the Romans in 188 B.C., the Seleucids became even more fearful of a Greek betrayal and even more dependent on the wealth derived from the sanctuaries. But the choice between a traditional Judaism (as had been established by Nehemiah) and Hellenization represented a real dilemma for many Jews, and not only in Judaea. We know very little of the settlement process of Jews in Asia Minor and in Europe. We learn from the evidence provided by Flavius Josephus that Jews had difficulties with local authorities and with public opinion in general due to their nonconformism. Hellenizing Jews from the Diaspora and Hellenizing Jews from Judaea must have encouraged each other. We possess an inscription from Iasos in Asia Minor that tells us that Niketas, the son of Jason from Jerusalem, donated a sum of one hundred drachmas for the feast of the god Dionysus (*Corpus Inscr. Jud.* 749), who was often identified with Yahweh by the pagans.

In Judaea Hellenization was clearly an attitude of the upper classes while social conflicts and rivalries were raging between groups: vague hints from Ecclesiastes and Ecclesiasticus become clear statements in later sources, such as the Book of Enoch 94–105 (end of the second century?). The final victory of the Maccabean brothers against what the contemporary Daniel defines as the abomination of desolation resulted in a social revolution in which priests from the lower ranks replaced higher-ranking priests, a part of the aristocracy had to flee to Egypt or to other countries, and Syrian inhabitants of Palestine were attacked without mercy with the obvious consequences deriving from the transfer of wealth and territory.

The aggressive behavior toward Transjordan, Idumea, Galilee, and the Greek cities of the coast, which was feeding a civil war, had to stop. When political independence was achieved by degrees with the help of the Romans, it became necessary to consider the reactions of Rome. The simple formation of new political ties implied a certain degree of acceptance of Greek ways of life. Preexisting legends on the common origin of Jews and Spartans were exploited. The Eupolemos who went to Rome to negotiate an alliance in the name of Judas Maccabean is probably the author of a Greek book on the kings of Judah, where Moses is portrayed as the inventor of the alphabet and Solomon pursues the expansionistic policy of the Hasmoneans. Even the oldest account of the Maccabean revolution, written in five books by Jason of

Cyrene (around 160 B.C.) and summarized in the work we possess under the name 2 Maccabees (around 124 B.C.?), is evidence of Hellenization: the story is told in Greek in the style of popular pathetic historiography. The penetration of Greek words, customs, and intellectual modes in Judaea during the rule of the Hasmoneans and the following Kingdom of Herod has no limits. Contradictory statements in Talmudic literature as to the value and legitimacy of the knowledge of Greek are based on the reality of the power and influence of Greek culture in Palestine. Rabbis adopted hermeneutic rules drawn from the Greek logical tradition and also borrowed Greek legal terminology. Greek was used for inscriptions on ritual objects in the temple, and a synagogue in Caesarea used Greek in its liturgy. A famous Talmudic passage (*Babilonese Sotah* 49b) mentions five hundred students of Greek wisdom and five hundred students of Hebrew wisdom in the school of Gamaliel II (around 100 A.D.), a symbolic indication of the penetration of Greek culture in rabbinic schools. Yet the results of the Maccabean revolt did not run counter to the anti-Hellenic premises of the Maccabean movement. In the two centuries from 150 B.C. to 50 A.D., Jewish society is pervaded by two forces that, combined or in contrast with each other, draw a line between Judaism and Hellenism.

The first of these forces is apocalyptic. Prophecy in the common biblical sense no longer existed: there appeared no prophet to admonish and to guide the Jews during and after the Maccabean revolt. The absence of prophecy in fact may have contributed to the popularity of surrogates of an equivocal nature such as the Sibylline Oracles. Prophecy was dead because new expectations, considerably more dramatic and radical, extended to the territory of the Beyond, a territory that had not existed for biblical prophets. It is significant that apocalyptic writers claimed their inspiration from men of the past, such as Adam or Daniel. There is obviously no conformity of vision of the future between Daniel, Enoch (a composite work), the Book of Jubilees and the Testaments of the Twelve Patriarchs, on the one hand, and the various texts known as the Dead Sea Scrolls on the other. But they all more or less agree in dividing the history between "this world," where Belial reigns, and "the world to come," belonging to the sun of justice. For apocalyptic writers, the notion of the Messiah was associated with the end of time, when the dead will arise to receive their final compensation. In this apocalyptic literature, the end of time is often identified with a return to the time of creation. The great contribution the discovery of the Dead Sea Scrolls has made to our knowledge of apocalyptics consists in having revealed to us the existence of one of the centers of dissemination of these beliefs: a monastic community with a strong hostility for the ruling class in Jerusalem, with a detailed code of daily conduct and a dualistic vision of things. It matters little that this community is that of the Essenes, which we know from Flavius Josephus and from other sources.

The second force that separated Hellenism from Judaism was Pharisaism, a movement closer to the main current of Jewish life after Esdras and Nehemiah. First the Hasidim (the pious men)—and later their successors, the Pharisees—developed in opposition to the aristocracy (the Sadducees) that again had formed around the Temple once the Maccabean revolution began to die out. Unlike the Sadducees, the Pharisees believed in the immortality of the soul and in the resurrection of the dead; they were all but insensitive to apocalyptic expectations. The Pharisees respected *ante litteram* Hillel's rule (late first century B.C.) of not separating from the community. Typically enough, when they succeeded in controlling Jewish religious life (starting after the destruction of the second Temple) they excluded all apocalyptic books, except Daniel, from the canon of the sacred Scriptures. Their main intention was to use the synagogue and the school to regulate the santification of daily life through a series of precepts. The Pharisees insisted on the importance of oral tradition, of learning and work; they differed from the Sadducees who controlled the Temple, upheld the literal interpretation of written Law, and were reluctant to accept the proliferation of commandments or *mitzvoth*.[1] The Pharisees looked with contempt at the "people of the earth," that is, at those Jews who were not concerned with learning, ritual purity, and the scrupulous payment of sacred tithes. The Pharisees had faith in God and felt that God trusted them directly with no intermediary outside the Law (Torah). They were ready to live and to die for the Law. For the first time in history, martyrdom became an ideal, and the ideal was tested as such. Although there is no exclusive connection between Pharisees and "wise men"—that is to say, those teachers and scholars who acquired authority individually or as schools from the end of the second century B.C. to the end of the second century A.D. and beyond—wise men were often Pharisees, and their ethos slowly became identified with the Pharisaic ethos.

The wise men rarely underestimated the power and force of attraction of Greek civilization. In general, they did not behave too strictly with those who yielded to it. The great Rabbi Elisha ben Avuyah, who

1. *Mitzvah* (pl. *Mitzvoth*) is the comandment, the religious obligation. Traditionally, there are 613 mitzvoth divided into 248 positive comandments and 365 prohibitions. Mitzvoth were also grouped into two main categories: the *mitzvoth de-oraita*, or biblical comandments, and the *mitzvoth de-rabanan*, or rabbinic comandments.

came under the influence of Greek thought at the beginning of the second century A.D., is looked upon with sadness rather than contempt by the Talmudic tradition. It is stated explicitly that his pupil Rabbi Meir never broke his friendship with him. But what the wise men thought about God, about the Law, about the relations between Jews, and about the relations between Jews and Gentiles represented a rejection of Greek culture altogether. The choice was represented by the Torah, given that "also a Gentile, if he practices the Law, is equal to the High Priest" (*Sifra* 86B).

Apocalyptic seers or mild rabbis (two groups, as we shall continue to repeat, that were not easily separable) represented a different world from that of their fellow Gentiles. There was no serious economic conflict between Jews and Gentiles. Jews were employed in too many different professions to cause trouble in any one of them in particular. We possess only one papyrus with a specific complaint regarding Jewish usury (*Corpus Papyr. Judaic.* 152) from the first century A.D. The dividing line was exactly between Jews and Gentiles. Given Greek apathy in supplying evidence about foreign tongues and traditions, it is perhaps not entirely surprising that ever greater voices expressing contempt for the Jewish cult frequently were being raised. Greek intellectuals' initial sympathy for Jews at the end of the fourth century B.C. was certainly being replaced by underground currents of hostility or at least of irony. Manasseh (second century B.C.) is the first author known to us who speaks of the cult of the Donkey in connection with the Temple of Jerusalem. Around the same period we find the first mention of ritual sacrifices of foreigners. (These two innuendos were, of course, later extended to the Christians.) The accusation, against Jews, of ritual homicide appears to have received little credit, but the curious idea that the Jewish God was iconographically comparable to the figure of Tifone-Seth enjoyed some credibility in the eyes of an admirer of Moses such as Posidonius, and is found repeated in Tacitus.

## VII

We have little news regarding Babylonian Jews, who had come under Parthian rule in the two centuries before and after Christ. From the little that we know, we can presume that, for the most part, they followed the religious guide of the Jews of Palestine and increasingly became imbued with Pharisaic principles. What matters to us here is their submission to the Greek Diaspora, particularly to the Diaspora of Egypt.

We know that Palestinian leaders were concerned with obtaining the approval and the following of the Jews of Egypt. For a long period of time they had needed the support, or at least the neutrality, of the Ptolemies in their struggle against the Seleucids. When one of the members of the Oniad family, the previous high priests, founded a Jewish temple in Leontopolis in Egypt, and turned it into a center for the recruitment of Jewish mercenaries at the service of Egypt, it became absolutely necessary for the men in Jerusalem to put an end to the competition of Leontopolis without offending the Ptolemies. They were rather successful in doing so. The introductory letters of 2 Maccabees indicate the repeated attempts of the authorities of Jerusalem to persuade the Jews of Egypt to join the Jews of Palestine for the celebration of the feast in memory of the reconsecration of the temple of Jerusalem after the profanation by Antiochus IV (Hanukkah). Similar propaganda for new feasts was a common feature of the Hellenistic world in general. Palestinian wise men accepted Greek as *one* of the languages into which the Bible could be translated; at least one wise man was convinced that it was, indeed, the only language (Mishnah, *Megillah* 1.8).[2] Around 132 B.C. a Palestinian Jew who had moved to Egypt translated Ecclesiasticus into Greek, thus making it possible for the conservative ideas from Jerusalem to become known in the Diaspora. Translations from Hebrew (or from Aramaic) into Greek were common: a further example is the translation of 1 Maccabees, a very pious account of the Maccabean revolt written in biblical style around the end of the second century B.C.

Egyptian Jews appear to have been eager to follow the Palestinian guide. The Letter of Aristeas stresses Jerusalem's approval of the Septuagint: the translators themselves had been chosen by the high priest of Jerusalem. The book 3 Maccabees (first century B.C.?) is an imitation of 2 Maccabees; it tends to show that the Jews of Egypt, like the Jews of Palestine, were persecuted under Ptolemy IV Philopator. There appears to be no historical basis for this legend, which must be seen as a document of solidarity between the Jews of Egypt and the Jews of Palestine. The third book of the Sibylline Oracles, a Hebrew-Egyptian composite work that recounts the Maccabean revolt all the way to the time of Augustus, favors the Jews of Palestine in their struggle first against the Seleucids and later against the Romans. No element from

---

2. The Mishnah represents the codification of the Jewish tradition and of the oral Law in all its aspects. The Mishnah, divided into six sections, was written around the beginning of the third century A.D. by Judah ha-Nasi.—Ed.

this book can be interpreted in favor of the schismatic temple of Leon-topolis. To the extent that it spoke in favor of Jews, the sibyl was cer-tainly not a paladin of Alexandrine Judaism.

## VIII

In fact, it has become very difficult to define the notion of Alexandrine ("Hellenistic") Judaism, which scholars from the nineteenth century opposed to Palestinian (normative) Judaism, and its consequences for the development of Christianity.

Given the loose and fluid nature of the organization of the Jewish Diaspora, it is necessary to acknowledge a wide range of Jewish attitudes—personal, class, local—vis-à-vis the surrounding world, which was not at all homogeneous. We learn from Alexandria that two rival Jewish factions sent two different legations to Rome (*Corpus Papyr. Judaic.* 153). Different types of documentation cannot but recount dif-ferent stories. It is hard to say whether the epitaphs in the cemetery of Leontopolis testify to a deeper process of Hellenization than the docu-ments of Jewish manumission for which Panticapaeum in Crimea is famous. Who can say to what extent the Greek sermon on martyrdom, entitled 4 Maccabees (first century A.D.), is typical (typical of what?). Although many Jews indulged in magic activities and enjoyed reputa-tions as sorcerers among the Gentiles, it would be absurd to suggest that they were not Orthodox Jews. E. R. Goodenough has attempted to bring to this notion of Alexandrine Judaism the massive support of ar-chaeological documentation, which he collected so admirably in his twelve-volume *Jewish Symbols in the Greco-Roman Period*. The most Goodenough was able to reveal was that Jews did not systematically avoid objects with pagan symbols; they lived, in fact, in a pagan world.

Philo of Alexandria (first century A.D.) presents a different prob-lem, one that does not lend itself to generalizations. He accepted the Law, the Torah, in the form in which he knew it and recommended obedience to it. Although he personally made wide use of allegorical interpretation, Philo did not approve of Jews who made a pretext of the symbolism of the Law in order to avoid the literal observance of the Law (*Migrat. Abrah.* 88–93). But Philo did not make considerable contri-butions to Jewish Law: he read the Pentateuch as a navigation chart in his voyage to God; he really loved God and felt that every good thing was a gift from heaven. For Philo, knowledge was based on revelation, and he experienced revelation personally through the ascent of his soul toward God, through the mediation of the Word, the Logos (*Somn.* 1.65ff.). He readily describes the object of his contemplation in the language of Greek philosophers he admired (Plato, the Stoics), and this correspondence reassured him. His mysticism contained but few elements that could recommend him to those Jews who read the Bible to learn about God's commandments or to pray to God. It is interesting to note that Philo was not too concerned with Psalms and the Prophets. Nor was there much in Philo to make him appealing to the Gentiles. Those Gentiles who were seeking a philosophy could draw from one closer to their own tradition; those who were seeking salvation would not find it in Philo's message. Philo's presentation of the facts, a commentary on biblical texts, was likely to prove incomprehensible to readers not acquainted with the Bible. Although the anti-Christian Celsus (end of the second century A.D.) read Philo, he did so to polemicize against the Christians. Thus Philo, whose writings were directed at Greeks and Jews (but most probably Jews), was not of great interest to either of these peoples. He found his readers mostly among Christians, especially the author of the Epistle to the Jews. Hellenizing Christians acknowledged him as their predecessor in the attempt to bring Greek philosophy to the support of Revelation. Clement of Alexandria and Origen studied Philo attentively. In the fourth century, Eusebius (*Hist. Eccls.* 2.17.1) knew the legend according to which Philo had met with St. Peter in Rome and had become converted. Jews forgot Philo even before they forgot Greek. They later rediscovered Philo in a sixteenth-century Latin translation by the Italian Jew Azariah de' Rossi, but, even so, he never accounted for much in Jewish thought.

Thus we have reached the conclusion that among the Greek-speaking Jews, only a very few can be defined as Hellenizing Jews. One of these was probably Jason of Cyrene, the source of 2 Maccabees; another, as we might expect, was Flavius Josephus, a historian (first century A.D.).

Flavius Josephus was a Palestinian Jew of priestly descent who began writing history in Aramaic, but never succeeded in achieving sufficient command of this language so that he could manage independently. He drew from Jewish sources, both biblical and extrabiblical, and brought to his work a considerable knowledge of the Jewish oral tradition. But given his intention to write a history of the Jews for the pagans (the Romans), Josephus was compelled to resort to Greek models of historiography. Further, he chose to write his autobiography and to refute the theories of certain pagan authors regarding Jews. This, too, implied that he had adopted Greek models. Like Philo, Josephus was read by Christians, but unlike Philo he enjoyed a certain reputation among the pagans (Porphyry in the third century, Vegetius probably around 400 A.D.). Josephus was also read indirectly by Jews in the Middle Ages: a part of his work was utilized for a compilation (the so-called Josippon) by an anonymous southern Italian Jew in the tenth century.

Yet the destiny of philosophy and of Greek historiography among Jews was to a large extent similar. With the development of the interpretation of the Torah as a basis for private life and for the community—and as a source of joy and sanctity—neither philosophy nor historiography as conceived by the Greeks could appeal to the Jews. In the case of historiography, other elements made it superflous even in its biblical form, preserved (although with modifications) in 1 Maccabees. A comparison with other cultures shows that there is no strong stimulus to the writing of history when one's national, religious center is destroyed, and this is precisely what happened to the Jews in 70 A.D. More specifically, the triumph of Pharisaism led to the virtual disappearance of the sense of providential direction—from the most remote past to the present and beyond—so typical of biblical history. The Pharisees (unlike Kohelet) replaced history with an exclusive concentration on the yearly repetition of events taken from the past, an attitude that had always been typical of Hebrew worship. Jews remained in touch with selected episodes of their past through Passover, Simchat Torah, the four fast days connected with the first destruction of the Temple, Hanukkah, and so on. But historical continuity was lost. In difficult times, the celebration of feasts replaced the enigmatic and often tragic view of historians and biblical prophets with an optimistic and contemplative vision. It is sufficient to note that Greek philosophy again became a concern for Jews through their connection with Arabs in the tenth century; Greek historiography would have to wait until the nineteenth century.

# 3

## Daniel and the Greek Theory
## of Imperial Succession

### I

The notion of a succession of empires is as old as Herodotus. Herodotus was aware that the Persians had succeeded the Medes in the imperial rule (1.95, 130) and, in his history, he promises to devote a special treatise to the Assyrians (1.184) (this treatise, however, never appears in his work). A few decades later, Assyria, Media, and Persia reappear as successive empires in the work of Ctesias. We are certain, then, that these three empires epitomize all that a historian has to say on the subject of a history of Asia. Given that first in Herodotus, and later in Ctesias, Egypt necessarily appears as a province of the Persian Empire, it should not come as a surprise if, at least in its conclusive phase, Egyptian history is absorbed within the great history of the great empires of Asia. For both Herodotus and Ctesias, only the Greeks truly exist outside of Asia. Both writers are, of course, Greek, and because they come from territories that have experienced or continue to experience Persian rule, they are also aware that the exclusion of the Greeks from the Asian empires is problematic, stemming from elements (such as differences in constitution and habits, and an ensuing will for independence) that are ultimately volatile. Beyond the empires of Asia, and outside of Greece, other peoples and other states exist, but such peoples and states are not important enough to warrant the historian's political consideration. In other words, what lies at the heart of the historic investigation of both Herodotus and Ctesias is the issue of imperial succession, and of the problematic exclusion of the Greeks from that succession. This accounts for the special nature of their historic inquiry, which unfolds, for the most part, as a series of military and institutional events. It is difficult to say how frequent similar descriptions of human events were in the new historiography of the fourth and fifth centuries. Historians such as Thucydides, Xenophon, and Theopompus evidently devoted little or not attention to imperial successions. But Polybius, who was very attentive to imperial successions, and for whom this study ultimately coincided with that of universal history, considered Ephorus a predecessor worthy of mention (5.33.2). Thus, in one form or another, it is likely that Ephorus was more concerned with the issue of imperial successions than existing fragments lead us to believe. It is also Polybius who tells us that, toward the end of the sixth century, Demetrius of Phalerum had meditated on the fall of the Persian Empire and on the subsequent advent of the Empire of Alexander and the Diadochi (29.21). As might be expected, his contemporaries soon became aware not only of the existence of the new empire, the fourth in the series, but of the fact that Greece was no longer a complete outsider. Indeed Greece had joined imperial history.

Hence it is certain that in the Hellenistic period the notion of imperial succession represented a pattern of general history known to the Greek historiographic tradition, and was even typical of Greek historiographic thought. The Greeks had arrived at this notion because of their specific interest for political and military phenomena. A strange gloss in the work of Velleius Paterculus informs us that a Roman, Aemilius Suras, in a work entitled *De annis populi romani*, added the Roman Empire to those of Assyria, Media, and Macedonia (1.6.6). A close analysis of the passage suggests that the document is probably dated earlier than 168 A.D., that is, earlier than Polybius. As a historian, not only is Polybius very much aware of writing within the context of imperial successions; he also entertains the very interesting point of view that what makes it possible for him, Polybius, to write a truly universal history is the very fact that the Roman Empire is much more universal that preceding empires. For Polybius, preceding universal histories are defective not so much because of the incompetence of their authors, but because they are premature. Like Hegel, Polybius believes he was born at the right time. But we must add that Assyria and Media are little more than names to him, and that Persia, too, is distant (38.22). On the other hand, the Empire of Sparta (not Athens) is seen as the real predecessor of the Empire of Alexander.

It is likely that for two centuries after Polybius, historians, especially in Rome, were all somewhat aware of the notion of imperial succession. In our opinion, the idea is formulated with special clarity in the work of one of the universal historians of the age of Caesar, Trogus Pompeius (handed down in the summary of Justin, dating probably from around the second century A.D.). But the idea is developed by

Diodorus, who typically follows Ctesias in this regard, and we can assume that it was mentioned in the work of Nicholas of Damascus. It also comes up in the writings of Dionysius of Halicarnassus (1.2; 2.4). Thus, we can be certain that the theory of imperial succession was a constant in Greek political and historical thought.

Here we come to a main feature of the Book of Daniel. The author of this book is the only non-Greek and non-Roman writer who formulates the imperial succession theory as a pattern of history, albeit a history that does not end in a conventional fashion, the way a reader of Greek or Latin histories was in the habit of expecting. The Book of Daniel, as we have it, was put together toward the end of 164 or in the early months of 163 B.C. The author had not yet learned of the death of Antiochus IV, which, according to the well-known cuneiform text (published in *Iraq* 16 [1954]: 212), took place around November 164. On the other hand, he is aware of the restoration of the cult in Jerusalem (8.14), which occurred at approximately the same time.[1]

While this is the date that has been established for the text, it has often been remarked that the material itself is heterogenous and may not all necessarily date from the same period. Leaving aside the complications inherent in the bilingual nature of the text (chapters 2–7 are written in Aramaic while chapters 8–12 are written in Hebrew), it is obvious that the first six chapters are not concerned with the rebellion of the Jews against Antiochus Epiphanes, for they do not even hint at the event. The final chapters, on the other hand, are rooted in this struggle—in the episode of the profanation and subsequent reconsecration of the sanctuary of Jerusalem. Among the early chapters, one chapter is of special concern to us here: chapter 2.

This is the chapter in which Daniel interprets Nebuchadnezzar's dream of the statue made up of different metals (and where iron is mixed with clay). The interpretation is that the four metals represent four kingdoms. Following both independent and contextual analysis, more sensible readers of antiquity were already persuaded that the dream involved not four kingdoms within one dynasty but four empires—Babylon was certainly the first (indeed this was the kingdom over which Nebuchadnezzar reigned) while the last was certainly the Empire of Macedonia, created by Alexander the Great (iron) and his successors (iron and clay). The two intermediate kingdoms are, allegedly, those of Media and Persia. The text contains a hint, which appears to be certain, to the marriage, disrupted by warfare, between the

1. A recent introduction to the problems of the Apocalypse as a literary genre is in *Semeia* 14 (1979).

Seleucid King Antiochus II and Berenice, daughter of Ptolemy II, around 250 A.D. The hint is made as if to a conclusive event, a fact otherwise inexplicable in a text written much later that date. Therefore, it is wise to date this text around 245 B.C.[2] Although this date does not apply equally to the dates of the remaining chapters (1, 3–6) in the first part, it does suggest that they are part of a group of texts written before 200 B.C. in connection with events concerned more with the religious integrity and the political thought of Jews at the service of Hellenistic (or Parthian) sovereigns than with the purity of the cult in Jerusalem. Chapter 2 is distinguished from this group of chapters because of its apocalyptic and universalistic inspiration: history is seen here as a succession of empires, and the end of history as a direct intervention of the God of Israel (stone), who replaces the kingdoms of men with the Kingdom of God.

The theory of the succession of the empires (four) is, as we know now, a Greek notion. It is found in chapter 2, where the events being described are Hellenistic, and because it dates from the middle of the third century B.C., the obvious inference is that the author has learned this theory from the Greeks. Around 200 B.C. there were Jewish historians, such as Demetrius (whom Flavius Josephus stupidly mistook for Demetrius of Phalerum), who were writing in Greek. It should not come as a surprise that the notion of the four empires, not a very farfetched notion after all, should have been received by the author of the Book of Daniel and adopted as a starting point for his apocalyptic vision. The interest of this chapter lies precisely in the fact that the writer adopts the Greek notion of imperial successions and reacts to it not only by effecting partial corrections here and there (Babylonia in place of Assyria), but also by positing a radical opposition between the history of the empires of men and the advent of the Kingdom of God.

## II

Against this simple solution, it is obviously possible, indeed legitimate, to bring into question a text such as the "dynastic prophecy," recently published by A. K. Grayson (*Babylonian Historical-Literary Texts*, 1975, pp. 24–37), where, in the guise of a vision of the future, a list is given of the kings who have governed Babylonia, and emphasis is placed on each dynastic and territorial change. The text contains an al-

2. The most recent scientific commentary to Daniel that I know of is that of L. F. Hartman and A. A. Di Lella, Anchor Bible, Garden City, 1978. For further information, see John J. Collins, *The Apocalyptic Vision of the Book of Daniel*, Missoula, 1977.

lusion to an Assyrian army (1.10), a reference to Cyrus the Great as king of Elam (2.17), and Alexander the Great appears to be heading an army of Ḥanû (3.9); thus, the text is Hellenistic. As in Daniel's book, it is certain that historic events are presented here in the form of a vision of the future, and that the Babylonian writer is very much aware of the shifts of power from one people to the next. If further proof were necessary that the Jewish people were not the only ones in the East who realized what was happening around them, this text would suffice. I am not convinced, however, that this document provides an accurate formalization of imperial successions, as Daniel's book does. The essential point is that Daniel looks at these empires from the outside, and isolates each one of them. The "dynastic prophet" assumes that Babylonia remains, while its conquerors, good or bad, change. The "dynastic prophecy" does not account for a universal history but for a local one. It is possible that the part of the "dynastic prophecy" that has not reached us contained a reference to the future fall of the Seleucids. An allusion to a future empire of peace centered in Uruk appears to be contained in another late Babylonian text, first known in a provisional publication by H. Hunger, *Vorläufiger Bericht . . . Uruk-Warka* 26–27 (1972): 86–87, and now in *Spätbab. Texte aus Uruk* 1 (1976): n. 3. This, too, would confirm what was already clear from the Sibylline Oracles 3.381–87, namely, that the Jewish people shared with the Gentiles the expectation of revolutionary and apocalyptic changes. (Sibylline Oracles 3 is, precisely, a Judaic text imbued with pagan elements.) Thus far, what is not found in these Babylonian texts is a notion of history that develops as a sequence of human, universal empires and ends with a divine empire. If the existence of an explicit Babylonian theory of imperial succession could be verified because of a better interpretation of Babylonian texts dating from the Hellenistic period, either known to me or otherwise existing, the question would arise, as it does with Daniel, whether such a theory has undergone Greek influence. Only the discovery of pre-Hellenistic Babylonian texts containing a clear formulation of the theory of imperial succession would compel us to radically change the terms of the matter, and would lead us to wonder whether Herodotus or Ctesias had any knowledge of Oriental imperial theories.

The most difficult point to be explained analytically remains the association, made by the author of Daniel 2, of the notion of imperial succession with that of the succession of metals. From Hesiod on, the Greeks were familiar with the idea of a succession of ages typified in metals of decreasing worth—a symbol of human decadence. But, as far as we know, no Greek had ever associated the imperial successions of the East with a succession of ages typified in a succession of metals, nor was this likely to happen. As political thinkers, the Greeks would have found it awkward to meditate on and evaluate past empires in mythical terms. The truth is that there is something incongruous about the very association that appears in chapter 2 of the Book of Daniel. The author can very well pay homage to the kingdom of Nebuchadnezzar by having Daniel say that a less glorious kingdom will follow (2.39), but in general he does not present the empires in order of decreasing degeneration. Further, if we consider that the writer is a Jew, one wonders how he honestly could prefer Babylonia, cause of the first destruction of the Temple, to Persia, instrument of God in rebuilding the Temple. The association is awkward and not very convincing. It does not seem either to belong originally to Daniel or to have been taken from the Greeks; we must assume that it was derived elsewhere.

Thus, it is possible that we should turn to Persia for a more satisfactory explanation—possible though not certain. As we know, the events described in the text do not help. Medieval commentaries of a lost Book of the Avesta—the *Vohuman Yasn*—reveal that this book presented a succession of metallic ages corresponding to a succession of Persian rulers (or periods) in relation to Zoroastrian religion. While details necessarily remain dubious, it appears certain that a version of this book containing a succession of ages was known in Hellenistic times in areas influenced by Zoroastrian religion. Unlike Hesiod's account, where a succession of ages was followed by normal human history, this particular version contained a history of men, and specifically the history of a singe people, the Persian people.[3] If this version really did exist, then it is possible that "Daniel," the author of chapter 2, found in the Persian tradition the example of the adaptation of the succession of metals to a succession of kingdoms or historical periods. But what he could not possibly have found was a precedent for the adaptation of a succession of metals to the interpretation of a universal history as a succession of different empires (Babylonia, Media, Persia, and Macedonia). After all, no one in Persia would have ranked Persia second to Babylonia in order of decreasing prestige. Hence the awkwardness inherent in the attempt to apply a classification, such as the Persian one, which was meant to express value judgments, to a succession of empires for which the writer does not express a preference. So far, this further step can be found only in Daniel 2, and I do not see why we

3. See D. Flusser, "The Four Empires in the Fourth Sibyl and in the Book of Daniel," *Israel Oriental Studies* 2 (1972): 148–75. I do not share Flusser's view in the hypothetical part.

should not attribute it to the author of Daniel 2 as his original thought. So far, this writer from around the middle of the third century B.C. appears to be the inventor of the opposition between the notion of the Kingdom of God and that of the four empires theorized by the Greeks, as well as of the association of metallic ages with universal empires.

That the author of Daniel 2 was, in any case, a serious thinker is proved by his reaffirmation, in chapter 7, of the basic idea of imperial succession. Chapter 7 is a later text, and, as I was saying, must be seen as part of the history of resistance against Antiochus IV. The author of this chapter (who is probably the author of the following chapter as well) uses different images. He prefers monsters to metals in designating the empires, thus freeing himself of the less convincing part of the fantasies present in chapter 2 and replacing it with images of monsters, which have at least partial justification as astrological symbols. Seventy years ago, F. Cumont had already observed that the ram symbolizes Persia in astrological texts (*Klio* 9 [1909]: 265–73). The compiler of the Book of Daniel—who, in my opinion, is certainly different from the author of chapter 2 and may not be identical with the author of chapter 7—reaffirms the importance of the opposition between the four empires and the Kingdom of God by placing these two chapters in their present positions, as introductions to the two sections, the pre-Maccabean (chapters 1–6) and the Maccabean (chapters 7–12).

Many other things remain to be said about these two chapters, about the overall vision of the book, and about its influence on later Hebrew and Christian thought. For the time being, we only wish to draw attention to what is ultimately obvious. Daniel 2 got the theory of imperial succession from Greek historiography and, in adopting it, he opposed to it his own expectations for an imminent Kingdom of God. The "enlightened ones" (*maskilim*) who repeated Daniel's prophecies at the time of the resistance against Antiochus IV found in them both the inspiration for and the reaffirmation of their beliefs. In their eyes, the struggle against Antiochus IV was justified by the conviction that the kingdom of men, as exemplified and theorized by the Greeks, was soon to be followed by the Kingdom of God.[4]

4. W. G. Lambert, *The Background of Jewish Apocalyptic*, London, 1978, pp. 10–13, corrects A. K. Grayson on the point concerning the dimensions of the "dynastic prophecy." See D. Mendels and H. Tadmor in *Amer. Journal Phil.* 102 (1987): 330–37.

# 4

# The Second Book of Maccabees

## I

The second book of Maccabees is unique in ancient historiography.[1] The author, who remains anonymous, introduces himself as an epitomist of a work by Jason of Cyrene. He explains with care the difference between a work of entertainment and edification on the one hand, and a work of research and erudition, filled with statistical data, on the other. The compiler's preface is preceded by two letters addressed to the Jews of Egypt by Jewish authorities in Judaea. Both letters invite the Jews to participate in the festivities of 25 Kislev (*Encaenia*) for the celebration of the purification of the Temple of Jerusalem after its profanation by Antiochus IV of Syria and his followers. The first letter is dated at a year from one of the Seleucid eras: 188 (around 124 B.C.); according to the most probable interpretation, it refers to a letter of the year 169 (around 143 B.C.) on the same subject. The second letter is dated indirectly from the very recent death of Antiochus IV. From the cuneiform tablet, British Museum 35603, we learn that Antiochus's death took

1. A bibliography until 1966 is included in the reprint of my book *Prime linee di storia della tradizione maccabaica*, Amsterdam, 1968; first ed., Rome, 1930. The classical research work is E. Bickerman, *Der Gott der Makkabäer*, Berlin, 1937. For further information, see M. Stern, *Enciclopedia Miqrait (Encyclopedia Biblica)*, Jerusalem, 1968, 5:292–98 and 303, and J. G. Bunge's excellent dissertation, "Untersuchungen zum Zweiten Makkabäerbuch," Bonn, 1971. Another important recent book is D. Arenhoevel, *Die Theokratie nach dem 1. und 2. Makkabäerbuch*, Mainz, 1967. For the proem, see Hubert Cancik, *Mythische und historische Wahrheit*, Stuttgart, 1970, pp. 108–26.

There is a critical edition of 2 Maccabees by R. Hanhart (Göttingen, 1959). The best commentary is by F. M. Abel (Paris, 1949). We are expecting a new commentary by C. Habicht [published in 1976]. My debt to E. Bickerman and M. Stern is obvious. My discussions with C. Habicht have also been useful. I would like to add to my acknowledgments the names of my teachers and friends who are now dead: E. Artom and B. Motzo.

place in the eighth or ninth month of the Seleucid Babylonian year 148, that is around November–December of 164 B.C. (A. J. Sachs and D. J. Wiseman, in *Iraq* 16 [1954]: 202–11). The second letter appears to imply that the purification of the Temple took place immediately after the death of Antiochus IV, but we cannot exclude another interpretation, according to which the event of 25 Kislev is the celebration of the (first) anniversary of the purification of the Temple.

No effort is made to connect these letters with any part of the narrative text that follows. In fact, the account of the assassination of Antiochus IV in the second letter is in complete disagreement with the story of the natural death of the king recounted in chapter 9. Further, 2 Maccabees ends with an account of the institution of a festivity of 13 Adar to celebrate the victory of Judas over Nicanore in the Seleucid year 151 (160 B.C.). This feast, of course, could not fall within the range of the author of the second letter (*ex hypothesi*, around 148 Sel.) and is ignored by the author of the first.

The epitomist clearly implies in 2 Macc. 2:23 that he has summarized the entire work by Jason. From his statement in 2 Macc. 15:37, it appears instead that he presents the choice of the ending as a personal choice: "From that time on the city was in the hands of Jews and my story ends here." But there is no real contradiction between the two passages, and we can assume that 2:23 is more accurate and reliable: "All that Jason of Cyrene has reported in five books we will try to epitomize in one." If anything, difficulties lie elsewhere.[2] Aside from the documents quoted in the text, only in 13:1 and 14:4 do we find absolute dates instead of the relative dates normally used by the epitomist. What is more, in chapter 13, the style is unusually paratactical. In this case, too, it is difficult to find convincing arguments in support of the hypothesis that chapters 13–15 were added by another epitomist. We should be cautious and treat 2 Maccabees as a whole, except for the preliminary letters, as a work by someone who has epitomized Jason. As to whether it is a competent summary, this is an altogether different issue. To quote a safe example, the account of Judas's campaigns against Timotheus and Bacchides is not narrated in the exact chronological sequence: 8:30–33 is an awkward insertion in the different story of Nicanore's expedition, and in 10:37 Timotheus is killed but reappears ready to fight in 12:2 (where it cannot be a question of a *different* Timotheus). It is also possible that the epitomist has inverted the sequence of events we find in 1 Maccabees (where the purification of the

---

2. See the excellent study by M. Zambelli, "La composizione del secondo libro dei Maccabei," in *Miscellanea greca e romana*, Rome, 1965, pp. 195–300.

Temple precedes the death of Antiochus) under the influence of the second introductory letter (which he may have interpreted in the sense that the ceremony of 25 Kislev in 148 Sel. was indeed the actual purification of the Temple, not its commemoration).

That he did so, however, cannot be proved. In other words, we cannot prove that Jason of Cyrene considered the purification of the Temple as an event that preceded the death of Antiochus IV. Nor is there any proof that the chronology 2 Maccabees gives for these two events is wrong. The date given for the death of Antiochus IV provided by the tablet BM 35603 neither confirms nor denies the priority of the purification of the Temple. The Book of Daniel could be decisive, since it has some knowledge of the end of the persecution but no knowledge at all of the death of Antiochus (about which it provides an entirely false prophecy). The problem is that we are uncertain as whether (a) Daniel identifies the end of the persecution with 25 Kislev in 147 or 148 Sel., and (b) Daniel or anyone else in Jerusalem was readily informed of the death of Antiochus in November 164 B.C. The only evidence that news arrived quickly in Jerusalem is contained in the second letter of 2 Maccabees, which, as we shall see, is of doubtful value.

## II

Given that no explanation is provided for the two introductory letters, all we can do is make conjectures as to their relationship with the epitome of Jason's work. The simplest conjecture is that someone was asked to compile a summary of Jason that could be sent to Egypt in support of the invitation contained in the letters. We can imagine the following situation. In 124 B.C. an officer of the Council of Jerusalem was asked to reiterate the invitation to Egyptian Jews to participate in the feast of 25 Kislev. This person not only referred to a preceding letter dated 143 B.C., but also transcribed a letter from 164 B.C. attributed to Judah and his followers. Further, he persuaded a writer who was familiar with the techniques of pathetic historiography to make an epitome of the great work of Jason to be sent to Egypt. The second book of Maccabees, as we know it, is supposedly the result of a joint effort by an officer of the Jewish community in Jerusalem, whose mother tongue was Hebrew or more probably Aramaic, and a writer whose mother tongue was presumably Greek. In this case, there is no place for an editor (*der Redaktor*) who follows the epitomist, as D. Arenhoevel and others have suggested.

We can examine the advantages and the disadvantages of a similar hypothesis. There appears to be a long interpolation in the second letter, supposedly written in 164 B.C. The text is spoiled in 1:18, where a long excursus of miracles dating from the time of Nehemiah begins. In 2:16, where the excursus ends, there appears to be a clear intention to continue the first part of the sentence from 1:18. The excursus intends to stress the holiness of the Temple of Jerusalem and to create a parallel between the events from the time of Nehemiah and events from the time of Judah. If the excursus is an interpolation, it can be attributed to the joint efforts of the author of the first letter and the epitomist. This supposed collaboration makes it pointless to examine whether the language of the excursus, deeply imbued with Hebraisms, is compatible with the linguistic peculiarities of the epitomist.

Another advantage of this hypothesis is that it supplies the epitomist with a date and an intention. He supposedly wrote around 124 B.C. with the intention of offering Egyptian Jews an attractive epitome of the splendid and often miraculous events that preceded and followed the reconsacration of the Temple of Jerusalem by Judas Maccabean and his followers. Like the introductory letters, the epitome attempts to retain the Jews in Egypt within the influence of the Temple of Jerusalem as against the competition of the Temple of Leontopolis. This temple also appears to have been a center for the recruitment of Jewish mercenaries at the service of Egypt; it played an important role in the dynastic struggles raging around 124 B.C. (Josephus, *Ap.* 2.49–56; *AJ* 13.65). While the leaders of the party in support of Cleopatra II, Onia and his sons, Chelkias, and Anania were the builders of the Temple of Leontopolis, many Egyptian Jews turned with growing sympathy toward the Temple in Jerusalem, which was not involved in dynastic struggles.

The Letter of Aristeas, which combines an apology of the Greek translation of the Bible with an idealized view of the Temple of Jerusalem, probably comes from those same years and belongs to the same intellectual climate. The Jews in Alexandria were especially subject to regal resentment and to the popular hatred for the actions performed by the mercenaries of Leontopolis.

These positive aspects of the hypothesis that 2 Maccabees was written in 124 B.C. in order to be sent to Egypt should not make us forget that this does not explain the precise form given to this book. We would expect there to be something more final in the preface: this is evident if we compare this text with the preface to the Greek translation of the Book of Sirach or to the postscript of the translation of Esther in the Septuagint. As I have said, we are not told that the first letter is followed by a second one and by Jason's epitome.

Despite these difficulties, I continue to believe that the hypothesis that the work was written in 124 B.C. is more satisfactory than any other. In any case, 2 Maccabees cannot have been written after Pompeius (see 15:37); the Romans are distant friends (4.11; 11:34).

## III

I assume the first letter to be an authentic message from the Jews in Jerusalem to their brothers in Egypt, but I am not as certain of the authenticity of the second letter, written by "those who are in Jerusalem and in Judaea and the Senate and Judas" to "Aristobulus, teacher of King Ptolemy, who is also of the stock of consecrated priests, and to the Jews in Egypt." I will leave aside what I have called a probable interpolation (1:18b–2:16) and will confine myself to the rest. It is not altogether impossible to think that Judas and his followers thought they could associate the Jews of Egypt either with the purification of the Temple or with its first anniversary. But the account of the death of Antiochus IV in this letter is entirely forged. In order to preserve the authenticity of the letter, we must assume that those who wrote it had accepted a false version of the death of Antiochus before learning the truth about it, or that the authors stuck to the false version of the facts even after the actual version as known. In the latter case, the senders of this letter would have been discredited immediately. But the first hypothesis, which implies the good faith of the epitomist, also presents some difficulties. We cannot understand why Judas and his followers should have received an entirely false version of the death of Antiochus and then readily transmitted it to the Egyptian Jews. I would like to keep open the possibility that the author of the first letter was deceived by what he considered an authentic letter by Judas.

There are two other documents included in 2 Maccabees that I consider doubtful. In chapter 9, the letter by Antiochus IV recommending his son to the Jews is certainly less fantastic than the preceding story, according to which the king, in despair and on the point of death, promises that he will convert to Judaism. In the letter, however, we find that the king hopes in heaven (see the Hanhart edition, p. 27), writes a prescript that is impossible for a king to have written, and does not take into account the real situation in Judaea. Part of the letter is undoubtedly modeled after an authentic document, perhaps a letter of Antiochus IV to the citizens of Antiochia. If this text is forged, it cannot be attributed either to Jason or to the epitomist, since they would have attempted to work out something in agreement with the surrounding text. If this letter is not authentic, and if it precedes Jason, this strengthens our belief that there exist forged letters (as, for example, the second introductory letter) circulating independently in those years of struggle.

We now come to the third case of this possible forgery: the letter of Antiochus V to Lysias, which appears in chapter 2 as the second of a group of our letters. The other three letters appear to be above suspicion, even if there is controversy as to their absolute and relative chronology. The first letter by Lysias to "the Jewish people" (2:16–21) appears to have been sent to the followers of Judas; it constitutes a cautious opening. We should note that this letter does not mention Judah or the Council. The third letter is sent by Antiochus IV (?) to the Council and to other Jews, evidently the loyal ones, those whose institutions are acknowledged. The letter promises amnesty to the rebels who agree to return to their homes before a set time. The amnesty has been negotiated by the high priest Menelaus, who, for a certain period of time, was a favorite of Hellenizing Jews. The Temple is not mentioned in the letter. This implies that nothing is being done to regain the Temple for "orthodox" rites. The fourth letter, written by two Roman legates to the Jewish people is an offer of Roman mediation. Here, too, the recipients of the letter are necessarily followers of Judas. B. Niese's observation that the text from Codex V enables us to recognize the Titus Manius from most manuscripts as the Manius Sergius of Polybius 31.9.6 increases the credibility of the letter.[3]

These three letters were evidently preserved in the archives of Jerusalem. This direct evidence is missing for second letter, which is a recommendation from King Antiochus V to Lysias guaranteeing complete religious freedom to the Jews and the restitution of their Temple. If the letter is authentic, we can assume that it was written later than the other three, and that it represents a later phase in the withdrawal of the Syrians. R. Laqueur won great approval in dating this letter to 163 B.C., a year after the other letters.[4] But the letter could have been communicated to the Jews only with an accompanying letter by Lysias. Now, it is noteworthy although understandable that this accompanying letter is missing. Further, the letter appears to be a touch too beautiful. The letter appears as a document produced (certainly by an excellent drafter of legal deeds) in order to prove to the followers of Menelaus that Judas had obtained better conditions. Moreover, although the letter is major document, it is unknown to 1 Maccabees,

---

3. *Hermes* (1900): 485. For a different opinion, see O. Mørkholm, *Antiochus IV of Syria*, Copenhagen, 1966, p. 163.

4. R. Laqueur, in *HZ* 136 (1927): 234.

which, in 6:57–59, clearly implies that there were only verbal decisions on the abolition of Hellenizing laws. Finally, it appears that this letter has left no trace on following events. What 1 Maccabees tells us about the momentary isolation of Judas and the election of the new high priest Alcimus is explained better without this letter: a similar document would have strengthened Judas's authority. All of these reasons (together with the fact that the *Megillat Ta'anit* does not register the event)[5] are not decisive, but they should lead us to be cautious. The second letter, because it was received by Lysias and not by Jewish leaders, has a different status from the others.[6]

## IV

The epitome is a rather loose conglomerate of six main elements: tribal war spirit; miracles, especially interventions of supernatural beings in events concerning the Temple; some fundamental beliefs in God's intervention in history; the solitary leadership of Judas Maccabean; mixed attitudes toward foreigners; and the importance of martyrdom. These six elements are hard to reconcile because they belong to different cultural strata, some of which were originally non-Jewish.

To a certain extent, 2 Maccabees represents a revival of the ancient warrior spirit of the old Hebrew religion. The considerations in 2 Macc. 6:12–17 (probably due to the epitomist) are clearly aimed at reproducing the atmosphere of the Book of Judges. Yet there appear to be new elements as well. The Jewish state is identified with the city of Jerusalem under Greek influence. God distinguishes between Jews and other nations to the extent that Jews are punished immediately for their iniquity, thus having time to repent, while other nations are punished at the height of their iniquity. This same principle can be found, more or less, in chapter 12 of the Wisdom of Solomon.

The fact that Judas Maccabean is a solitary figure can be a sign of archaism. Judges were not surrounded by their families. Conse-

---

5. The *Megillat Ta'anit* (or "scroll of fasting") is a list of the thirty-six days on which there were significant victories and happy events in the history of the Jews under the Second Temple. For this reason, in those days the rabbis prohibited fasting. Hence, the name should be understood as "scroll of the days on which fasting is prohibited." Written in Aramaic, the scroll has reached us in the present state from the period of the destruction of the Second Temple, or, at the latest, from the period of the revolt of Bar Kokhba against Rome (132–35 A.D.)

6. I share some of the doubts of K.-D. Schunk, *Die Quellen des I. und II. Makkabäerbuches*, Halle, 1954, pp. 103–5. W. Mölleken's complex study of 1 Maccabees 6–7, in *ZATW* 65 (1953): 205–28, although very sophisticated, is not convincing.

quently, the hero's relatives play a very minor role compared with what 1 Maccabees has to say about them. This is especially true of Judas's father, Mattathias (see 1 Macc. 2:17ff.). Significantly, 2 Maccabees ends with the victory of Judas over Nicanore and thus avoids the sad story of his death. If Jason's account also ends at the same point, we can assume that the entire portrayal of the personality of Judas is based on Jason. Judas is the model of the Jewish warrior, loyal to the laws of his people and ruthless with the enemies of his nation. But Judas's solitary condition is not only due to the influence of the Book of Judges. It is also a consequence of the entirely new concept of martyrdom. Not Mattathias but Eleazar and the seven brothers begin an open resistance against the decrees of Antiochus. Judas withdraws to the desert as a sign of quiet protest (5:27), and it is only after the martyrdom of the seven brothers that he comes out as the leader of the resistance (chap. 8). The legend of the seven brothers, where the emphasis is placed on the resurrection—an important motif in Daniel (around 164 B.C.)—may very well be one of the oldest motifs of the tradition adopted by Jason of Cyrene. Its popular character is indicated by the presence of the king at the martyrdom, a detail that raised problems of localization for ancient readers as well (see Abel's commentary).

The glorification of the Temple is not in itself a prominent feature of biblical historiography. Miracles and interventions by angels do not play a great role in preceding stories concerning the Temple. What 2 Maccabees has to say from this point of view can hardly be separated from well-known genres of Hellenistic historiography. For example, we find a chronicle of the Temple that listed the miracles performed by the local god and the gifts received. Occasionally this took the form of an inscription open to the inspection of visitors of the Temple, as we can see from the Chronicle of Lindos, dated to 99 B.C. Hellenistic literature also included collections of *epiphaneiai* of a given god. One of the most respected pupils of Callimachus Istro of Paphos wrote at least two books on the *epiphaneiai* of Appollos (A. Tresp, *Griech. Kultschriftsteller*, p. 198).

Although 2 Maccabees alludes to the Greeks as barbarians (2:21; 4:25; 5:22) and appears narrowly nationalistic in its religious perspective, it is not hostile to non-Jews as such. The death of Onia causes the indignation of many Gentiles (4:35). Antiochus IV himself is moved and compassionate (4:37). The citizens of Tyrus are sympathetic with the Jewish victims of an unfair punishment (4:49). The Scitopolitans are spared by Judas because they have helped the Jews on previous occasions (12:30). The common origin of Jews and Spartans is declared openly, without scruples.

The collective ethics of the battles of Yahweh are now supplemented, so to speak, by acts of individual martyrdom. The new ethics of martyrdom support (and receive support from) the new faith in individual resurrection reserved for devotees. It is a woman who carries the new message (7:9; 22:29), the mother of the seven brothers. She is not a leader like Deborah nor a defender of Judaism (through feminine ways) like Esther and Judith; she is a mother of martyrs. The epitomist (if not Jason) adopts the idea of resurrection in 12:43–45. The text we possess is confused at times and perhaps interpolated (see Abel's commentary), but its essence is not in question. Not only does the author believe in resurrection; he also believes in the effectiveness of sacrifices for the dead. On the one hand, the old faith in the immediate intervention of God for or against the chosen people is enriched with the accessory of miracles of the Temple and the *epiphaneiai* in battle, which are unusual in biblical historiography; on the other, it is connected with a new faith in the resurrection. The discovery of martyrdom as an autonomous value mediates between the old beliefs and the new.[7] Thus, 2 Maccabees combines with difficulty but very effectively old and new motifs. Its ethics is nationalistic but not blindly so; devotion to the Temple is expressed in a manner far more naive and rough than in its biblical predecessors. The notion of obedience to the Law is transformed by the introduction of the interdependent values of resurrection and martyrdom.

If we consider the importance Jews and Christians later ascribed to martyrdom, this feature of 2 Maccabees appears as the most important. This book introduced martyrdom as a value in historical writing. The influence of 2 Maccabees can be acknowledged more directly in the Christian, tradition where the book continued to be read. In the Hebrew tradition, where the Greek translation of 2 Maccabees soon ceased to be authoritative, the elaboration of the concept of martyrdom took on new forms: it became the highest expression of the "Sanctification of the Name." The original protomartyrs, the seven brothers, however, were not forgotten. "Those marvelous young men, the sons of the pious Hannah, in the days when the priests could come close to the presence of God," were still the models Abraham ben Eliezer ha-Levi invoked as an example for the generation that was experiencing the expulsion of the Jews from Spain.[8] The name of Hannah, as the mother of the seven brothers, appears in the Vulgate text of the Josippon (although other

7. This point is neglected in the interesting study by B. Renaud, La loi et les lois dans les Livres des Maccabées," *RBi* 68 (1961): 39–67.
8. Y. Baer, *A History of the Jews in Christian Spain*, Philadelphia, 1971, 2:430. On the seven brothers, see E. J. Bickerman, *L. Ginzberg Jubilee Volume*, New York, 1945, pp. 105–12, and E. Bammel, in *Theologische Literaturzeitung* 78 (1953): 119–26.

names had been used previously). The Fathers of the Church persuaded their flock with effort that the seven "Maccabean" brothers deserved to be treated as Christian saints. Saint Augustine adopts a circular argument: "Sanctorum Machabaeorum basilica esse in Antiochia praedicatur . . . haec basilica a Christianis tenetur, a Christianis aedificata est" (*Sermo* 300; Migne, *PL*, XXXVIII; 1379).

What remains exclusively Jewish in 2 Maccabees, and may very well have caused Christian readers to hesitate, is the very great importance ascribed to the Temple and its purification by Judas Maccabean. To the extent that the notion of individual martyrdom is strictly connected with the purity of the Jewish cult, 2 Maccabees could be read with full appreciation only by Jews.

## V

With the inclusion of the preliminary letters (whether or not they were inserted by the epitomist) 2 Maccabees was combined with the Book of Esther as a festive book and probably served as a model for another festive book, 3 Maccabees. In festive books, history was written with the intention of explaining, justifying, and celebrating a given religious ceremony or feast. Historiography was enacted not only to interpret the intervention of God in a series of events but also was used to justify the institutional commemoration of the happy conclusion of these events in the form of a religious feast.

Festive books were not entirely unknown in the Greco-Roman world: it is sufficient to mention the *Fasti* by Ovid. But perhaps no pagan book (at least none of those written in the pre-Christian era) developed the implicit theology of a divine intervention underlying the individual feasts. Moreover, no pagan festive book appears to have been used for public readings on the day of a given feast. In Judaism, it was possible for a festive book to be read in the synagogues. The Book of Esther, which remained the model for such festive books, is known to have been read in synagogues during the first centuries of the Christian era.

We can ask ourselves whether the aspiration toward being considered a festive book did not reduce the popularity of 2 Maccabees among Greek-speaking Jews as well. There is no evidence that 2 Maccabees was read publicly during the feast of 25 Kislev. It is also questionable whether the book was disseminated among private readers. There is no clear sign that Philo knew 2 Maccabees (*Quod omnis probus liber sit* 13.88 does not constitute evidence), and Flavius Josephus, who used 1 Maccabees as a source, ignored 2 Maccabees.

Other texts soon began to compete with 2 Maccabees II. The fourth book of Maccabees (first century A.D.?) was more adequate for the mere moral edification of cultivated Greek readers: it derived from 2 Maccabees and developed the philosophical implications of martyrdom. At an uncertain date, the Scroll of Antiochus, in its Hebrew and Aramaic versions, provided a brief popular indication of the feast of the *Encaenia*, for those who were familiar with either one of these tongues. What is interesting for us in this regard is that the Scroll of Antiochus does not know either 1 or 2 Maccabees and was itself seldom used for readings in the synagogue.

Perhaps this type of feast did not require a specific book after all. It is also possible that the complexity and the very layout of 2 Maccabees made it inadequate for both private readings and readings in the synagogue. The episodes of martyrdom were connected only indirectly with the purification of 25 Kislev, and the accounts of warfare culminated with a different feast, the Day of Nicanore, which the introductory letters ignored. While Jason chose the Day of Nicanore for the ending of his work (perhaps in order to recommend this feast), he was partly responsible for the fact that the epitome did not succeed in becoming a convincing festive book for the *Encaenia*. The second book of Maccabees handed down to posterity not the justification for a given feast but paradigmatic episodes of martyrdom: the book became "known" rather than "read," at least among Jews. Later, the language in which it was written made it twice as inadequate.[9]

The disappearance of 2 Maccabees from Hebrew literature is obviously only a particular case of the overall rejection of history and historiography by Jews after the destruction of the Second Temple. Even if it was originally written in Hebrew and was not a festive book, 1 Maccabees shared the destiny of 2 Maccabees. Also, the work of Flavius Josephus was left to Christian readers. Occasional exceptions such as the compilation of the Josippon in tenth-century Italy, do not change the basic fact that from the second century on Jews lost interest in their history—especially in the Persian and Hellenistic period of their history.

But the case of 2 Maccabees can help us to understand how such a rejection of history took place. First, the revival of Jewish historic writing in the period 200 B.C. to 100 A.D. is inseparable from Greek influence. In the previous three centuries, there appears to have been little interest in keeping a record of events of Jewish history. Moreover, al-

9. I do not see any references to either 1 or 2 Maccabees in the Jewish liturgy mentioned by S. Stein, "The Liturgy of Hanukkah and the First Two Books of Maccabees," *Journal of Jewish Studies* 5 (1954): 100–106, 148–55.

though new feasts were being introduced to commemorate new historical events, the relationship between the feast and the event that inspired it was transformed to the point of becoming unrecognizable. The *Encaenia* became the commemoration of a miracle rather than the celebration of a religious and political struggle, as 2 Maccabees had described it.

# 5

# Problems of Method in the Interpretation of Judeo-Hellenistic Symbols

*For the seventieth birthday of*
*Giorgio Levi della Vida*

Thirty years have passed since the publication of G. F. Moore's admirable work *Judaism,* and it now would be pointless to praise his orderly and well-documented reconstruction of Tannaitic Judaism. It is also clear that the work of the Harvard professor has all the merits and the defects of a perfect systematic reconstruction, somewhat in the style of Mommsen. It is not surprising that the most resolute opponent of the reduction of postbiblical Judaism to normative Judaism described by Moore has come from America, from the rival Yale (but after having attended Moore's seminary). Since 1935, when he published that unique book *By Light, Light: The Mystic Gospel of Hellenistic Judaism,* E. R. Goodenough has resorted to Philo to present us with a different kind of Judaism, one imbued with Greek elements, closer to the Fourth Gospel and, so to speak, to Hermetism. "Judaism in the Greek-speaking world, especially in Egypt, had been transformed into a Mystery. The objective of this Judaism was salvation in the mystical sense" (p. 7). In his new work, *Jewish Symbols in the Greco-Roman Period,* Goodenough explains even more clearly the meaning of salvation: "Salvation from bondage to the flesh and its desires, and release to share in the freedom of immaterial reality" (4:211). But, already in 1935, he added that if one accepts this thesis, it is also possible to explain "that revealing Jewish art, which the Yale expedition has now discovered at Dura under the direction of Professor Rostovtzeff" (p. 9).

This work, of which Goodenough now presents the first four volumes (and promises three more), represents the development of a thesis he outlined briefly in 1935. While Philo is the theorist of this Judeo-Hellenistic mystery, figurative representations found in hun-

Review of E. R. Goodenough, *Jewish Symbols in the Greco-Roman Period,* vols. 1–4, New York, Pantheon Books, Bollingen Series 37, without a date but around 1954.

dreds of tombs, synagogues, amulets, and Jewish lamps from the Hellenistic-Roman age are its figurative symbols. According to Goodenough, these figurative symbols make it possible to confirm and to extend that Hellenistic version of Judaism we acknowledge in Philo. Goodenough's new work cannot help but have the character of an answer to the objections raised specifically against *By Light, Light* and more generally against the overall interpretation of Philo contained in various books and articles summarized in *An Introduction to Philo Judaeus* (1940). The objections had been raised from several sources that Philo should be considered unto himself and not as a representative of a religious current, and that Philo himself cannot be interpreted as a mystical philosopher outside of the normative Judaism of his age.[1] Goodenough's new work, with its insistence on questions of method and principle, cannot be understood clearly without these polemic concerns.

Whatever the reaction to Goodenough's thesis, the first four volumes of his work should be welcomed with admiration and recognition. Goodenough's research does not deal with minor issues. His theme is vast and important, and he has examined it with all of the necessary information of symbolics and religion. He has contributed, as he intended, both to the history of Judaism and its Christian origins and to a more general theory of human symbolism. The chapters in volume 4, where he describes his methodology, are largely but not exclusively of Jungian derivation (see, for example, 4:110) and must be read with care by anyone wishing to utilize the preceding volumes. The vastness of the approach goes hand in hand with the accuracy of the information. What we have here is an exceptional quantity of iconographic material, little known and at times even unedited (and photographically documented in volume 3). As a scholar, Goodenough is a creative, original, and deep mind. I do not know to what extent he may be considered a pupil of Rostovtzeff, but his work testifies to the open perspective of the Russian master at Yale.

---

1. See A. D. Nock's review in *Gnomon* 13 (1937): 156–65. Nock has now written a fundamental review of *Jewish Symbols* in *Gnomon* 27 (1955): 558–72. I recommend this review for its detailed observations, which reveal Nock's vast knowledge, as well as for its methodological objections. My debt to Nock in questions of method is obvious throughout the present article. For a point of view closer to Goodenough, see H. Masurillo in *Theological Studies* 15 (1954): 295–300, and in *Traditio* 10 (1954): 577, n. 1. As to Philo, the three most important recent studies are M. Pohlenz, *Nachr. Göttingen*, 1942, pp. 409–86; H. A. Wolfson *Philo* 1947 (see my review in *Ricerche Religiose* 20 [1949]: 199–201); and A. J. Festugière, *La révélation d'Hermès Trismegiste*, 1949, 2:521–86. See also the discussion of Wolfson's book by I. Heinemann in *Theol. Zeitschrift* 6 (1950): 99–115, and S. Sandmal, "Philo's Place in Judaism," *Hebrew Union College Annual* 25 (1954): 208–337 and 26 (1955): 151–332, which stresses the opposition between Philo and the rabbis.

## II

Anyone who like me has never believed that Goodenough has interpreted the allegory of Philo correctly, inevitably tends to see a circular argument in his new book: Goodenough wants to confirm an old thesis on Philo by using figurative materials, and he interprets the figurative material presupposing his interpretation of Philo. Further, it is impossible not to feel that when Goodenough speaks of normative Judaism he is inspired by Moore's book rather than by original Hebrew and Aramaic texts. There is nothing wrong with not being a Talmudist, but it becomes dangerous not to be one when one studies the contraposition between Talmudic Judaism and so-called Hellenistic Judaism. This is all the more true since it has been years since G. Scholem (*Major Trends in Jewish Mysticism*, 1941; 3d ed., 1955) has made us laymen aware of the antiquity of mystical currents within so-called normative Judaism. Moreover, the later discovery of gnostic books (see, for example, the book edited by F. L. Cross, *The Jung Codex*, with essays by H. C. Puech and G. Quispel, London, 1955) has increasingly confirmed the rightness of Scholem's idea and the need to analyze the mystical material in Hebrew. Is it possible that two types of mysticism coexisted without mutually affecting each other—the mysticism known to Jewish sources and the mysticism Goodenough wants to reconstruct from Philo and from Judeo-Hellenistic monuments? We must bear in mind that, according to Goodenough, Judeo-Hellenistic mysticism does not express itself exclusively in Greek: one of its formulae is supposedly the very Hebrew word for *peace*, "the symbolic expression of that mystic hope."[2]

But these are all generic considerations. The real issue Goodenough raises is that of the interpretation of the figurative representations themselves.

And here, at the cost of being tedious, we must repeat that as soon as we enter the world of the interpretation of figurative symbols, the earth beneath our feet begins to shake.[3] From the Renaissance onward,

2. E. Stein, *Die allegorische Exegese des Philo aus Alexandreia*, 1929, p. 51, n. 1 claimed, "das hebräische Schalom bezeichnet mehr als εἰρήνη [eirene]."

3. See my remarks in *Contributo alla storia degli studi classici*, 1955, p. 91, and *X Congresso Internazionale di Scienze Storiche, Relazioni VI*, 1955, p. 36. A model essay on the criticism of symbols is A. D. Nock, "Sarcophagi und Symbolism," *Amer. Journ. Archaeol.* 50 (1946): 140–70.

Also by Hock compare "Hellenistic Mysteries and Christian Sacraments," *Mnemosyne* 4 (1952): 177–213, n. 5, and the essay he inspired, by B. M. Metzger, "Considerations of Methodology in the Study of the Mystery Religions and Early Christianity," *Harv. Theol. Rev.* 48 (1955): 1–20. The introductory part of C. H. Dodd, *The Interpretation of the Fourth Gospel*, Cambridge, 1953, pp. 3–130, is full of wisdom; on Philo, see pp. 54–73.

the problem of interpreting symbols by the ancients, or symbols believed to be by the ancients, has become a matter of concern for antiquarians and historians. The problem is not substantially different from that of interpreting literary and epigraphic texts. But while for the latter it gradually has become possible to develop, with the help of grammar, a generally accepted hermeneutics that only geniuses and crazy people can ignore, in the case of figurative arts such an agreement has not yet been reached. Now that archaeology has come to play a major role in the reconstruction of all aspects of ancient life, uncertainty in the interpretation of ancient figures has even greater consequences. Until we decide on the rules of the game, what now is happening before our very eyes will continue to happen: scholars of great renown and value present interpretations of the same momument—for example, the subterranean Basilica of Porta Maggiore or the Villa dei Misteri—interpretations different to an extent that would be unthinkable in the case of an epinicion by Pindar or a tragedy by Aeschylus. Moreover, when the interpretation concerns a vast group of figurative documents, such as the Pompeian paintings (K. Schefold) or the contorniates (A. Alföldi), the chances for agreement between experts are reduced to zero.[4] We can only hope that someone will come along and write a new treatise on the interpretation of ancient paintings and coins.[5]

In the case of symbols or figurative symbols presumed to be Judeo-

4. See, for example, J. M. C. Toynbee's review of A. Alföldi's *Die Kontorniaten* in *Journ. Rom. Stud.* 35 (1945): 115–21, and A. Rumpf's review of K. Schefold's *Pompejanische Malerei. Sinn und Ideengeschichte* in *Gnomon* 26 (1954): 353–63 [and Ch. Picard, in *Rév. Archéol.* 6 (1956): 114–22]. Note also I. Sonne's review of R. Wischnitzer's *The Messianic Theme in the Paintings of the Dura Synagogue* (1948) in *Amer. Journ. Arch.* 53 (1949): 230–33. A systematic study of divergent interpretations and their presuppositions would be very useful. For a recent general orientation, see C. Schneider, *Geistesgeschichte des antiken Christentums*, 1954, 2:109–70, 351–53.

5. On monetary symbolism, see A. H. M. Jones, *Numismatics and History, Essays in Roman Coinage Presented to H. Mattingly*, 1956, p. 32: "If numismatists wish further to assist historians, I would suggest that they pay less attention to the political interpretations of the coins." This can appear wrong if we compare the brilliant essay by Alföldi, "The Main Aspects of Political Propaganda on the Coinage of the Roman Republic," not to speak of the more general essay by J. M. C. Toynbee, "Picture-Language in Roman Art and Coinage." But Alföldi's essay, although very rich in interesting details, reveals the danger of an uncontrolled interpretation of monetary symbols. A serious criticism of Alföldi's essay comes from C. M. Kraay, "Caesar's Quattuorviri of 44 B.C. *Munismatic Chronicle* 14 (1954): 18–31. For a discussion of late Roman and Byzantine symbolism, see G. B. Ladner in *Traditio* 10 (1954): 579. See also R. A. Carson's review of Alföldi in *Gnomon* 28 (1956): 181–86. (Alföldi's reply to my observations in *Centennial Publication of the American Numismatic Society*, 1958, p. 41, may express a misunderstanding. I am not stressing the differences of opinion among numismatists as such, but the lack of a rigorous and controllable method of interpretation.)

Hellenistic, difficulties increase for reasons of time, space, and the co-existence of different cultural traditions. These documents cover about eight or nine centuries; they often are not dated and extend from Spain to Mesopotamia. Even when they are unquestionably Jewish, they are the product of variously educated groups and of subgroups that have even different educations. Jews from the Hellenistic-Roman period were often bilingual, if not trilingual to some extent, but the literary, artistic, and religious elements in this polyglotism are very hard to determine. The variety of the figures with which Jews decorated their tombs, their synagogues, and many objects of common use, not to mention the magic formulas some Jews used and lived by, is, of course, connected with this polyglotism. In general, it is also evident that Jewish figurative arts from the Hellenistic-Roman period are the sign of a cultural atmosphere that is very different both from that of the preceding Persian period and from the following Talmudic period. But when we claim that these figures can be divided into three groups—those that are clearly Jewish, those common to Jews and non-Jews, and those of certain pagan origin—we are immediately tempted to ask, for example, to what extent and with what spatial and chronological uniformity were pagan figures fitted into a system of Jewish religious symbols? To what extent did figures of pagan origin represent decorative elements, or did they merely express conformity with the surrounding world? What meaning did Jewish symbols assume when they became part of this new context? What role did non-Jewish donors, architects, and decorators play in the choice of decorations?[6]

## III

In order to answer these and other questions, we would have to possess solid criteria of judgment.[7] Now, as we have stated briefly, the

6. On non-Jews participating in the building of synagogues—a fact made famous by Luke 7:5—see S. D. Schwartzman, "The Synoptic Evangelists and the Synagogue," *Hebrew Union College Annual* 24 (1952): 119–25. This essay, however, does not go into great detail. For example, it does not mention that the Capitolina, who contributed to the building of the synagogue of Tralles in the second and third centuries (E. Groag, in *Jahresh* 10 [1907]: 283), was not Jewish but came from a highly aristocratic pagan family (L. Robert, in *Etud. Anatol.* [1937]: 410). More generally, see L. H. Feldman, "Jewish Sympathizers in Classical Literature and Inscriptions," *Trans. Amer. Phil. Ass.* 81 (1950): 200–208.

7. As we can see from the Goodenough's bibliography as well, the philosophical discussions on the nature of symbols are much more frequent than the discussions on the method of determining the significance of specific symbols. A great deal of material for future elaboration into a manual on the method of interpreting symbols is available from

simplest criterion appears to be missing: the existence of literary texts that unquestionably attest that Jews from the Hellenistic-Roman period used certain figures or figurative groups to express certain precise religious ideas. Philo can confirm that certain objects and certain figures from the Bible assumed a symbolic value, but he is of no help to Goodenough when it comes to the interpretation of symbols that are not specifically Jewish. Here I would mainly like to emphasize the difference between the allegory of Philo and the type of symbolism postulated by Goodenough, because Goodenough appears to presuppose too easily that what he postulates is similar to Philo—that it "is far more intelligible if understood in Philonic terms" (2:10). Philo presupposes that the Scriptures can be interpreted allegorically, that is, that certain passages from the Bible can have more than one meaning. But, according to Goodenough, Jews who attached a mystical value to the symbols of Nike, the zodiac, or the seasons did not interpret the Scriptures; instead they created a system of symbols outside of the allegorical interpretation of the Bible. If it is true, as H. A. Wolfson writes, that at the bottom of Philo's thought is "the conception of Scripture as mistress of which philosophy is to be the handmaid" (*Philo*, 1:164), for the Jews Goodenough postulates, symbols often do not come from biblical sources. Nor can Goodenough find support in the Dialogue with Tripho by Justin, which he uses to reinforce his thesis. First, it is doubtful whether Tripho's Judaism ever existed or whether, like sophistics in Plato, Judaism is a polemical disguise. But even if Tripho's Judaism did exist, the fact remains that Tripho does not speak in a symbolic language comparable to the one Goodenough postulates.

Another possible criterion is the constant repetition of certain symbols in certain buildings or objects to indicate that a precise symbolic

---

the studies of the Warburg Institute (*Vorträge, Journal*, etc.) and the *Eranos-Jahrbuch*. It may also help to remember that a two-volume anthology of *Eranos-Jahrbuch* studies was published in an English translation by Pantheon Books, Bollingen Series, without a date but from around 1954, under the titles *Spirit and Nature* and *The Mysteries*. M. Schlesinger's *Geschichte des Symbols*, Berlin, 1912, is a remarkable work to this day, but a fundamental contribution is E. H. Gombrich's "Icones Symbolicae: The Visual Image in Neo-Platonic Thought," *Journ. Warburg Instit.* 2 (1948): 163–92. Recent American studies are mentioned in the anthology by L. Bryson et al., *Symbols and Value, An Initial Study*, New York, 1954, where, among others, we find a weak essay by L. Finkelstein, "Judaism as a System of Symbols," pp. 87–108. The most important recent studies on the philosophy of symbolism are Susanne Langer's penetrating books (*Philosophy in a New Key*, 1941; *Feeling and Form*, 1953; the first has an exhaustive bibliography). Langer acknowledges her debt to A. N. Whitehead and E. Cassirer (see her contribution to the anthology *The Philosophy of E. Cassirer*, 1949, pp. 381–400). See also *Umanesimoe Simbolismo*, Padova, 1958, and E. Wind, *Pagan Mysteries in the Renaissance*, London, 1958.

language was known. This constant repetition has made it possible to reconstruct, at least in part, the symbolic language of medieval Christian art. But aside from the most obvious Jewish symbols or certain non-Jewish elements, which can be simply decorative or roughly evocative (Nikes, crowns, zodiacs), we find no common language in the illustrations Goodenough studies.[8] Despite Goodenough's efforts to show that its symbolism is of a conventional type after all (4:231–32), the synagogue of Dura is obviously unique. But several types of Palestinian synagogues exist as well. The Talmudic passage Goodenough quotes (1:183), wherein it is stated that the outside of a pagan temple might pass as a synagogue, is very significant. The tombs of Sheikh Ibreiq (1:89ff.) display a quantity of figures that are absolutely unique. The synagogue at Dura and the tombs of Sheikh Ibreiq are the major elements in support of Goodenough's theory. The two monumental complexes differ from each other in terms of the symbolism they employ; they also differ from the mysterious Roman catacombs of Vigna Rondanini. The differences can be interpreted in terms of a variety of religious beliefs, or more simply in terms of a variety of social customs, but they do not permit us to presuppose a uniform religious language on the part of those who erected these monuments.[9]

The third major difficulty with Goodenough's interpretation of documents is that just as there is no uniform Judaism, there is also no uniform paganism. As we have already said, the exact symbolic value of most pagan figures is still *sub iudice*. Even if we accept the presupposition that a given Jewish symbol of Hellenistic origin should have a meaning not too different from the original meaning, the original meaning of these figures has yet to be established. Goodenough speaks of a lingua franca of Dionysian symbols circulating in the Hellenistic world (4:46). But did this lingua franca actually exist? The only syncretistic material we possess consists in amulets and magic formulas, and even after the excellent book by Campbell Bonner, Goodenough shows that much remains to be said. From this material Goodenough draws the conclusion that Judaism "accepted the best of paganism (including its most powerful enchantments) given that paganism oriented itself to-

8. It has not been demonstrated that the zodiac always implies "a belief in the influence of the planets on the affairs of this world," as E. L. Sukenik claimed in *The Ancient Synagogue of Beth Alpha*, Jerusalem, 1932, p. 56.

9. When it comes to details, Goodenough is at times naive. See, for example, his interpretation of a grotesque lamp from Naples (4:1 144, fig. 112). He also believes that πίε ζήσαις ἀεὶ ἐν ἀγαθοῖς [*pie tessis sei eu agatois*] on a glass means "drink and thou shalt live forever among the good" (that is, "among the saints"), and he comments, "the phrase is definitely eschatological" (2:117).

ward the supreme Iao Sabaoth and found its significance in it" (2:295). But it remains to be seen how many of these amulets were produced by Jews for Jews, how many were produced by the pagans for the Jews, how many by Jews for the pagans, and how many by pagans for pagans with Hebraistic tastes. The fundamental question remains open if in the mind of a person using a certain amulet religion was "something different." It is "something different" for many modern people, and, if human nature has not changed, it must have been "something different" for many ancient people as well.[10]

In the books he has published so far, Goodenough has not yet carried out a thorough analysis of the so-called non-Jewish symbols; he has only presupposed the results of his research. But he has discussed exclusively Jewish symbols, such as the candleholder (menorah), the closet for the scrolls of the Law, the tuba (shofar), and so on. This should be the simplest case of symbolism. Yet as soon as Goodenough goes beyond the most elementary data—that is, that Jews used these symbols to designate something that is theirs, almost like a flag—his conclusions become extremely conjectural. We realize that even the allegorical interpretation suggested by Philo, and in some cases by Flavius Josephus, is useful to him only in part. No one can say for sure if the complex allegory of the candleholder presented by Philo, and alluded to by Flavius Josephus (4:82–88), was present in the mind of the Jew who placed the candleholder on the tomb of a loved one. And who can say what was being evoked through the symbol of the shofar, which every Jew heard echoing on certain solemn occasions such as Rosh Hashanah and Yom Kippur? It is clear that local situations and individual reactions must have accounted for a great difference in the interpretation of these symbols if in times of "normative Judaism" (tenth century) Saadya Gaon was able to provide ten different interpretations of the sound of the shofar (4:194).

## IV

In the present state of things, this material raises more problems than it solves. Sure criteria for interpretation are still lacking. I believe that at this point I should concentrate on a preliminary element that Goodenough appears to have neglected: the study of the overall life of a Jewish community in the Hellenistic-Roman period. It is obvious that the symbols of a religious community can be understood better when one has a clear idea of the community as a social group. We should begin by

10. See M. Simon, "Superstition et magie," *Verus Israel*, 1948, pp. 394–431.

asking: who were these Jews who decorated their synagogues and their tombs with obvious inconsistency?

For example, Goodenough mentions (2:143) one of the two famous inscriptions of the Jewish politeuma of Berenice (Bengasi), but he does not appear to know the second one, and he certainly does not appreciate its importance. These two inscriptions—which originally were published by Scipione Maffei and the study of which has been renewed by J. and G. Roux in *Rev. Ét. Grecques* 62 (1949): 280–96[11]—belong, as is known, to the time of Augustus and Tiberius (See *IGRRP* 1:1024 and notes). One of them is a decree in honor of the Roman governor M. Tittius on the part of the Jewish politeuma assembled during the feast of the Tabernacles; the second inscription is in honor of a member of the same politeuma, the Roman citizen Decimus Valerius Dionysius, "who painted (ἐχονίασεν) [the pavement] and the amphitheatre at his own expense as a voluntary contribution for the community." What we have here is a Jewish politeuma that apparently possesses a building called an amphitheatre, which is painted by a member of the politeuma itself. The process of Hellenization is considerable, but the politeuma celebrates traditional Jewish feasts. Should we expect a mysteriosophic religion from this politeuma? Or, rather, is it not the case with these Jews that they behave similarly to the Jews from Miletus, who reserved for themselves a sector of the local theater and in the inscription proudly declared themselves to be "believers in God" (A. Deissman, *Licht vom Osten*, p. 391)? These Jews appear to be mixing Greek and Jewish ways of life, but without achieving a particularly deep synthesis. We should now ask whether Philo, instead of representing the surrounding Jewish world, does not in fact react to the superficiality of that culture. After all, as his *De Congressu eruditionis gratia* shows (ed. Wendland, 3:71–109), he is not the theorist of an immediate and direct knowledge of the divine but the theoretician of a complex education, where the encyclopedia precedes and prepares philosophy.

Philo did not prevail. A different, much more radical reaction prevailed: the creation of an intellectual discipline, of a Jewish form of education, which gradually and consciously opposed itself to the Greek one. As S. Lieberman (*Greek in Jewish Palestine*, 1942) has shown, the rabbis of Palestine, who created the basis for this education, all but ig-

---

11. G. Caputo, "Note sugli edifici teatrali della Cirenaica," in *"Anthemon" in Honor of C. Anti*, Florence, 1955, pp. 283–87 (to which P. Fraser has drawn my attention), again claims that the "amphitheatre" was not a property of the Jewish politeuma, but the difficulties mentioned by J. and G. Roux appear to persist. See also M. Grant, *From Imperium to Auctoritas*, 1946, p. 142.

nored the Greek language and culture. A new form of Judaism emerged, a form more nationalistic and exclusive but founded on the awareness of intellectual values, of mental discipline, and of devotion to learning—a form that appears unthinkable without the Greek example. Here I shall repeat the conclusion to a very beautiful but little-known essay by E. Bickerman: "Judaism adopted the most important idea of Hellenism, that of *paideia*, of perfection through liberal education." Bickerman adds that the difference between Jewish and Hellenistic *paideia* is that the first was aimed at producing "the scholar versed in the Holy Writ," the latter, "the athletic gentleman of the gymnasion."[12] It is from this perspective rather than that of religious mysteries that I believe we should consider the true result of Greek influence on Judaism. Thus, we should consider, as a reasonable working hypothesis, that the symbols Goodenough studies should be interpreted in the context of a superficial process of Hellenization against which both Philo and the rabbis reacted rather than in terms of a mysteriosophic religion not otherwise documented.

12. E. Bickerman, "The Historical Foundation of Postbiblical Judaism," in *The Jews, Their History, Culture and Religion*, ed. L. Finkelstein, 1949, 1:70–114. For Hellenized Jews among the ephebes, see L. Robert in *Rev. Étud. Juives* n.s. 1 (1937): 86. An important collection of information and attentive judgments on the process of Hellenization is found in S. W. Baron *A Social and Religious History of the Jews*, vol. 2, 1952, pp. 3–56 and relative notes. (For all the questions discussed herewith see E. Bickerman in *Antiq. Class.* 25 [1956]: 246–51; A. D. Nock in *Gnomon* 29 [1957]: 524–33, and 30 [1958]: 291–95; and Goodenough's reply in *Jewish Symbols*, 8:218–32. On 8:224 we find a clear statement of his presupposition, "When Jews adopted the same lingua franca of symbols, they must, it seems to me, have taken over the constant values in these symbols" on Berenice; E. Gabba, *Iscrizioni greche e latine per lo studio della Bibbia*, Turin, 1958, pp. 62–67).

# 6

# An Apology of Judaism:
# The *Against Apion* by Flavius Josephus

A religious apology is not only a defense; it is, above all, a confrontation. This is its interest. An apology compels the believer to justify himself in the eyes of the world and to find, outside of idle custom, reasons
of faith that have a universal value. A belief is opposed to a different
belief in order to test its value and to see how it meets those demands
that opponents raise through their objections. Thus, an apology invariably implies an examination of conscience, even when the din of war
and love for oneself are not conducive to a calm consideration and tend
to corrupt the debate by resorting to lawyerlike arguments. But a conscious reader understands, from what the apologist says and from
what he does not say, that which appears to be the highest, unquestionable and original content of his religion, so that it can be offered
without fear to the criticism of adversaries. Thus, an apology invariably
points to those elements that in a given time and for a given current of
thought appear to be basic to a religion, those elements that have been
affirmed as its reason to thrive and to be appreciated, if not followed,
by other men. The choice of such elements is then used to weigh how
the action of adversaries or, better, of currents of thought in the surrounding world, have affected apologists by imposing their presuppositions to a greater or lesser extent, thus compelling the apologists
themselves to deal with those very presuppositions.

To study Judaism through its apologetics thus means to understand
it in its effort to take a stance before the surrounding world and its effort to define itself in relation to that world. A good account of Jewish
apologetics could make a precious contribution to the understanding
of the development of Judaism; in fact, from a particular but vast point
of view, Judaism might be identified with the very history of this development. The greatest concern of Judaism today is its function in modern civilization: whether this function exists and, admitting that it

does, how can we define it. The problem of this function, if we have to weigh the ideals of Judaism against those of the surrounding world, has its source precisely in apologetics. Thus we must return to apologetics in order to gain an accurate sense of the difficulties with which our predecessors were confronted, difficulties we want to avoid in all forms.

One of the most important periods for Jewish apologetics is once again that of the Hellenistic-Roman world. The unsettling diversity of the Hellenistic world, its longing for truth and new ideals of beauty, and the richness of its phenomena were such that they prevailed even upon those Jews who were the most loyal to the simple and rigid line of tradition. Whether they liked it or not, in defending the spiritual patrimony of their people, Jews had to deal with the strength of the civilization that lay before them. Although for Jews "paganism" could appear immoral in religion and custom, Greek culture, given its dialectical nature calling for discussion and refutation of ideas, could not be simply rejected. But diversity often conceals similarities. Jewish ideals and conceptions—above all, monotheism—appeared to echo in Greek philosophy under different forms. Such ideas appeared to lead to consequences that, although alien to Orthodox Judaism, seemed inevitable. Having become involved in a Greek mentality, Judaism could not avoid changes in its development. The travail of Hellenistic-Roman Judaism wavered between opposition and agreement with Greekness. Now I would like to examine, briefly, the *Against Apion* by Flavius Josephus, one of the most important documents we possess of this travail.[1]

The greatest difficulty one experiences with the writing of a Jewish apology lies in the very nature of Judaism, whose living element lies not in dogmatics but, for lack of a better word, in preceptism, better still, in the daily practice of the Law felt as a manifestation of the Divinity. Hence the task of the Jewish apologist is not to defend a speculative attitude or given articles of faith, but rather a very detailed norm of life. Consequently, the dangers of a similar apology have been either in theorizing the Law too abstractly, to the point of rarifying it into a metaphysical conception, or in becoming lost in a minute justification of its

---

1. I am using Reinach's edition, *Flavius Josèphe, Contre Apion*, Paris, 1930, which is recommended for its widely informed introduction as well as for its accompanying French translation by Blum. I am using this edition as a basis for an article "Sul Contro Apione," *Rivista di Filol. Classica* 59 (1931), in which I am dealing with the very problems mentioned in the text. Little has been written on Flavius the apologist; much of it is not very good. See P. Krüger, *Philo und Josephus als Apologeten des Judentums*, 1906; B. Brüne, *Flavius Josephus und seine Schriften in ihrem Verhältnis zum Judentume . . .* ,Gütersloh, 1913; J. Guttmann, *Die Darstellung der jüd. Religion bei Fl. J.*, Breslau, 1928.

individual precepts. In the former case, the result is a philosophical treatise; in the latter, a commentary to a code, or worse, to a manual of hygiene. Flavius Josephus is one of the few writers who has managed to avoid both dangers by presenting Judaism as an organic legislation: he presents Judaism as the Law, not the laws or the theory of the law. We now shall see how he has managed to achieve this result and whether his work maintains the characteristic mark of the Law as it is conceived by Judaism: its divine origin.

I believe I have shown elsewhere that Flavius Josephus did not begin his *Against Apion* with the intention of writing an apology of Judaism. As far as the end of book 1, he simply wanted to refute the objections raised against his major work, *Archaelogia Judaica*, concerning the antiquity of the Jews. In the second book, while discussing the opinions expressed on the subject by the Alexandrine and anti-semitic grammarian Apion, Flavius was led to defend not the antiquity of Moses and his legislation, but the intrinsic value of the legislation. This explains why, among other things, the apology itself is confined to the last part of the second and final book (145ff.), and why the whole work gives the impression of not having a well-established economy. It is certain, however, that the defense of Jewish antiquity is directly related to the apology of the Law. We shall see clearly how Flavius has lost, in part, the exact sense of the originality of Jewish law; consequently, he does not have the vigor to extol Judaism as a moral edifice that does not pale in comparison to more recent religious constructions, regardless of the more or less ancient time in which it originated.

First, Flavius needs to establish that Moses precedes the famous Greek legislators: "Thus, I declare that our legislator surpasses in antiquity all known legislators: Lycurgus, Solon, Zaleucus of Locri and all of the others admired by the Greeks appear to have been born yesterday, or before yesterday, compared to him" (2:154). And while he simply hints at the idea that the Greek philosophers themselves depend on Moses, a rather common idea in the Jewish apologetics of his time, he insists that they have done nothing else but appropriate and develop the Jewish conception of God "unbegotten, eternally immutable" (2:167).

> Indeed, the wisest among Greek men learned to think these things about God by adopting his principles (Moses), that these are beautiful and becoming to the nature and greatness of God, it is certain that they can bear witness. Indeed Pythagoras, Anaxagoras, Plato and all or almost all of the later philosophers of the Stoa seemed to have such thoughts on the nature of God. (2:168; on Plato, see 2:257).

This connection between Jewish Law and Greek philosophy required that the priority of the former be established over the latter so that it would become impossible to invert the reasoning. But this is evidence, as we were saying, of the limited originality Flavius attaches to the Law.

Indeed, in the *Against Apion*, the apology of Judaism becomes an apology of Moses the legislator. It is hardly worth mentioning that Flavius does not distinguish at all between the prescription of the Pentateuch and later prescriptions: all are traced back to Moses in compliance with a well-known Pharisaic theory, as is formulated, for example, in extreme terms in the famous passage of *i. Peah*, 17a: "Whatever shall be taught in the future by an intelligent disciple before his teacher has already been said to Moses on the Sinai." This detail has surprised a few critics, whereas it should have appeared very natural. The basic point has not been observed: for Flavius, it is not God who imposes the Law on Israel through Moses; it is Moses who imposes God on Israel through the Law. Compare the following:

> The differences peculiar to the customs and to the laws of men are infinite, but they can be summarized thusly: some entrusted political power to a monarchy, others to an oligarchy, others to a democracy. Our legislator did not heed any of these and created a theocracy, as one would say, by violating language, by *placing all power and strength in God*, and persuading everyone to address him as the cause of all good. . . . He showed God unbegotten and immutable over time, different in beauty from all mortal things, knowable to us through his strength but unknowable as to his essence." (2:164–69)

The truly characteristic point of this apology is that the legislator comes before god while all of the action is concentrated on the legislator. True, the legislator in turn should be considered as inspired by God so as to appear as God's speaker. What is lacking in Flavius, however, is precisely the ability to define this inspiration. The curious formula with which the author attempts to clarify the divine origin of the Law has already been noted, but it has not been appreciated fully:

> Because his plan was beautiful and his great works were fortunate, (Moses) truly believed that his leader and counselor was God, and having persuaded himself that everything he thought and operated was through God's will, he believed he should impart this conviction to the people, because those who are persuaded that God watches over their lives do not dare err in any way. (2:160)

Hence, Moses did not experience the divine intimately, but convinced himself he was inspired by God through a cautious and well-considered reasoning. This point is interesting not because it is attributed to Moses, but because it reveals his way of judging the divine inspiration of the Law. Divine inspiration is present as a rational presupposition, not as a fulcrum and intimate force of the Law. In the act of legislating, Moses is not inspired: the inspiration appears after the fact. Thus, the original Jewish relationship between God and Moses, which lies in prophetic inspiration, is missing in Flavius.

At the beginning of the second of his life of Moses, Philo acknowledged in Moses the king, the legislator, the priest, and the prophet. Flavius acknowledges only the legislator and considers him higher than Lycurgus, Solon, and Zaleucus, although he remains substantially similar to them. Flavius himself compares Moses to Minos.

> Such was our legislator, neither a sorcerer nor an impostor, as he is called unfairly by those who insult him, but such as the Greeks have boasted that Minos was, or, after him, other legislators, some of whom trace their laws back to Zeus, others to Apollo and the Delphic oracle, be it that they hold this to be the truth, be it that they believe they can persuade better this way. (2.162)

Both Moses and the legislators create legislation that leads to a divinity. The difference lies, of course, in the fact that while the divinity of the latter is false, that of Moses is real. But what really matters here is that Moses has been compared to Greek legislators, and that he has been placed among them.

Flavius's conception of Moses can be understood better if seen in the context not of Judaism but of a common Hellenistic mentality. Just as all ancient people without distinction were unable to conceive the gradual, material development of a city without postulating a hypothetical founder, so they never succeeded in comprehending the constitutional formation of a city. Here, too, there had to be a deus ex machina, a legislator endowed with unique foresight, an almost divine being who offered men a hidden good by creating a political order. Given this mentality, it is only natural that a tradition of Egerian nymphs and Numa Pomilia appeared, and that in the Roman Hellenistic period these traditions were strengthened by the cult of the monarch or of the emperor as the expression of the sense of infinite superiority attached to a leader. Hence, it is generally recognized that divine inspiration existed in the pagan world as well, but here it was expressed through evocations, order, and outer momentum, and did not consist in a direct contact between the will of God and human action, as in prophetism. Since God was not conceived as a moral will, the dialogue between man and God in the solitude of man's conscience—where man surrenders to the will of God and becomes the expression of this will—could not be conceived. In Flavius, the inspiration of Moses is not of a Jewish but of a pagan type, and Moses is represented as a legislator in the Hellenistic sense.

Now I wish to anticipate an easy—and for this very reason, pointless—objection. It was believed, and many continue to believe, that Flavius would rally on the side of his adversaries so that they could appreciate the value of Judaism. This remark apparently contains a contradiction in terms. By assuming the point of view of his adversaries, Flavius could no longer defend that Judaism which, for this very reason, had already disappeared. Neither Tertullian nor Saint Augustine ever renounced the presuppositions of Christianity in polemicizing with their enemies. In the field of Judaism, Profeit Duran, in writing his apologetic letter to Buen Giorno, did not place himself on the side of the Christians in order to discuss the Trinity. The apologist feels, indeed must feel, the necessity of defending the specific values of his faith, otherwise the very reasons for his polemic disappear. Flavius does not give up any conviction for apologetic ends; only those who have no convictions can give up a conviction. The conclusions we have obtained from our study of the *Against Apion* may be viewed as only the most typical evidence of Flavius's basic lack of religiosity. This is not an accusation; indeed, it helps us to attain a more human perspective on his political conduct. We cannot deal with this problem here as it is rendered more complicated by the presence of partisan feelings, noteworthy but harmful in current opinions, the only reaction to which has been to bury Flavius's personality under the "search for sources." But it is certain that Flavius was substantially alien to the religious zeal that led his fellow men to the final struggle with Rome, and led him to appreciate the situation realistically. In other words, he held it pointless to fight Rome, given that Jews were facing a sure disaster. His attitude proves, despite his apparent orthodox loyalty to the Law, his detachment from the soul of his people. This distance, invariably accompanied by loyalty to the Jewish life, can be felt in the *Against Apion*.

From a superficial perspective, we find in Flavius's work the most strenuous defense of Judaism. Yet we cannot be deceived. Flavius's Pharisaism, together with the Essenic experiences that are part of his background, finds expression in his legalism, and there is no trace of a rich inner religiosity. We find in Flavius a very distinct sense of Judaism as Law, so much so that the prophets are not even mentioned because they represent a religious *creativity*, an intimacy with God that is very far from Flavius's ideal of the full, passive obedience to the eternal norm. Flavius can respond to those contemporaries who would accuse Jews of scarce theoretical and practical inventiveness by answering, not without acumen, "We believe that the only wisdom and virtue consists in not doing and not thinking anything contrary to the original Law" (2.183). But not even once in the *Against Apion* do we find those words that reveal the most common Jewish Pharisaic religiosity: prayer, love and fear of God, sin, messianism, resurrection. In order to understand the *Against Apion*, we first must read some studies on Judaism, such as *The Pharisees* by Herford or *Judaism* by Moore. Only then will we be able to understand what is missing in the *Against Apion*. Indeed, what we find missing in the *Against Apion* is all that the people of Israel consider reasons for life and hope—the struggle against sin, the aspiration to absolute justice, the invocation of the Kingdom of God, and the suffering for the tragic destiny of Israel. In the *Against Apion*, we have the legislator who has ordered all things in the most excellent manner and who "has not left one thing, not the slightest one, to the free initiative of those who use it" (2.173). But no God sheds His light over this legislation, no God is its origin and end. God is only one of the aspects, perhaps the most conspicuous one, of the Mosaic legislation; it is not its very soul. At a certain point Flavius says, "all our works, our cares, our speeches express our devotion to God" (2.171). Then he explains why "devotion" to God lies at the center of the Law: "The fact is that, due to the nature of our legislation, which is concerned with what is useful, (the legislator) invariably surpasses by far all other men; he did not make devotion a part of virtue, but all other virtues a part of this virtue, and I mean justice, temperance, fortitude, the agreement of all citizens in all things" (2.170). The devotion to God is not the prime mover of legislation but a consequence of the legislation itself. What is being extolled here is the concept the Law has of God, not the concept God has of the Law. Whereas Jews have always felt that the Law was the highest gift from God, that gift for which, according to the famous Talmudic apologist, Moses had to contend with angels, Flavius postulates the Law itself as a distant object. It is not the vision of the perfect God that leads to the perfect Law, but the perfect Law that leads to the perfect God. "What (legislation) could be more beautiful and more just than that which places God above all things?" (2.185).

In this direction Flavius has certainly to some extent been preceded by Philo, whose work *Hypothetica*, which we possess in a partial summary by Eusebius (*Praeparatio Evangelica* 8.6–7), must be considered, despite recent objections, a direct source of the *Against Apion* because of its exposition of Mosaic Law. But we cannot reconstruct the overall aspect of the work from Eusebius's summary; all we can say, judging from the overall spirit of Philo's thought, animated by the contemplation of God, is that, however important Moses must have been to him, God had to be present to a much greater extent than in Flavius's elaboration. This is confirmed by Philo's "Life" of Moses, and deserves to be examined in a special study on Philo's attitude with regard to the Law. Only after a similar study will we be able to gauge how much Flavius owes to the Neoplatonic philosopher, not in the details but in the general spirit of his apology.

Through the extrinsic appreciation of Pharisaic legalism, severed from its intimate religiosity, Judaism inevitably must have appeared to Flavius only as legislation, and Moses only as a legislator to be associated with Minos, Zaleucus, and Solon. Thus, it looks like Flavius's defense of Judaism resolves itself into a discretionary surrender to paganism. This is so, in theory, because Jewish faith disappears; in practice, however, this attitude proves to be a conservative force of Jewish life by justifying devotion to the Law as obedience to the best of legislations. Moreover, it is obvious that this attitude, notwithstanding faith, indeed presupposes faith, because without faith not one word of the Law, which from the beginning to the end is a divine service to God, would remain standing. In essence, throughout his apology, Flavius presupposed not only the generic existence of God but also the specific existence of the God of Israel, that is, of a God who is such because he wants a particular legislation and no other. It is only because of this tacit presupposition that Flavius can speak easily about Moses, who establishes the Law in the name of God without being concerned whether God exists or whether God approves the Law itself. In the *Against Apion*, we find the objects of faith without the faith itself. This is a curious point of view, which can be explained only by considering how rooted such beliefs must have been in the Jewish soul. They believed because a centuries-old tradition, even when the religious experience was not there to suggest the immediate presence of the divine.

Thus, although the *Against Apion* is founded on the material data of Judaism, it does not possess Jewish religiosity itself and interprets Judaism with a Hellenistic mentality. This situation was unbearable because it was absurd. Had it become widespread, it would have led to the disappearance of Judaism once its presuppositions were no longer sustained by religious experience and were splintered by doubt. This has not prevented the situation from repeating itself substantially nineteen centuries later, however, when scholars have shown with wisdom and doctrine that Judaism can provide the perfect response to the thought of Kant, Hegel, or even Jesus, as though it were not simpler, in such a case, to prefer the real Kant, Hegel, and Jesus to their Jewish copies.

If Judaism is to be appreciated by resorting to categories drawn from a different system of thought, it is inevitable that one ends up realizing that its truth lies in the thought that provides the criterion for such appreciation. In general, one ends up realizing that an apology has no value if it is heteronomous. This basic absurdity has prevented the *Against Apion* from exercising any effective influence on Jewish thought, so much so that it has come down to us only in the Christian tradition, due to the interest of its erudite information. This absurdity, however, concealed the deep logical need of comparing Jewish civilization with Greek civilization, just as the absurdity of interpreting Judaism through Kantianism deforms the necessity of appreciating it at the level of the highest modern thought. Flavius attempted to situate Judaism within the patterns of Greek thought, but most Jews were aware that their values could not be confused with those of the "peoples." Johanan ben Zakkai and Paul of Tharsos did not think differently on this point.[2]

2. For recent literature on Flavius Josephus, see L. H. Feldman, *Scholarship on Philo and Josephus (1937–1962)*, New York, (around 1963). G. Bertram, "Josephus und die abendländische Geschichtsidee," in W. Grundmann, *Germanentum, Christentum und Judentum* Leipzig, 1942, 2:41–82, should be studied attentively by historians of Nazism.

# 7

# What Flavius Josephus Did Not See

## I

The author of this book, a book born out of an introduction to a French translation of the *Judaic War* by Flavius Josephus, now has a definite place among the scholars who have joined J.-P. Vernant in renewing the interpretation of Greek thought. Starting from nondogmatic premises in which historic psychology, Marxism, and structuralism converge (both in the Dumézil and the Lévi-Strauss variety), this group of scholars, known and powerful in Italy as well, has aroused fresh interest in mythology as well as in poetry and in various philosophical currents as the expression of a taking possession of reality in Greek culture. Out of this group of scholars, Pierre Vidal-Naquet, born in 1930, is the most interested in direct research of political and social history. This is evident from his book *Clisthène l'Athénien* (1964), with P. Lévêque, and from the penetrating pamphlet *Le bordereau d'ensemencement dans l'Égypte Ptolémaïque* (1967) as well as from the essential role he has played in presenting and developing for the French public the economic and social research of his friend M. I. Finley.[1] This can be explained, in part, simply by his orthodox background as a classical and historic philologist of antiquity, a pupil of H.-I. Marrou, Victor Gold-

---

1. P. Vidal-Naquet, "Économie et Société dans la Grèce ancienne: l'oeuvre de M. Finley," *Archives Européennes de Sociologie* 6 (1965): 111–48; an introduction to the French translation of *Democracy Ancient and Modern* [*Tradition de la Démocratie Grecque*] Paris, 1976. For the work written in collaboration with J. P. Vernant, see *Mythe et tragédie en Grèce ancienne*, Paris, 1972 (Ital. trans., 1976). It is impossible to provide here a bibliography of even the most important of Vidal-Naquet's writings which would be necessary given the difficulty of tracing the numerous contributions he made to anthologies and the original introductions he provided for other books. We will simply mention the excellent and fortunate selection of texts written in collaboration with M. Austin, *Économies et sociétés en Grèce ancienne*, 1972, which was translated into English in an enlarged version.

PART ONE

schmidt, L. Robert, A. Aymard, and that curious Socratic figure, Henri Margueritte. But, as is generally recognized, the interests of Vidal-Naquet the historian cannot be separated from the major role he has played (without particular party affiliations) in two decisive episodes of recent French history: the Algerian crisis, when he opposed the methods of repression used by the French government (see *Lo stato di tortura*, Bari, 1963), and the student uprising of 1968, where he was a participant and later a historian in collaboration with Alain Schnapp in the documentary book *Journal de la Commune étudiante* (1969), which has been translated into English.

In 1960–61, Vidal-Naquet, then an assistant professor in Caen, was suspended from university teaching for having signed the Statement of the 121 on the right of *insoumission* in the Algerian war. More recently, in both France and Italy, he was attacked by scholars from the right and from the left (B. Hemmerdinger and V. Di Benedetto).[2] After a few years at the CNRS and at the University of Lyon, he was appointed vice-director of studies (1966) and then director of studies at the École Pratique des Hautes Études (1969), a successor to A. Aymard. He is also involved in the editorship of the *Annales* and has had especially close collaborative ties with the medievalist J. Le Goff.

While it is not surprising that Vidal-Naquet's historiographic interests should include Judaism, his book on Flavius Josephus surprised the author himself, even before it reached the common readers of his works on Greek subjects. Indeed, Vidal-Naquet has not forgotten and will not forget that he is Jewish, one of those Jews from the Arba' Kehillot, from the "four communities" of the Contado Venassino, whose center is in Carpentras; ever since the Middle Ages, generations of rabbis and doctors, and more recently musicians, politicians, writers, and scientists, have come from Carpentras in very high proportions compared to their small numbers. Both Vidal-Naquet's father, who participated in the Resistance in 1940, and his mother, were deported and killed at Auschwitz by the Nazis.

Vidal-Naquet's involvement in support of the Algerian Arabs (and Berbers) has its root here. So too, does his constant preoccupation with the problem of Israel. Although this preoccupation cannot be described briefly, the main point about it is that Vidal-Naquet believes that Israelis and Palestinians can have a dialogue.

Nor can we peremptorily define the relationship between his concern, as a French Jew, for the future of Judaism and his interpretation of

2. See, for example, V. Di Benedetto in *Belfagor* 33 (1978): 191–207, an essay filled with valid objections, and the strange piece by B. Hemmerdinger, in *Belfagor* 31 (1976): 355–58.

the position of Flavius Josephus during and after the Jewish War of 66–67 A.D. It is enough to stress here the deep emotional root from which a new—and perhaps more personal—Vidal-Naquet the historian has emerged, as is revealed in a chapter on Hellenistic-Roman Judaism in the second volume of *Rome et la conquête du monde méditerranéen* (1978) from the collection "La Nouvelle Clio" by Claude Nicolet and his collaborators. We can tell that this historiographic activity is just a beginning.

## II

There is one point, however, where Vidal-Naquet's current preoccupation, as a Jew of the modern Diaspora, and the narration of the Jewish War of 70 A.D. takes on a more precise aspect. This is the attention he devotes to the ancient Diaspora before, during, and after the war of 70 A.D. while at the same time stressing two elements in the cultural formation of Flavius Josephus: the rabbinic (Jewish) and the rhetorical (Greek) as variants of the same phenomenon. These two points are unquestionably connected. The Diaspora (or at least most of it) remained absent from the war of 70 A.D.. The Jews of the Diaspora fought and were bled white in the heroic and furious rebellion under Trajan, to which the Jews of Palestine appear to have been almost entirely foreign. The latter, in turn, were alone in defying the legions of Hadrian in the revolt of Bar Kokhba, the final disaster. As to Flavius Josephus, the historian of the war of 70 A.D., he is a Jew who speaks Aramaic and writes first in Aramaic. It is only after he has acquired Roman citizenship and settled in Rome that he begins, with some difficulty, to write in Greek. By adopting Greek patterns of thought, Flavius signified his distance from Palestinian Jews, but at the same time he wrote an apology of Judaism, which in many ways reflects the situation of the Diaspora. Indeed, the *Against Apion* is a reply to a Greek-speaking Egyptian detractor.

The condition of being a refugee was not new. Polybius had experienced it. But, as Vidal-Naquet accurately points out, Polybius had to deal with his Achaean fellow citizens, not with God. Unlike Polybius, Flavius Josephus justifies himself in front of the God of the Fathers. He thus not only writes a contemporary history like Polybius, but also an account of the past of his people and a defense of their religious traditions. The case of Flavius Josephus, who, while becoming a refugee remains loyal to his God and to his people, is not in its objective elements all that different from the case of the Jews of the Diaspora who did not fight in the war of 70 A.D. and, although scattered in different linguistic areas, remained Jewish. A traitor to his fellow fighters in Palestine, Flavius takes refuge among those who did not fight in the war, or who ignored that they will fight one.

## III

In speaking of Flavius Josephus's solitary condition, we are not inspired by a moralistic prejudice. Flavius does not appear to comprehend the synagogue, an institution that bound Jews together even before the destruction of the Temple. He appears to comprehend even less that the apocalyptic enthusiasms he opposed involved not only Palestinian revolutionary groups but also Jews from the Diaspora, not to mention Christian groups. Finally, apocalyptics was rooted in the burning soil of the hostility against Rome raging in the provinces. And here my interpretation of these facts begins to differ from that of my friend Vidal-Naquet.

1) The history of the survival of national cultures in the Roman Empire is a history that does not admit generalizations. It includes the opposite cases of Greeks who become Romans when they become Christian (and would address the pagans as Hellenes) and the Egyptians (or Syrians) who reacquired the best of their national conscience when their language (respectively Coptic and Syrian) became the language of their religion after their conversion to Christianity. In the Latin West, old regional cultures appear to have lived a subterranean life, until they reemerged (at least to a certain extent) in Latin or Neo-Latin form after the fall of the Western Empire.

As for the Jews, their national life before 70 A.D. consisted in associations that the Greek language designated primarily by the word "synagogue."[3] Synagogues existed in Palestine as well as in the Diaspora. We do not know where and when (certainly at least by the first century B.C.) synagogues began to develop wherever Jews were to be found. In Palestine, as long as the temple of Jerusalem existed, and indeed as long as the majority of the population remained Jewish, the synagogue was not used to distinguish the Jews from the Gentiles and thus to pre-

---

3. See *The Synagogue*, ed. J. Gutmann, New York, 1974. Three different trends in the study of Judaism in the first century A.D. can be exemplified by *The Jewish People in the First Century*, ed. S. Safrai and M. Stern, 2 vols. (published until now), Leiden, 1974–76; E. Rivkin, *A Hidden Revolution: The Pharisees' Search for the Kingdom Within*, Abingdon, 1978; and *Approaches to Ancient Judaism: Theory and Practice*, ed. W. S. Green, Missoula, 1978. On the educational theme, see J. Goldin in *Ex Orbe Religionum. Studia G. Widengren*, Leiden, 1972, 1:176–91. It would be interesting to compare a sociological study of the modern American synagogue: S. C. Heilman, *Synagogue Life*, Chicago, 1973.

serve the Jews as Jews. But in Palestine, as well as in the Diaspora, the synagogue involved the existence of a cult founded on the reading of and commentary on the Bible (in particular, the Pentateuch), the direct or indirect care of the education of children and adults, and an administrative and assistance-giving organization. Because each synagogue was founded by private initiative, it was possible for various synagogues to exist in the same city. These synagogues were free to establish ties and to communicate with each other. The religious service of the synagogue presupposed that the biblical text was accessible even to those who did not know Hebrew: hence, the oral and written translation of the Bible into Greek, Aramaic, and later Latin, a unique phenomenon in the ancient world. Through the synagogue, the Jews became the people of the book for the first time, although they were still far from accepting as an ideal model the rule of Maimonides—that every Jew, rich or poor, young or old, healthy or ill, until the day of his death has the duty to reserve a portion of his everyday life to the study of the Torah. The synagogue provided the opportunity to express, and up to a point resolve, existing economic, social, and specifically religious conflicts. The synagogue maintained and developed the unity of the cult where there was no linguistic unity. But the large number of synagogues would have led to chaos were it not for the existence of authoritative interpreters of the Law; thus, synagogues began to rely on rabbinic schools.

We learn this from texts such as the Gospels, Acts of the Apostles, and Letters of Saint Paul. But Flavius Josephus speaks very little of the synagogue. He only mentions the practice of studying the Law on the Sabbath, as introduced by Moses (*Ant. Jud.* 16.43: *Contra Apionem* 2.175). The synagogue as a functioning institution does not appear in his works.

2) Today, perhaps, we need not insist on the fact that the internal social conflicts of the Jewish people around 70 A.D., which Vidal-Naquet analyses so well, were in part generated and in part contained by the presence of Rome. As such, they are inseparable from the situation created by Rome and from the hostility Rome aroused throughout the Empire. The ruling class exploited and essentially despised the common provincials, from whom it attempted to separate a limited number of rich people by Romanizing them and gradually admitting them to public posts. The presence of Roman authorities sharpened the contrast between rich and poor in the provinces, without entirely winning the heart of the privileged provincials. Plutarch cannot help but allude to the boots of Roman soldiers that stand on the head of the Greeks (*Praecepta gerendae reipublicae* 813 E). It is impossible to isolate the revolt of

the Jews in the years 66–70 from other provincial revolts, especially because these were years of general commotion in the Empire. But Flavius Josephus tends to separate the events in Palestine from those
taking place in the rest of the Empire (*Bellum Jud. 7.75ff.*). More generally, Josephus does not appear to realize that the apocalyptic expectations of certain revolutionary groups in Judaea, which were very
familiar to him (*Bellum Jud. 2.258, 6.285*), were shared by Jews of the
Diaspora, adopted by Christian groups, and finally did not differ substantially from the expectations of provincial pagans who were hoping
for Nero's return to avenge the Oriental and Greek provinces against
the tyranny of Rome.[4]

For information on this particular state of mind, we must turn not to
Flavius Josephus but to the Apocalypse of John: the Apocalypse of John
transforms the return of Nero, awaited by large pagan circles, into the
advent of the Antichrist, for whom the destruction of Rome as a new
Babylonia is the sign of the advent of the millennium.[5] The Apocalypse
gives an extreme messianic expression to the resentment against
Rome. It is characteristic that it was written by a Christian, because
Eusebius's tradition (*Hist. Eccl. 3.5.3*) tends to separate Christians from
Jews completely, for the latter refused to rebel against Rome. The exact date of the Apocalypse, which Irenaeus placed under the rule of
Domitian (*Adv. Haeres. 5.30.3*), matters relatively little compared with
its anti-Roman and specifically anti-Neronian content. But we should
not forget that there are two specific signs that lead us to think that the
Apocalypse was written between 68 and 69 A.D., that is, that it is con-
temporaneous with the Jewish revolt. The Apocalypse presupposes
the existence of the Temple of Jerusalem (2:1), and it mentions seven
Roman emperors, the last of whom had a short reign (chap. 17). If we
begin with Caesar, as Suetonius does, the seventh emperor is Galba,
whose reign was very short. This cannot be a coincidence.[6]

4. On the legend of Nero, see A. Yabro Collins, *The Combat Myth in the Book of Revelation*, Missoula, 1976, pp. 170–206, supplemented in certain points by J. J. Collins, *The
Sibylline Oracles of Egyptian Judaism*, Missoula, 1974, pp. 73–90.

5. Among the best commentaries on the Apocalypse of John are W. Bousset (1906);
R. H. Charles (1920); B. M. Allo, 3d ed. (1933); G. B. Caird (1966); H. Kraft (1974). The
commentary by J. Massyngberde Ford (1976), which essentially transforms the Apocalypse into a pre-Christian work from the circle of John the Baptist, appears to be more
cunning than true. For the social and religious background, see S. E. Johnson, "Unsolved
Questions about Early Christianity in Anatolia," in *Studies in New Testament and Early
Christian Literature . . . in Honor of A. P. Wikgren*, Leiden, 1972, pp. 181–93.

6. The Neronian date of the Apocalypse (which I adopted in *Cambridge Ancient History*,
1934, 10:726) is minutely defended by J. A. T. Robinson, *Redating the New Testament*, London, 1976, pp. 221–53. On the situation of Jews and Christians at the time of the Flavii,

These expectations, both political and messianic, were not limited to Judaea and to the year of the four emperors (thus the question of the date and place of origin of each apocalyptic document is relatively important). In the collection of Sibylline Books we possess, texts that are considered prophecies by pagan sibyls were composed outside of Paletine by Jews and Christians between the second century B.C. and the third century A.D. (if not later). Books 4 and 5 are a less evident but nonetheless clear expression of the state of mind that gives rise to the Apocalypse of John. Both books are of Jewish origin, but some Christian interpolations in book 5 (lines 68, 256–59) show that the book was accepted and adopted by a Christian group. Book 4 alludes to the eruption of Vesuvius in 79 A.D., which corresponds to the date of the text. Book 4 accepts and modifies the notion of imperial succession as it was introduced in Jewish thought by the Book of Daniel,[7] and awaits the imminent end of the fifth empire (Rome) due to a rebellion in the East, where the return of Nero is supposed to represent the central episode. In book 5, which appears to have been modified after the rule of Marcus Aurelius but has a core dating from 76 A.D.,[8] the expectation of the end of the world is explicitly connected with the expectation of the end of Rome. It is not by chance that the date of composition of book 8 of the Sibylline Books, which in its present form is entirely Christian, takes us back to Marcus Aurelius. In this book, too, the fall of Rome was predicted and awaited.

At the time of Marcus Aurelius, the Jews were exhausted from the three messianic rebellions and had already repressed, if not abandoned, the messianic and eschatological hopes that had sustained them in the period of their armed struggle against Rome. The rabbis, whose thought was devoted to the great juridical compilations of the third century A.D. (the Mishnah and the Tosefta),[9] generally discour-

---

see, for example, Bo Reicke *The New Testament Era* (2d English ed. of *Neutestamentliche Zeitgeschichte*, 1964), London, 1969; P. Keresztes "The Jews, the Christians and Emperor Domitian," *Vigiliae Christianae* 27 (1973): 1–28. H. Kreissig, "Rom und die Entwicklung der judäischen Kultur" in *Atti CeRDAC* [Milan] 10 (1978): 83–97 appears to me to be out of focus.

7. I have already developed this point in my essay "The Origins of Universal History," presented at the University of Chicago and at the Chr. Gauss Seminars at Princeton University (1979).

8. Verses 155 and following refer to a comet circa 74 A.D., which very probably corresponds to the one Pliny dates to 76 A.D. (Nat. Hist. 2.89).

9. The Tosefta ("addition") is a collection of Tannaitic *beraitot*, arranged according to the order of the Mishnah. The term *baraita* (pl. *beraitot*) designates all of the special written laws as well as the interpretations of the Law, and the historic or haggadic tradition not included in the Mishnah by Judah ha-Nasi.—Ed.

aged messianic speculation, especially if it implied revolutionary activity. After 130 A.D., the composition of strictly apocalyptic works by Jews tends to slow down (we possess, however, later texts: for example, chapters 15–16 of 2 Esdras, also called 5 Esdras, are often dated to 270 A.D. by modern scholars). These works were gradually handed down to Christians. Medieval Christian groups helped to preserve these texts of Jewish origin. In neglecting this literature, Flavius Josephus does not follow the advice of the rabbis, whose roles were not to be historians; he neglects these texts simply because he does not appreciate their importance.

## IV

We will now define more accurately the meaning of Flavius Josephus's double indifference to the synagogue and to the wider Jewish and Christian apocalyptic currents of his time.

As a refugee, Josephus feels the need to justify himself. Yet his historical works, which ripened gradually between two cultures, are accurate in their construction and attention to details, and reveal a serious commitment to historiography.

Flavius Josephus writes his works in Greek especially for the readers of the Greco-Roman ruling class (*Bellum Jud.* 1.16), but he cannot help bearing in mind Greek-speaking Jews as well (more than he is willing to admit). The fact that he writes in Greek implies—as Vidal-Naquet does not fail to point out—the acceptance of criteria of exposition and explanation inherent in the Greek historiographic tradition. Jewish sects are characterized in the Greek style, and dominant figures are described with abundant rhetorical means unparalleled in contemporary Aramaic and Hebrew prose. It is impossible for linguistic reasons alone to express the emotions of the apocalyptics or, vice versa, the normal activities of the frequenters of the synagogue in a Greek historiographic prose. Outside of historiography, "John," author of the Apocalypse, is an original artist who, because he feels involved, succeeds in translating apocalyptic emotions into Greek despite breaking grammar and syntax.[10] Within the historiographic tradition we learn about the synagogues, and the churches that derived from them, from "Luke," author of Acts of the Apostles, but only because he manages to create a new type of prose that is in keeping with the revolutionary situation he wants to represent. For Flavius Josephus, the adoption of the

10. G. Mussies, *The Morphology of Koiné Greek as Used in the Apocalypse of St. John*, Leiden, 1971.

Greek language has the opposite meaning of manifesting the longing that Judaism, as he conceives of it, live within the Greco-Roman civilization. But apocalypse and synagogue are foreign to that model of Judaism which, right or wrong, he draws from the Bible, from a few other documents, and from his own experience and offers to his Gentile, or if Jewish, Hellenized readers.

By blaming the disaster on the ruling class of his people (for example, *Ant. Jud.* 1.23), Flavius Josephus is far from secularizing his categories of judgment. He, of course, refuses to share those messianic hopes that had sustained the fighters. Going beyond a generic loyalty to the religion of the fathers (as expressed in *Ant. Jud.* 3.317–22 and elsewhere), Flavius is convinced that the prophets had already predicted Roman rule and the limits of its duration. Theoretically, there is space for agreement between Flavius and his coreligionists. He agrees that the destiny of the Roman Empire was included in the prophecy of Israel, both from the point of view of its present success and for its future fall, which is inevitable as the condition, or one of the conditions, of the instauration of messianic rule. For Jews as well as for Christians, there was no *Roma aeterna*. But Flavius Josephus prefers to stress past events, that is, the rule of Rome, and to foreshadow future events. Flavius's diffident attitude toward the apocalyptic enthusiasms of the zealots is mixed to some extent with caution: he feels he is being watched. On the one hand, he tells us clearly that Roman rule had been predicted by Jeremiah, Ezekiel, and Daniel (*Ant. Jud.* 10.79, 10.276) as well as by the much older Azariah (*Ant. Jud.* 8.294–96, *2 Chron.* 15.1); on the other hand, he eliminates certain aspects of the prophecy of Daniel. He omits the vision of the beasts, that is, of the empires in Daniel 7, whose reference to Rome is attributed to God himself in a very original passage from 2 Esdras 12.10ff. (an apocalypse from the end of the first century A.D.) For the same reason, and betraying some embarrassment, Flavius Josephus refuses to explain the prophecy of the divine stone, which breaks the statue of the empires in Daniel 2.34. He knew it had been reinterpreted as an oracle on the fall of Rome (*Ant. Jud.* 10.210).[11]

11. The passage from Flavius Josephus, *Ant. Jud.* 10.276 is mutilated, but it is quoted more fully (although not necessarily more accurately) by John Chrisostomus in *Adv. Judaeos* 5.9 (*PG*, 48, 897). The defense of the texts by Flavius Josephus attempted by J. Braverman, *Jerome's Commentary on Daniel*, Washington, 1978, pp. 109–10, does not appear possible to me. On Flavius Josephus and Daniel, see V. Nikiprowetzky, *Hommages à André Dupont-Sommer*, Paris, 1971, pp. 461–90, and A. Paul, in *Recherches de Science Religieuse* 63 (1975): 367–84, already quoted by Vidal-Naquet. See also U. Fischer, *Eschatologie und Jenseitser-wartung im hellenistischen Diaspora-Judentum*, Berlin, 1978.

He applies the same procedure to Alexander the Great. When Alexander visits Jerusalem, he enters the Temple and is informed by the Book of Daniel up to the point of learning about his imminent victory over the Persians (*Ant. Jud.* 11.337); but Alexander is not told anything about the later destruction of the empire he had founded.[12] In essence, in Flavius Josephus, Jewish prophets appear above all to be promising the empire to non-Jewish rulers. As to Cyrus, regarding whom Isaiah's prophecy was explicit, Flavius Josephus manages to add on his own account that Cyrus read the prophecy in person 210 years after it had been formulated (*Ant. Jud.* 11.5) and was led to act accordingly.

Flavius Josephus preserves the prophetic value of biblical books and at the same time deprives them of any subversive tendencies by showing that foreign rulers were satisfied with them. Among the prophets of the past, he prefers Daniel (*Ant. Jud.* 10.267): Daniel is a prophet of good tidings and accurate in the timing of events. We get the very strong impression that at some level of his conscience, Flavius Josephus has established an equation between Daniel and himself. Flavius is convinced that he possesses the gift of prophecy and dream interpretation and that he has demonstrated this not only in predicting the reign of Vespasian (*Bellum Jud.* 3.400–408) but at the time he betrayed his fellow men (3.351–54). He ascribes the gift of prophecy to the Pharisaic sect to which he had belonged (*Ant. Jud.* 17.43) and to certain Pharisees in particular (*Ant. Jud.* 15.3). What is more, he holds himself to be a descendant, on his mother's side, of the Hasmonean John Hyrcanus, endowed with a prophetic spirit (*Ant. Jud.* 13.299; *Bellum Jud.* 1.68).

Relying on his prophetic talent, Flavius predicts a Roman victory, and thereby justifies his decision to surrender rather than to commit suicide. As Vidal-Naquet points out, this is the opposite attitude from the one he ascribes to the leaders of the defenders of Masada: there the leader recommends committing suicide rather than surrendering to the enemy (*Bellum Jud.* 7.320–88). But perhaps it is arbitrary to define, as Vidal-Naquet does, Eleazar's speech as an apocalypse with no way out, as an apocalypse of death. Eleazar's speech, in its form and content, has nothing in common with an apocalypse: it is an exhortation to suicide based on arguments more comprehensible to a Greco-Roman

---

12. See my article "Flavius Josephus and Alexander's Visit to Jerusalem (this volume, chap. 8). See also W. C. van Unnik, *Flavius Josephus als historischer Schriftsteller*, Heidelberg, 1978, and the remarks by M. I. Finley in the introduction to Flavius Josephus, *The Jewish War and Other Selections*, London, 1966, which in its brevity is one of the best evaluations of the historian.

than to a Jew. In fact, Flavius Josephus's representation of the episode implies that Eleazar opts for suicide because he realizes that imminent apocalyptic hopes have proved wrong.

Trusting in his prophetic talent, Flavius Josephus predicts the future and survives. As a survivor, he professes his loyalty to the God of the Fathers and to the laws of the Bible. But he is cut off from the two vital currents of the Judaism of his time: the apocalypse and the synagogue. These two currents appear to us to be heading in opposite directions, as they do beginning in the second century A.D. But in the first century A.D. they often converged and nurtured each other. The same thing happened with primitive Christianity, which derived from Judaism both its eschatology and its ecclesiastical organization.

Flavius's Judaism is flat, not false or trivial but rhetorical and generic.[13] It has many similarities with the religious attitudes and practices of the group of rabbis, led by Johanan ben Zakki, that attempted to recreate the structures of the Jewish people after the disaster of 70 A.D. These rabbis, too, repressed apocalyptic hopes, stressed the exemplary character of biblical narration, and tried to reach an agreement with the Romans and seeked their support. In a way, Johanan ben Zakki was a refugee, and it is symbolic that the rabbinic tradition attributed to him the prophecy of Vespasian's assumption of the throne, which Flavius Josephus (confirmed by Suetonius, *Vesp.* 5) claims for himself.[14] But these similarities are superficial. What one finds lacking in Flavius Josephus is the act of rejoicing in the Law, the sense of a disciplined community life, the love and concern for younger generations, and a faith in God that—together with a high degree of intellectual freedom, juridical competence and obsession with norms of purity—characterize the rabbis who emerged as leaders of a nation without a state, without a territory, and without linguistic unity.

Well before the Jews had lost the Greek in which Flavius Josephus wrote as one of their cultural tongues, Flavius's works had already ceased to interest his coreligionists.[15] When contact was reestablished between Jews and Flavius Josephus in the Middle Ages, it took place

13. See my comments on the *Against Apion* from 1931 ("An Apology of Judaism: The *Against Apion* by Flavius Josephus, (this volume, chap. 6), which still appear to be substantially correct.

14. For a difficult reconstruction of the figure of Johanan ben Zakki, see J. Neusner's self-correction to his previous writings on the subject in *Journ. Jewish Studies* 24 (1973): 65–73.

15. See H. Schreckenberg, *Die Flavius-Josephus-Tradition in Antike und Mittelalter*, Leiden, 1972.

with the mediation of redactions that retain little of the spirit of the original. The authentic text was saved and used by Christians as an independent witness of the destruction of the old Israel in favor of the new: a much greater and certainly more authentic *testimonium flavianum* than the brief passage of *Jewish Antiquities* (18.63–64) where Jesus is mentioned and for which this title is usually reserved.

# Flavius Josephus and Alexander's Visit to Jerusalem

## I

In the *Jewish Antiquities* as a whole, Flavius Josephus makes evident his sensitivity to the new atmosphere of discredit, harassment, and self-questioning in which the Jews had to live under Domitian. Though the disputes about the chain of events that had led to the catastrophe of 70 A.D. were far from subsiding—Josephus would still have to defend himself in his autobiography—there were now far more radical questions in the air about the relations between God and Israel and about the relations between Jews and Romans. Add to these the relations between Jews and Christians, about whom the Jews spoke little then—and have traditionally spoken little ever since. One of the ironies of the situation was that Jewish proselytes qualified for persecution for the first time under Domitian, while the rival Christian proselytes derived some prestige from the destruction of the Temple without, however, ceasing to be in the front line of the enemies of the Empire. What exploded in the Jewish rebellions under Trajan and Hadrian, with their messianic overtones, must be correlated with the vigorous apocalyptic writing of the previous decades. But of course there was no unanimity of feeling among Jews. It was arduous enough to maintain some communal spirit in the face of linguistic, social, and geographical barriers. There must have been people who looked back to the reconstruction of the Temple after the Babylonian captivity as a more realistic model of hope for Israel. I would suggest that Josephus was one of these Jews, though from an unusual personal point of view. He had an interest in and understanding of Greek historiography (as the preface of the *Jewish Antiquities* shows) which has no obvious counterpart in the surviv-

Originally published in English in *Athenaeum*, n.s. 57, no. 3–4 (1979): 442–48. Reprinted by permission of Giulio Einaudi editore s.p.a.

ing Greek writings by Jews. He was familiar with the Hebrew Bible and
with Palestinian biblical exegesis, yet he was an admirer of the Septuagint when its reputation was beginning to decline among Greek-
speaking Jews. He wrote not only for educated Jews and proselytes of
the Greek-speaking world, but for inquiring pagans, such as we meet
in Plutarch and may suspect in that other bookworm from Chaeronea,
the freedman Epaphroditus. This Epaphroditus is very probably the
man to whom Josephus dedicated both the *Antiquities* and the *Against
Apion:* quite a comedown from the lofty protectors to whom he was accustomed. But, as Josephus himself admits in his preface, the *Antiquities* were partly dictated by personal needs. He took from the Bible
what he could—with the ominous omission of the classical prophets
and a telling preference for Daniel and Esther. The worldly success of
the courtier Mordecai and the optimistic prophecies of Daniel ("to
whom everything happened in a most unexpected way," 10.266) fasci-
nated Josephus. After all, in the good old days of Vespasian he himself
had been something of a courtier and a successful prophet.[1]

## II

But Daniel and Esther were not enough. Josephus had to fill the gap
between the end of the Bible and the Maccabaean age in order to give a
picture of the rebirth of the Jewish nation after the exile. As the *Against
Apion* shows, he was aware that there were problems of evidence—not
so much a shortage as unreliability of sources (1.41). He made the most
of the Letter of Aristeas, picked up some official documents such as the
letters of Antiochus III, and dug out from somewhere a few interesting
stories like that of the Tobiad Josephus.[2] Alexander the Great had to be
included. What is remarkable is that the story of Alexander's visit to
Jerusalem should be inserted between two episodes of the contacts between this king and the Samaritans.[3]

1. It will be enough to refer to the bibliography of the recent book by H. W. Attridge,
*The Interpretation of Biblical History in the Antiquitates Judaicae of Flavius Josephus,* Montana,
1976, esp. 103–6. See F. F. Bruce, "Josephus and Daniel," *Ann. Swedish Theol. Inst.* 4
(1965): 148–62; M. de Jonge, *Festschrift für Otto, Michel* Göttingen, 1974, p. 207; D. Daube,
"Typologie im Werk des Flavius Josephus," *Sitzb. Bayer. Akad.* 6 (1977), 14–18. I have developed my interpretation of Josephus in the introduction to the Italian translation of P.
Vidal-Naquet, *Du bon usage de la trabison,* Paris, Les Editions de Minuit, 1979 (Rome, Edi-
tori Riuniti) to appear in 1980 ("What Flavius Josephus Did Not See," this volume, chap.
7).
2. See J. A. Goldstein, "The Tales of the Tobiads," in *Studies for Morton Smith,* Leiden,
1975, 3:85–123.
3. The essential bibliography in *Josephus,* ed. Loeb, 1958, 6:512–13, in a very useful appendix on "Alexander the Great and the Jews" by R. Marcus. See especially the impor-

I shall say immediately and dogmatically that I assume there is no truth in the visit of Alexander to Jerusalem. It is not recorded by any respectable ancient source on Alexander and is full of impossible details. The defenders of the story—the latest I know of is Arieh Kasher in *Bet Miqra* 61, no. 2 (1974): 187–208 ("Massa' Aleksander ha-gadol be-Eretz Israel")—have not been able to overcome the objections to its credibility. The story of course was not invented by Josephus. Until a few years ago one could speak of three versions of the legend: the one told by Josephus, a second transmitted in a scholium to the rabbinic *Megillat Ta'anit* under the date of 21 Kislev[4] and in a passage of the Babylonian Talmud, *Yoma* 69a, and a third in Pseudo-Callisthenes 2.24, a chapter which was generally believed to be of Jewish origin. Now Pseudo-Callisthenes seems to have lost the value of an independent witness, because the passage in question is a late addition to the romance of Alexander in the ε-version of Pseudo-Callisthenes (critically edited by J. Trumpf in 1974) and appears to have been taken over from Josephus.[5] There are obscure points in this theory about Pseudo-Callisthenes, which need not detain us here. As for the rabbinic texts, I shall only say that, interestingly enough, they too involve the Samaritans, but in a way that seems independent of Josephus.

Josephus first tells how the Samaritans led by Sanballat[6] passed to the side of Alexander while he was besieging Tyrus. In this way they obtained permission to build a temple of their own. They chose as a high priest Manasses, the brother of Jaddus, the High Priest of Jerusalem, with whom he had quarreled. Jaddus and the other priests of Jerusalem had preferred to remain faithful to their oath of loyalty to Darius of Persia. Alexander, therefore, decided to march on Jerusalem with no kind intentions. But God reassured the anxious Jaddus in his sleep and ordered him and his fellow priests to open the gates of Jerusalem to Alexander and to meet him in their white priestly robes. The

tant essay by A. Büchler, "La relation de Josèphe concernant Alexandre le Grand," *Rev. Ét. Juiv.* 36 (1898): 1–26. Also see J. Gutmann *Tarbiz* 11 (1940): 271–94 (in Hebrew), and M. Simon in *Rev. Hist. Phil. Rel.* 21 (1941): 177–91.

4. See the critical edition of this text by H. Lichtenstein, *Hebrew Union College Annual* 8–9 (1931–32): 257–351. See also the Jerusalem edition, 1964, with a commentary by B. Lurie.

5. See R. Merkelbach, *Die Quellen des griechischen Alexanderromans*, 2. Auflage unter Mitwirkung von J. Trumpf, Munich, 1977, pp. 136–37.

6. The discovery of a new Sanballat in the Wadi Daliyeh papyri (F. M. Cross, *Harvard Theological Rev.* 59 [1966]: 201-11) does not make any difference to the question of the historicity of Alexander's visit to Jerusalem; it is also hardly relevant to the relations between Alexander and Samaritans. The essential questions are: Did Alexander originate the temple of Garizim? Was its first high priest a Jewish refugee with a story very similar to that of Jehoiada in Nehem. 13:28?

effect was immediate. Alexander prostrated himself before the high priest and explained to his companion Parmenion that he had seen the same man in the same robes in a dream when he was still in Macedonia: the man had promised him the empire of Persia.

Alexander was now shown the Book of Daniel, in which his victory over the Persians was prophesied with sufficient clarity. The priests did not tell him that he was mentioned in Daniel. He was apparently left to make the discovery for himself: "When the book of Daniel was shown to him, in which he had declared that one of the Greeks would destroy the empire of the Persians, he believed himself to be one of the indicated, and in his joy he dismissed the multitude for the time being" (11.337). The next day he granted the Jews the right to live under their law and be exempt from tribute in sabbatical years when the land would rest. Jews volunteered to serve in Alexander's army and contributed to his victory. The Samaritans could not leave matters there. They reappeared before Alexander and invited him to visit their sanctuary, which was apparently in full operation, but at the same time declared themselves Jews in order to share the Jewish privileges. Alexander asked some questions that compelled them to admit they were not Jews, but he postponed his decision until his next visit to Palestine: a remarkable anticlimax.

As they stand now, the two accounts about the Samaritans, which precede and follow Alexander's visit to Jerusalem, are mutually exclusive.[7] The second account, prima facie, presupposes that Alexander had not met the Samaritans before: it assumes that they had never asked to be allowed to build a temple of their own in order to weaken the Jews. One must add (though this is not a point to be pressed in fairy tales) that ancient temples were not built in a few months. If Alexander had given Sanballat permission to build the temple, it could not have been ready to receive him so soon. The first account has the look of a genuine Samaritan story that tries to connect the temple of Mount Garizim with Alexander; the second story is definitely anti-Samaritan, though in a mild tone—a point to be retained for future reference. Neither story is necessary to explain the Alexander's visit to Jerusalem; but the second story presupposes this visit and may well have been its appendix from the time in which the visit to Jerusalem was invented. The first story, being favorable to the Samaritans, is incompatible with the Jewish story of Alexander's visit to Jerusalem and must have been joined to it later in special circumstances: it may or may not have some truth.

7. See A. Büchler in *Rev. Ét. Juiv.* 36 (1898): 18.

## III

The story of the great friendship between Alexander and the Jewish priests of Jerusalem, if it originated in Palestine, should be dated either before the Maccabean rebellion or much later, perhaps under the Romans, when the Macedonian name was less odious to the Jews. Needless to say, the Book of Daniel, in its final version of about 165 B.C., is firmly anti-Macedonian. Michael the prince of Israel fights against both Persia and Greece, that is, Macedonia (10:13, 20). The first lines of 1 Maccabees, if read with an ear to its Hebrew substratum and its biblical allusions, are a condemnation of Alexander: "The land was silent before him, and he became arrogant and his heart was uplifted." As Daniel 11:12 had warned: "his heart shall be exalted . . . but he shall not prevail." The original Hebrew text of 1 Maccabees was almost certainly written before the end of the second century B.C. Elsewhere I have given reasons for a date of composition about 129 B.C.[8] The LXX version of Esther turns the villain Haman into a Macedonian (*E.* 10; 9:24). Though the absence of consistency in this transformation leaves room for doubt, the Macedonian note may well go back to the translation of Esther made in Jerusalem and sent to Egypt in 78–77 B.C., according to the best interpretation of the colophon of the book by E. Bickerman.[9] It is difficult to imagine Palestinian Jews inventing a visit of Alexander to Jerusalem between 170 and 70 B.C.

But the story of Alexander's visit to Jerusalem may have been invented in Egypt, where the Jews may have thought differently of Alexander and the Macedonians even during the struggles of the Palestinian Jews against Syria, to which they were not indifferent. Now Josephus has in book 13, 74–79, the rather extraordinary story that under Ptolemy VI Philometor Jews and Samaritans disputed in Alexandria about which of the temples had been built in accordance with the Laws of Moses. They requested King Ptolemy Philometor to hear their arguments and to punish by death the speakers for the defeated side. Andronicus, the advocate for the Temple of Jerusalem, presented a persuasive case based on the Law, on the priestly succession, and on the international reputation of the Jewish sanctuary, and carried the day. I agree with Peter Fraser (*Ptolemaic Alexandria*, 1:286) that it is difficult to reject this story as mere invention. Ptolemy Philometor had on

8. See "The Date of the First Book of Maccabees," *Mélanges J. Heurgon*, Rome, 1976, 2:657–61 [also in *Sesto Contributo*, 1980].

9. E. Bickerman, "The Colophon of the Greek Book of Esther," *Journ. Bibl. Liter.* 63 (1944): 339–62, repr. in *Studies on Jewish and Christian History*, Leiden, 1976, 1:225–45. See ibid., p. 263, n. 54 on Haman as a Macedonian.

his hands the resettlement of the Jews who had left Palestine under the leadership of a member of the family of the previous high priests, the Oniads. They founded a dissident temple in Leontopolis. The new settlement was bound to produce legal questions about the rights of Jerusalem, to which the Samaritans could not remain indifferent. The Jewish philosopher Aristobulus, who on the one hand is known to have dedicated a book to Ptolemy Philometor and on the other hand was in touch with the Jews of Jerusalem who sent a letter to the Jews of Alexandria, now in 2 Maccabees, may well have advised the king to find for Jerusalem.[10] If the debate took place in any form at Alexandria, it was a natural occasion for both sides to produce pamphlets on the reputation of the rival temples and therefore on their relations with Alexander. Until a better suggestion is offered, this hypothesis, put forward by Jacob Freudenthal more than a century ago, provides the most logical explanation for the origin of the two versions Josephus used directly or indirectly. This hypothesis is not refuted by an argument Adolf Büchler produced in favor of the Roman date of at least the Jewish version. He thought that the alleged exemption of the tribute in sabbatical years granted by Alexander was an imitation of the real exemption granted by Caesar to the Jews of Palestine in 47 or 44 B.C. (*Ant. Jud.* 14.202). But there is no reason to believe that Caesar did something unthought of before. Exemption from tribute in sabbatical years must have been a recurrent request by the Jews to any foreign ruling power.[11]

## IV

It is tempting to believe that a date in the middle of the second century B.C. for the two versions of the story of Alexander in Palestine is confirmed by the detail of the consultation of the Book of Daniel by Alexander in Jerusalem. A reference to Daniel is indeed perfectly compatible with the reputation we know Daniel already had in Egypt

10. See J. Freudenthal, "Alexander Polyhistor," *Hellenistische Studien I.*, Breslau, 1874, p. 103. The Samaritan sources are difficult to use and seem to be a simple reply to Jewish sources without new facts. The *Adler Chronicle* depends for this episode of the controversy between Jews and Samaritans before a Ptolemy on Abu'l Fath's Chronicle, written in Arabic about 1352: the relevant passage is translated in John Bowman, *Samaritan Documents*, Pittsburgh, 1977, pp. 126–35. Neither J. A. Montgomery, *The Samaritans*, 1907, reprint New York, 1968, pp. 76–77, nor H. G. Kippenberg, *Garizim und Synagoge*, Berlin, 1971, p. 66, are very helpful.

11. 1 Macc. 6.53 is enough to show that the sabbatical year was taken seriously in the second century B.C. For other evidence and chronographic questions, see S. Zeitlin, *The First Book of Maccabees*, New York, 1950, pp. 254–57.

in the years immediately after the death of Philometor, whose reign ended in 145 B.C. Daniel was echoed in the third Sibylline Book, ll. 388–400, which are clearly Egyptian in origin, not much later than 140 B.C.[12] More generally, the Book of Daniel was authoritative among Jews in the second part of the second century B.C. There are allusions to it in 1 Macc. 1:54, 2:59, and there seems to be no reason to doubt that the author of the original Hebrew text was acquainted with Daniel. The contacts between Daniel and the Book of Dreams in Enoch (83–90) have been less easy to interpret since J. T. Milik (*The Book of Enoch*, 1976, p. 44) claimed to be able to date the Book of Dreams exactly in 164 B.C. In this case Enoch would have worked next door to Daniel in the excited Jerusalem of the early Maccabean days and would quite possibly have swapped prophecies with him in the small hours.

Tempting though it may seem to support the second-century Alexandrian origin of the story of Alexander in Jerusalem by the reference it contains to Daniel, I would suggest that this reference is not part of the original story but was added by Josephus.

In the story, both the high priest and the Macedonian king have a dream conditioning their behavior. The high priest does not consult the Book of Daniel to decide his line of conduct, nor does Alexander learn anything new from his perusal of the Book of Daniel. Daniel has no essential function in the story. This would not, of course, be decisive if the Book of Daniel were not an anti-Macedonian prophecy, which could hardly be put into the hands of Alexander as long as Daniel was read in a definitely anti-Macedonian key. The message of the book was that a Jewish messianic kingdom or empire would replace the Macedonian states. But Josephus was no longer in that mood. His paraphrase of Daniel in book 10 leaves out all that in the original is pointedly anti-Greek or anti-Macedonian. It correspondingly eliminates the expectation of the fifth, Jewish, kingdom. Furthermore, in a very intriguing short sentence, Josephus adds: "in the same manner Daniel also wrote about the empire of the Romans and that Jerusalem will be taken and the temple erased" (10.276). The text, as is well known, is here out of order and must be supplemented from an excerpt in John Chrysostom (*Adv. Jud.* 5.8): the general drift is not in question. It is difficult to say precisely what Josephus had in mind in making this remark. Some of

12. See my paper, "La portata storica dei vaticini sul settimo re nel terzo libro degli oracoli sibillini," *Forma Futuri: Studi in onore del Cardinale Michele Pellegrino*, Turin, 1975, pp. 1077–84 [also in *Sesto Contributo*]. See, in general, U. Fischer, *Eschatologie und Jenseitserwartung im hellenistischen Diaspora-Judentum*, Berlin, 1978. For the text of Josephus, *Ant. Jud.* 10.276, J. Braverman, *Jerome's Commentary on Daniel*, Washington, 1978, p. 109, which I cannot follow.

his Jewish contemporaries were beginning to introduce the Romans into their interpretation of Daniel's prophecies. In another passage (10.210), outwardly unconnected, Josephus seems to accept the reference to the Romans, but to deprive it of its immediate apocalyptic application by refusing to provide an explanation for the stone that breaks the statue, according to Daniel (2.34). I have no doubt that Josephus was aware that by extending Daniel's prophecies to the Romans he admitted by implication that Daniel's statue either included or represented the Roman Empire. As a believing Jew he was bound to expect that the Roman Empire would one day break up because of divine intervention. But not in any foreseeable future. For the present Daniel is the prophet of the Roman rule, just as he had been the prophet of the Persian and of the Macedonian rule. The insertion of the Daniel reference in the story of Alexander in Jerusalem, while unsuitable to the second-century B.C. version, fits well into Josephus's mode of thought as exemplified by these other references to Daniel. Josephus seems to say: Daniel foresaw both the Macedonian and the Roman Empire—do not ask for more in the present circumstances.

The bland and loose way in which the pro-Samaritan and the anti-Samaritan versions of the contacts between Samaritans and Alexander are fused in Josephus's account also seems to be characteristic of his attitude. Josephus did not like the Samaritans, but the Samaritans had joined the rebellion of 67 A.D. and had suffered heavily from the Romans. Josephus did not have the necessary magnanimity to forget the old feud, but his pen lost its bluntness in retelling what the sources told him. He left a door open—as Alexander was supposed to have done.

In one of the best books ever written on Jewish-Hellenistic literature (*Studi di storia e letteratura giudeo-ellenistica*, 1924) my regretted friend Bacchisio Motzo elaborated the theory that for most of books 11–13 of the *Antiquities* Josephus followed an anti-Samaritan chronicle. This chronicle would have used the Books of Ezra and Nehemiah, some apocrypha, the story of the Tobiads; it would have culminated in the story of the judgment by Ptolemy VI Philometor in favor of the Temple of Jerusalem. Their theory founders on the unlikelihood of the implication that Josephus would have turned to a chronicle for facts contained in the Bible. Furthermore, as we have seen, the text of Josephus includes chunks that are not anti-Samaritan, or at least are hardly compatible with a definite anti-Samaritan polemic. I remember telling Motzo, perhaps forty-five years ago, that his brilliant analysis of Josephus's account characterized Josephus rather than his alleged source. In these books we have Josephus pursuing the task of presenting a version of Jewish history that would provide a "consolation for the tribulations of Israel," to repeat the title of Samuel Usque's compendium of Jewish history written in Ferrara about 1550. Josephus wanted to show that the destruction of the First Temple had been followed by periods of prosperity of the Jewish people under the Persians and the Macedonians. He smoothed away the sharp corners of Jewish history. Recognition of the Second Temple, and respect for it by foreign rulers, had been answered with tangible manifestations of Jewish loyalty. What is more, Jewish sacred books foretold the future of the Persians, of the Macedonians, and of the Romans. Cyrus (Josephus emphasized without biblical authority) had been pleased to learn what Isaiah had prophesied about him 210 years before and had consequently tried to live up to the prophecy (11.2). Jeremiah, most probably as the alleged author of Lamentations, and Ezekiel are supposed to have composed writings "concerning the recent capture of our city" (10.79). Alexander, as we have seen, had appreciated his mention in Daniel. If Daniel was obscurely referring to the Romans, they too might well take notice. It was not a very deep consolation, because it was not a very deep message. The comparison with Samuel Usque's book, with its burning words of faith and courage for his fellow Marranos, would be damning for Josephus if we had the heart to pursue it. But Josephus was more or less consciously trying to discourage the apocalyptic expectations about which we know something from events he no longer lived to see. And he was trying to be understood by pagans, perhaps also by Samaritans—not by Christians, the only ones who ultimately read him.[13]

13. For Josephus's attitude towards apocalyptic thought, see the acute remarks by P. Vidal-Naquet, "Flavius Josèphe et Masada," *Revue Historique* 260 (1978: 3–21 (but I am not sure that Eleazar's speeches at Masada according to *Be. Jud.* VII can be described as an apocalypse. They are a straight invitation to suicide). For the apocalyptic reinterpretation of Daniel against the Romans, much evidence is collected by R. H. Charles in his *Commentary on the Revelation of St. John*, 1920, 2:75. The strange Talmudic evidence about Trajan's intention to rebuild the Temple is collected, but not critically evaluated, by L. Finkelstein, *Akiba* (1936, reprint Cleveland and New York 1962), pp. 217–34. See E. M. Smallwood, *The Jews under Roman Rule*, Leiden, 1976, p. 425. The mention of Trajan's Day seems to be missing in the best manuscripts of the *Megillat Ta'anit* on 12 Adar: see ed. Lichtenstein, p. 346. See also N. R. N. de Lange, "Jewish Attitudes to the Roman Empire," in *Imperialism in the Ancient World*, ed. P. D. A. Garnsey and C. R. Whittaker, Cambridge, 1979, p. 271, and, more specifically, V. Nikiprowetzky, *Hommages à André Dupont-Sommer*, Paris, 1971, pp. 461–90.

---------------------------------- *9* ----------------------------------

# Preliminary Indications on the Apocalypse and Exodus in the Hebrew Tradition

### I

A few elementary clarifications might be useful. I will assume, of course, Ernst Bloch, *Geist der Utopie*, Munich, 1918 which I know from the second version of 1923, and *Das Prinzip Hoffnung*, 1954–59; but, above all, I wish to refer to the recent *Atheismus im Christentum* from 1968 (2d ed., 1977), whose subtitle is directly relevant, *Zur Religion des Exodus und des Reichs*. I will also assume Norman Cohn, *The Pursuit of the Millennium*, 1961; Frank and Fritzie Manuel, *Utopian Thought in the Western World*, Cambridge (Mass.), 1979; and the very recent M. Walzer, *Exodus and Revolution*, New York, 1984. It is enough to observe here that Walzer, an American who is now at the Institute for Advanced Study at Princeton, draws, like Bloch, from the common Jewish tradition, but he appears to attach little importance to his predecessor. In this regard, the difference in generations (almost two generations separate Bloch from Walzer) and in their personal experience (Bloch experienced Nazism and Stalinism while Walzer was safe in America and in touch with the millenarian ideology of blacks and Hispanic Americans) have prevailed with respect to their common Jewish tradition as the starting point.

The term *apokalypsis* is unknown in classical Greek, as far as I know, and is found in Hellenistic Greek from the second century B.C., either with a profane meaning (for example, to uncover a part of the body) or in a vague religious sense (discovery of a mistake). In the strictly religious sense of "revelation" it is used by St. Paul (for example, in Gal. 1:12), but it owes its importance to the first line, which is also the title, of the Revelation of John. In essence, what we call the Apocalypse is

This essay was written as an introduction to a seminar at the University of Pisa in February 1985, headed by N. Badaloni, on apocalyptic currents in political thought.

the text that has consecrated the word as a religious term and has created the model for a certain type of book. In this sense, St. Girolamo was right in considering *apocalypse* as a biblical term: "proprie Scripturarum est . . . a nullo sapientium saeculi apud Graecos usurpatum" (ad Gal. I,II; VII, I, 387 Vallarsi). The Hebrew word that comes closest to having the same meaning is *galah*, "to uncover, to reveal," but I do not believe it has a technical value.

It so happens that the meaning of the term *apocalypse* extends from the Revelation of John to other similar books, both of Hebrew and of Christian origin, to manuscripts (for example in the case of 2 Baruch or 3 Baruch). What is more, the recovery of the Codex with the life of Mani has revealed to us a Manichaean custom (but probably not born out of Manichaeism) of speaking of apocalypses of Adam, Seth, Enosh, Shem, Enoch, and Paul, that is, of a genre of writing called Apocalypse. Thus, to a certain extent, there existed in Judeo-Christian and in Manichaean antiquity (and perhaps in pagan antiquity as well; see letter 54 by Sinesius) the awareness of the existence of a literary genre called Apocalypse.

But the formalization of this awareness of a theory of a genre appears to be modern: it is said to be consecrated by connecting the Apocalypse of John to the Book of Daniel and to various other texts in the *Codex Pseudo-Epigraphicus Veteris Testamenti* 2 by Johannes Fabricius (1722). In the critical research of the nineteenth century, the apocalyptic genre draws increasing attention beginning with F. Lücke, a pupil of Schleiermacher, in *Versuch einer vollständingen Einleitung in die Offenbarung Johannis und in die gesammte apokalyptische Literatur*, Bonn, 1832. It is accompanied by an emphasis on the eschatological character of the message of Jesus. But we should not forget the simple fact that the nineteenth century is also the century in which libraries are explored; increased knowledge of uncommon languages made it possible to put back into circulation, at least among the learned, apocalyptic texts that had disappeared from view, such as the first book of Enoch and the ascension of Isaiah, retrieved in Ethiopian translations, and the second book of Enoch, published in a Paleo-Slavic version in 1880. Certain discoveries, among which was the *Assumptio Mosis*, were made in less remote libraries, such as the Ambrosian. Moreover, that text was in Latin, a language that was still understood. Some of the texts that were rediscovered, such as 1 Enoch, had originally been written in Hebrew or Aramaic, undoubtedly for Jews, but were forgotten by the Jewish tradition and preserved instead by certain groups of the Christian tradition. This fact, very simple in itself, raises some serious problems as to the character and the effectiveness of the Jewish apocalypse in rela-

PART ONE

tion to the Christian one. We must bear in mind that similar problems exist with other works and other literary genres. A philosopher such as Philo and, to a certain extent, a historian such as Flavius Josephus were forgotten for centuries by the Jews and were essentially preserved by the Christians. And, adding to the difficulty, the same can be said for a text such as 1 Maccabees, which was originally written in Hebrew and was of interest almost exclusively for the Jews.

In any case, it is a fact that the Book of Daniel, from the second century B.C., is the only apocalyptic book that the Jews accept into their canon of sacred books—what we would call the Old Testament. Daniel is also the only apocalyptic book from the period 200 B.C.–250 A.D. that Jews continued to read and consider as their own. Texts of Hebrew origin adopted by Christians were obviously open to Christian interpolations. The presence and the extent of these interpolations cannot be estimated easily. There appear to be no Christian interpolations in the Assumption of Moses, but the date of the text, which scholars place between the second century B.C. and the second century A.D., is uncertain. In other cases, such as the Ethiopic Book of Enoch, Christian interpolations are probable, although the essential Jewish origin of the text is now assured by fragments of the original Aramaic text of Enoch, discovered in the fourth cave of Qumran. The question of the origin of a text, whether Jewish or Christian, is inevitably more difficult when there are good reasons to believe that the original text was written in Greek. The difference between a Jewish Hellenistic text and a Christian Hellenistic text is more subtle—hence the discussion about the origin of the testament of Job and especially about even the Slavonic Enoch, which supposedly was written originally in Greek and where specifically Jewish elements are hard to find.

Beneath these problems of attribution—whether to Jews or to Christians—of individual texts, we thus find a change in the Jews' attitude with regard to apocalyptic speculations, the cause of which may have been their reaction to Christian apocalyptic speculation. In the first six centuries of the Christian era, we find only one quotation from an apocalyptic text in a rabbinic text. This quotation does not come from a text that has been handed down to us; instead, it comes from a text that a Jewish soldier supposedly found in a Roman archive, written in Assyrian characters and in the Hebrew language as though it were a biblical text. This text is quoted in the Babylonian Talmud, *Sanhedrin* 97b,[1] and is so brief that we can translate it as follows:

1. The Babylonian Talmud is essentially an interpretation and reelaboration of the Mishnah, carried out in the great academies of Babylonia. It is dated approximately from between the first half of the third century A.D. and the end of the fifth century A.D.—Ed.

90

Rabbi Hanan ben Tahlifa sent a message to Rabbi Joseph: "I once met a man who had a scroll written in Hebrew in Assyrian characters. I asked him: 'Whence has it come to you?' He answered: 'I became a mercenary in the Roman army and I found it in the Roman archives.' In the text it is written that 4291 years after its creation the world will become orphan, some (of the following years) shall be years of war against the great monsters of the sea, others years of war between Gog and Magog, the rest will be a messianic era when the Blessed Saint shall renew the world after only seven thousand years." R. Abba the son of Raba remarked: "This statement was made after 5000 years (since creation)" (that is, there remain about 2000 years before the world will be renewed, and the messianic era, which is somehow connected with the end of the Roman Empire, should be about 5000 years after creation).[2]

There exists, however, a whole series of apocalyptic references in rabbinic texts beginning with the so-called "small Apocalypsis" in the treatise *Sota* in the Mishnah, that is, of the basic rabbinic text for Talmudic commentaries, whose approximate date is the third century A.D. In this small Apocalypsis, all the signs of decadence are assembled in order to indicate the imminent arrival of the Messiah. In this text, as well as in many others, it is assumed that the Messiah will come unexpectedly at the time of the greatest moral decline (for example, *Midrash Tehillin*, psalm 45.3). But opinions regarding the exact time of coming of the Messiah varied. In the Babylonian Talmud treatise *Sanhedrin*, which contains a mine of opinions on the Messiah, we find the opinion of Rabbi Johanan worth mentioning: "The son of David (that is, the Messiah) shall come only in a generation that is entirely just or entirely evil" (98a). The anti-Roman content of these messianic speculations is obvious from many allusions; it would become even more obvious if we were sure that the tradition that the Messiah awaits his hour among the poor and the lepers at the gates of Rome already appears in *Sanhedrin* 98a. But the present text, perhaps being cautious, reads only "at the gates of the city." On the other hand, distrust of messianic movements is clear from the *Sanhedrin* treatise itself, for example, from the well-known passage against Bar Cocheba or Bar Koziba, who had been acknowledged as the Messiah by some rabbis, such as Rabbi Akiba, at the time of the rebellion under Hadrian. *Sanhedrin* 93b reads: "Bar Koziba ruled for two and a half years and then he said to the rabbis: 'I am the Messiah.' They answered 'It is said of the Messiah that he rules by inclination. Let us see if this is your case.' When they saw that he was

2. For a textual criticism of this passage, see E. E. Urbach, *The Sages*, Jerusalem, 1:681. The whole content of this essay has been inspired by Urbach's work.

incapable of judging by inclination, they killed him." Thanks to Scholem, we know of another famous statement by three rabbis (*Sanhedrin* 98a): "The Messiah is welcome, but I do not wish to see him." In other words, rabbinic Judaism, which prevailed, does not deny the end of the world but ultimately acknowledges and appreciates the inconsistency between human action and the advent of the Messiah, and seldom encourages messianic activism. Instead, it does the opposite, which results in a bland representation of the figure of the Messiah. Strange as it may seem, the Jewish tradition does not deliver a clear picture of what the Messiah is supposed to be like.

Yet at the time of the second Temple, that is, until 70 A.D., a great variety of messianic figures existed. In the Bible, the Book of Zechariah mentions two figures: a high priest and a messianic king (4:13, 6:13). These two figures have taken considerable shape—although their picture is not any clearer—in the Dead Sea Scrolls, where the eschatological high priest appears to be more important than the Messiah son of David. However, the Messiah son of David prevails and becomes, for example, a central figure in Psalm of Solomon 17 from around 63 B.C., and then in 4 Ezra and in the apocalypse (Syrian) of Baruch from the first–second century A.D. A bland Messiah, son of Joseph or Ephraim (that is, from the tribe of Joseph or Ephraim), is sometimes considered the predecessor of the Messiah son of David and destined to die in the war against the enemies of Israel. Such is the case, for example, in the Babylonian Talmud, *Suk.* 52a, and in Targumim (*Pseudo-Jon. Ex.* 40, 11 etc.).[3] We should bear in mind, of course, that aside from speculations on the future Messiah, there were real pretenders to the position of Messiah in Palestine and the surrounding areas. We find a list of these pretenders in Acts of the Apostles 5:36–37. From Flavius Josephus we learn of a Menahem, son of Judas "Messiah," who, dressed in regal garments, was assassinated in the Temple of Jerusalem (Bell. 2.444–48). We have already spoken of Bar Kokhba. At the end of the sixth century and during the seventh century, in the Byzantine world threatened first by the Persians and later by the Arabs, we find messianic speculations documented in the so-called Book of Zerubbabel, a short pamphlet. The last king of Judah of Davidic descent narrates his vision of the advent of the Messiah, which is preceded by a king of Rome, son of Satan, called Armillus, that is, Romulus. Armillus conquers the world and everyone believes in him except the Jews. The war of the Jews against Armillus is conducted at first by the Messiah son of Joseph

---

3. *Targumim* (the plural of *targum*, "translation"); in rabbinic literature, the term primarily designates the translation of the bible into Aramaic, but it may also refer to the Aramaic parts of the Bible.—Ed.

together with a woman, Hephzibah (meaning "my delight in her"; the name of a queen in the Bible), who saves Jerusalem; later, the Messiah son of Joseph is killed by Armillus. The Messiah son of David, who appears to be the son of Hephzibah, defeats Armillus and begins the messianic era (ed. Jellinek, *Bet ha-midrash* 2.54–57). The Book of Zerubbabel was important enough to be summarized in the first Jewish medieval philosophical systematization, the Book of Faith and Opinions by Saadya Gaon (tenth century). It is undoubtedly true that medieval Judaism is to a great extent infused by messianism combined with kabbalistic beliefs. In times of serious political tension or persecution, messianic rebellions appear here and there. We will not forget the case of Obadiah, a Norman converted to Judaism, and his great surprise. In his autobiography, Obadiah recounts meeting around 1121 a Caraitic Jew of Aronid descent who proclaimed he was the Messiah. The poor proselyte Obadiah was dumbfounded: "I entered the covenant nineteen years ago (that is, I was converted) and I had never heard that a descendant of Levi, and not a descendant of David, can lead to redemption." This is the time of the basically anti-Arabic messianic movement of David Alroy. Another opportunity for messianic hopes was provided by the persecution in Spain, and even Martin Luther was considered a predecessor of the Messiah. The sixteenth and seventeenth centuries are filled with messianic expectations, with Messiahs such as David Reuveni and Sabbatai Zevi, ending with the Frankist movement of the eighteenth century and with Jacob Frank in Poland, who was converted to Catholicism in 1759. But within Judaism, messianism finds its limit in the statement constantly reaffirmed by major thinkers like Saadya Gaon, Maimonides (d. 1204), and Chasdai Crescas (fifteenth century)—that the Torah, the Law, remains valid for the messianic age also; in fact, it is strengthened by the joy of a contemplative life under the Law. And on Maimonides and Crescas depends, for example, Isaac Abarbanel, who represents the crisis of the expulsion from Spain, and Juda Loew ben Bezalel, the Maharal of Prague, in the climate of the Counter-Reformation (*The Victory of Israel,* 1599) with its miraculous elements. Hence, if anything, the anomic impulse is repressed by normative Judaism practically until the nineteenth century; anomie was brought back into fashion by G. Scholem in the twentieth century.

## II

Thus, it is sufficiently clear that the more intensely apocalyptic current—the one expressed in the Book of Daniel, included in the Bible (second century B.C.) and in a series of specifically apocalyptic writings—survives at the periphery of the Jewish tradition and cannot be excluded from it. Many of the texts in question have been adopted to a greater or lesser extent by the Christian tradition or, better, by the many Christian traditions. The best collection of texts today is probably the one J. H. Charlesworth edited in America for Doubleday in 1983. I will not list all readily accessible texts here; I will simply note that, aside from the decidedly apocalyptic texts, such as the books of Enoch and the various Ezra books (among which the most important is 4 Ezra from the late first century A.D.), it is customary, and I would say legitimate, to combine two other categories of similar texts: the testaments of biblical figures (the Testaments of the Twelve Patriarchs, perhaps second century B.C. if we consider the Christian elements as interpolations; the testament of Job, possibly first century B.C.; the testament of Abraham, possibly first century A.D.; the testament of Solomon, from before the fourth century A.D. because it has already been mentioned in the Dialogue of Timotheus and Aquila from around 400); and the Sibylline Oracles, a series of texts with dates and origins varying from the second century B.C. to the seventh century A.D., of Hebrew or Christian origin (if of Hebrew origin, with some Christian interpolations). Both Hebrew sibylline texts and Christian sibylline texts utilize pagan sibylline texts, mainly of a political nature, thus creating a link between Judeo-Christian apocalyptics and the political prophecy of the pagan world.

The sibylline texts are invariably spoken by sibyls, that is, pagan prophetesses. At this point, we have various problems. The sibyl who delivers the oracles is represented as a descendant of Noah and therefore is pre-Jewish. On the other hand, we know of other sibyls who are clearly pagan: thus, in some form, sybils are used to reveal through a pagan mouth a truth that is no longer pagan but Judeo-Christian. As pagan witnesses of Christian truth, the sibyls are utilized by apologists such as Lactantius (*Epit. Instit.* 68) and the Emperor Constantine (Discourse for the Saints). The influence of sibylline oracles on medieval millenarian thought (Gioacchino da Fiore) is known. The texts of sibyls, which are authentically pagan, appear for centuries to have contained punctual prophecies of events, not universal future histories. But Virgil's Cumaen sibyl already speaks of an *ultima aetas*. It is possible that Iranian influences are at work here. The Judeo-Christian sibyl, if we can give it that name, evidently develops the element of a universal history. It is also likely that there are other influences, such as prophecies of the Cassandra type, exemplified by the *Alexandra* by Licofrone, from the third or second century B.C.

As the example of the sibyl already shows, prophecies and apocalyptic visions are generally entrusted to a famous character from the past, such as Enoch, Abraham, Job, or Daniel, in the form of a report, a testament, or an oracle. While Jewish prophets such as Isaiah, Jeremiah, and Ezekiel spoke in the first person, the writers of apocalyptic books are concealed under illustrious and ancient names. The most important exception is the Apocalypse of John.

Further, these apocalyptic books appear to be books for the initiated. Isaiah's *Ascension* ends with a prohibition to King Hezekiah to reveal what the prophet has said. Moreover, as we were saying, all of history, or a large part of history, is included under apocalyptic consideration. Thus, past, present, and future history are considered in apocalyptic thought in a way that the prophet as such, dominated by the present or by the immediate future, does not have the possibility to express. But, in turn, the continuity of history is controlled—or, if one wishes, truncated—by a "day of the Lord," by a divine judgment, which is a divine intervention in history. The intervention may concern only the living or it may concern the dead as well: it can become a universal judgment. Another element essential to apocalypses is the existence of a mediator who is penetrated by a divine spirit and can predict what will happen before it is bound to happen. Thus, in 4 Ezra (14:39–48) the protagonist has been ordered to drink a potion that will give him the inspiration to write, seventy apocalyptic scriptures, among other works.

Dreams and ecstasies are part of the experience ascribed to a legendary author. Baruch, for example, is guided in the heavens by an angel. The heavenly world is described as being filled with angels and demons, but it is possible that this dualism is intrinsic to the apocalyptic vision. The force of evil will be destroyed by the force of good. God stands for the good and thus cannot stand for evil. The goodness of God is limited by the objective existence of evil, at least until evil is eliminated entirely. Enoch, 2 Baruch, and 4 Ezra are typical examples of this dualism. Different attitudes also exist because of the difference between a Judaism that considers the messianic age a future age and a Christianity that lives in the messianic age but awaits a second advent. Since, as far as I know, we do not possess any evidence of an apocalypse that can be verified as gnostic-Jewish, we shall leave aside the gnostic variety of the apocalypse without diminishing its potential importance.

Another characteristic of apocalyptic thought is the possibility of reinterpreting it when it does not materialize (as has been the case so far). Thus, the Book of Daniel, which considers Greece the fourth and last worldly empire, is reinterpreted both by 4 Ezra and by the Talmudic treatise *Aboda Zara* 2b as a reference to Rome. Long periods of time are divided into weeks, but the duration of the week can be interpreted freely. In this succession of weeks, other historic events can be taken into account. The notion of the imperial succession used by Daniel appears to be Greek in origin. Yet the preference for a notion of four ages may very well be Iranian in origin. What is typical of the apocalypse is the fall. The present world is opposed to the world to come. The Jewish contraposition *haolam hazze—haolam habba* corresponds to the Greek *aion houtos—aion mellon*. Equivalent, but not entirely so, are the contrapositions between the kingdom of light and the kingdom of darkness, between the kingdom of truth and the kingdom of error. But why should God enable a privileged few to have knowledge of the world to come? The question is a legitimate one, and the very people concerned have given different answers. Rabbis, of course, have discussed whether God was ready to reveal the future world. In a famous and controversial passage of uncertain date from a homiletic text, *Bereshit Rabba* 44, we find two opposite opinions expressed respectively by a rabbi from the first century A.D., Johanan ben Zakkai, and a rabbi and martyr from the second century, Akiba. According to what I believe is the best interpretation, Johanan ben Zakkai insists that God did not reveal to Abraham the future world, whereas Akiba believes that God revealed to Abraham both the present world and the future world. The divergence of opinion is interesting, but clearly God was persuaded to reveal to someone the future world and not only the present world.

The Apocalypse of John, canonized in the New Testament, is at the border between Judaism and Christianity. The date, the intention, and the unity of the work are still highly controversial, indeed increasingly controversial, so that we can speak of it here only with the utmost reserve. But there is an aspect of this text that strikes the modern reader. While the letters preceding the apocalyptic vision deal with the actual situation in Asia Minor—and in this context there is at least one anti-Jewish allusion to the synagogue of Satan in Smyrna (2:9)—the apocalyptic vision separates the martyrs and the faithful from their persecutors, not on the basis of Judaism but in relation to the Roman Empire. Babylon, as seen by the visionary John, is not the Jewish Jerusalem but pagan Rome, as is explicitly indicated by the reference to the seven hills of Rome (17:9); and Babylon, that is, Rome, is replaced in the end by the celestial and eternal Jerusalem where Jesus is present. But this is the Jerusalem of the future. For the present, the real Jerusalem continues to exist with a functioning Temple, even if it is on the verge of destruction

(11:1–2); this Jerusalem is temporarily transformed into Sodom or Egypt, "where the Lord was crucified" (11:8). The situation in Jerusalem is thus subordinated to that of Rome; we should have the courage to say that it was caused, albeit confusedly, by Rome. In any case, it is Rome, as an Empire, that is bound to pay the price; no celestial Rome is envisaged in the Apocalypse.

Internal references in the Apocalypse appear to suggest a date of composition slightly prior to the destruction of the Temple. The destruction of the Temple by the Romans was not yet considered inevitable by John, the seer who had taken refuge or was confined in Patmos and thus had to rely on the information made available to him there. It would not be difficult to prove that a date between 69 and 70 A.D. is compatible with the infamous allusion to the seven "kings," of which five have passed, the sixth "is," and the seventh will have a short reign (17:10), whereas the eighth "king," whose name is taken from one of the seven, has all the looks of a reviviscent Nero (Pseudo-Nero), a figure also dear to the Jewish-Christian Sibylline Oracles. The number 666 (13:18) is quite probably an allusion to Nero. If we begin with Augustus, the seventh king is Otho, and since John knows that the seventh king will have a short reign, it is likely that John writes shortly thereafter (but pretending he is still under the seventh king) while Vitellius and Vespasian are contenders to the throne.[4]

The idea that the Apocalypse was written under Domitian goes back to Irenaeus, but this is not decisive in itself. John is critical of the imperial cult as could be seen in the eastern part of the empire in general, not of those forms it took in Rome under Domitian. As has often been said, the very name "Sebastos" (the Greek for Augustus) involved the imperial cult. In John, the hostility against Rome absorbs the resentment against Judaism, which is also present. What is clear from all of this is that John expects the triumph of Christ as a consequence of the fall of the empire and considers this a premonition of the Jewish war. The habitual Jewish apocalyptic picture is rendered more complicated because what the author expects is not the final victory of the old Israel but that of the new Israel, an Israel that no longer needs the Temple. The dominant model in Jewish apocalyptics of revelation, the rebirth of Israel (or of part of it), is replaced by the promise of an entirely new world: perhaps the closest example in Jewish apocalyptics is that of the section of the so-called Celestial Luminaries in 1 Enoch (72–82).

---

4. For a date of the Apocalypse of John, regarding which I have already taken a stance in *Cambridge Ancient History* 1934, 10:726, see J. A. T. Robinson, *Redating the New Testament*, London, 1976, pp. 221–53.

## III

Since apocalyptic revelation includes both the past and the future, that which was and that which shall be, the end of history and the beginning of history are joined. It is therefore difficult to distinguish from apocalyptic books texts such as the life of Adam and Eve, preserved in various forms and languages, or the Book of Shem, preserved in a unique copy in Syrian, dating perhaps from the first century B.C., or the Book of Jubilees, known to the sect of Qumran, who writes the story of Genesis and part of Exodus. The revelation of the true end leads also to the revelation of the true beginning. The Eden that precedes original sin is joined with the Eden of redemption.

There exists, however, a past history that has a utopian, paradigmatic value, but it is not messianic and does not imply the end of the world: this model is Exodus, the exit from Egypt. Jews themselves celebrate and relive it every year in the ceremony of the seder at Passover.[5] Reminding the Jews that they were "slaves" in Egypt is a constant, biblical motif. The nonapocalyptic model of the exit from Egypt has had, as is generally known, a great influence on Anglo-Saxon Puritanism and is now one of the cardinal events in South American liberation theology. Ernst Bloch reproposed this model almost polemically within Marxism; perhaps he did not expect such a quick response from South America. See, for example, Severino Croatto, *Exodus: A Hermeneutics of Freedom*, which, as you can see from the quotation below, I know only from the English translation (New York, 1981). Cromwell, in the first session of his first Parliament, called Exodus "the only parallel of God's dealing with us that I know in the world."

However, the model of Exodus is not simple even if taken in itself. Negatively, it is not a prophetic model. Moses is not the prophet but the legislator. In the Hebrew tradition, however, Moses has the reputation of being the greatest of prophets, and, what is more important, he himself acknowledges in a rather polemical passage (Numbers 11) the right of other prophets to exist under the law. Further, Moses, legislator or prophet, is accompanied by that unwanted brother, Aaron, who in the absence of Moses builds the golden calf. A further complication: Moses must mobilize a minority of Levites, that is, priests, against the makers of the golden calf, but his brother Aaron is not involved in the repres-

5. The seder (meaning "order") is the ritual meal of Jewish families during the first two evenings of Pesach (Passover), a feast that commemorates the exodus from Egypt. The Haggadah, which is recited during the seder, recounts the slavery suffered in Egypt (according to Exodus 13:3, 13:8, 13:42, and other passages) and contains a prayer thanking God for the liberation.—Ed.

sion. The tension between the legislator and the priest remains unresolved. The tension between the priestly aristocracy and the plebeian majority also remains unresolved. Shortly after having declared in Numbers 11, "Would God that all the people of God were prophets," Moses must face the revolt of the Korah in Numbers 16.

There are more serious difficulties with the text. The government is theocratic. The form of acceptance of a theocracy is a pact, the covenant, which would become essential in democratic thought from Cromwell to Rousseau to the theory of popular plebiscites. But is the covenant confined to the generation that made it, or does it extend to future generations that have not been consulted? If it extends to future generations, must it be renewed from generation to generation? And in what form? And who decides who is the rebel? Who will play the role of avenger for Yahweh?

But let us suppose that there is no disagreement between the parties to the covenant. The covenant implies freedom from slavery in Egypt and the granting of the promised land. What were the characteristics of this slavery? In what sense were the Jews slaves in Egypt? And what is the promised land? What right do Jews have to conquer the promised land if it is occupied by other people? In other words, in what sense does freedom become a right to conquer when this involves the elimination or the submission of other people? Exodus is not messianic; indeed it is deeply antimessianic. As such, it has been appealing for all those who prefer a vision of liberation to a vision of radical, apocalyptic revolution. Exodus is the creation of a new state under the law. But what is the ultimate significance of the statement: "do not oppress a stranger, because you know the heart of a stranger, for you were strangers in the land of Egypt"? This is written in Exodus 23:9.

Exodus at first may appear easier than messianism. It has often been opposed to messianism. But, as is already evident from the work of medieval Jewish commentators, we do not have fewer problems with the ideal of Exodus than we do with a utopia of the end of the world. There is, however, one difference: the apocalypse can be left to the responsibility of God whereas, as Moses realized, the exodus is the responsibility of the heads of state, even if they are prophets.

## Bibliographical Note

These few notes will provide an orientation amidst the great amount of recent literature on the subject of the apocalypse and will indicate the names of people to whom I am particularly indebted.

The best general introduction may be the symposium held in Uppsala in

99

1979, published in Tübingen in 1983, *Apocalypticism in the Mediterranean World and the Near East*, edited by D. Hellholm. On the apocalypse as a literary genre, see J. J. Collins, "Apocalypse," *Semeia* 14 (1979), and *The Apocalyptic Imagination*, ed. Collins, New York, 1984. On the origins of the apocalypse, see P. D. Hanson, *The Dawn of Apocalyptic*, Philadelphia, 1975. On the apocalypse and theology, see L. Morris, *Apocalyptic* Eerdmans Publish., 1972; *Apocalypses et théologie de l'espérance*, ed. H. Cazelles Paris, 1977. On apocalypse and theocracy, see O. Ploger, *Teokratie und Escatologie*, Neukirchen, 1968. For the individual works: *Jewish Writings of the Second Temple Period*, ed. M. Stone, Philadelphia, 1984. For the Jewish tradition: D. S. Russell, *The Method and Message of Jewish Apocalyptic*, London, 1964; G. Scholem, *The Messianic Idea in Judaism*, New York, 1971. For the Christian tradition: D. S. Russell, *Apocalyptic Ancient and Modern*, Philadelphia, 1978; J. Carmignac, *Le mirage de l'eschatologie*, Paris, 1979. On individual points: G. Strecker, *Eschaton und Historie*, Göttingen, 1979. For modern research: K. Koch, *The Rediscovery of Apocalyptic*, London, 1972 (trans. from *Ratlos vor der Apokalyptik*, Gütersloh, 1970); J. M. Schmidt, *Die jüdische Apokalyptik. Die Geschichte ihrer Erforschung*, Neukirchen, 1976; various chapters in *Aufstieg und Niedergang der römischen Welt*, 1979. For a typological analysis, see also J. Schreiner, *Alttestamentliche jüdische Apokalyptik*, Munich, 1969. On Daniel, see the bibliography of my essay "The Origins of Universal History" in *Annali della Scuola Normale di Pisa* 3d ser., 12 (1982): 533–60, to which we should add A. Lacocque, *Daniel et son temps*, Geneva, 1983.

Among the recent works on the Apocalypse of John: M. Rissi, *The Future of the World*, London, 1972; E. Corsini, *Apocalissi prima e dopo*, Turin, 1980; A. Yabro Collins, *Crisis and Catharsis: The Power of the Apocalypse*, Philadelphia, 1984; E. Schüser Fiorenza, *The Book of Revelation*, Philadelphia, 1985. For the history of research: O. Böcher, *Die Johannesapokalypse*, Darmstadt, 1975. On recent commentaries: G. B. Caird (London, 1966); G. R. Beasley Murray (London, 1978); J. Massynberde Ford (New York, 1975); J. M. Sweet (Philadelphia, 1979); P. Prigent (Lausanne, 1981). The commentaries by W. Bousset (1906; reprinted Göttingen, 1966) and R. H. Charles (Edinburgh, 1920) are also memorable. The anthology edited by K. Koch and J. M. Schmidt, *Apokalyptic*, Darmstadt, 1982, is helpful in tracing classical research, such as that of J. Wellhausen, H. Gunkel, F. Crawford Burkitt, et al. A useful introduction to formal problems is U. Vanni, *La struttura letteraria dell'Apocalisse*, Rome, 1971.

For iconographic documentation, *La Gerusalemme Celeste*, a catalogue for the exhibition of the Università Cattolica del Sacro Cuore, Milan, 1983, is helpful. Useful, if consulted with caution, is the anthology *Messiah Texts*, available in English translation by R. Patai, New York, 1979. Finally, we should not forget E. De Martino, *La Fine del Mondo. Contributo all'analisi delle apocalissi culturali*, ed. Clara Gallini, Turin, 1977.

# *10*

# Prophecy and Historiography

## Preface

To be accepted at the Philipps Universität of Marburg means being accepted at the heart of the German classical tradition, an honor of which I am very proud and for which I am grateful. I am also pleased to say that the first person who spoke to me about the University of Marburg was Benedetto Croce, not long after he had received an honorary degree in 1927, and had been there as a guest of Leo Spitzer. In those days, for us Italians, the university represented, of course, a center of romance philology in Germany. Some time later, I was personally introduced to Ernst Robert Curtius and to Leo Spitzer. Curtius is the author of that book which, dedicated to Gustav Grober and Aby Warburg, reaffirmed the unity of European civilization after the war.

But to me the University of Marburg was also the University of Carl von Savigny, the man who at an early stage began to develop a relationship with scholars living and working in Piedmont, and who until my time exercised a decisive influence in the understanding of Roman and medieval law in Turin, my first university. But, as a scholar of ancient history, I am particularly grateful to men such as Rubino, Niese, Wissowa, Premerstein, and my friend Karl Christ.

This is not the time to dwell upon the difficulties of our past and the problems of our future, but it may be useful to recall that in ancient times the understanding of the past was expressed in forms that cannot be classified simply within the field of historiography or philosophy.

Lecture held at the University of Marburg on June 27, 1986, on the occasion of the award of an honorary degree.

## Prophecy and Historiography

The two means we have inherited from the Greeks for understanding religion and its development are philosophy and historiography. But we often tend to forget that the Greeks also left us a third means of understanding, a third way of access to history, specifically that of prophecy, and in particular the specific type of the oracle, or the Sibylline Books. Heraclitus is the first writer to mention a sibyl, but by the fifth century, Sibylline Books were rooted in the life of the Hellenic people, especially in the city of Athens. They were well known enough to be mocked by Aristophanes.

It was assumed that sibyls lived in certain cities both in Greece and in the barbarian world. In particular, it was believed that they lived for a period of one thousand years. But mortals seldom got to see a sibyl with their own eyes. Only Trymalchion, the hero of Petronius, claims he has seen a sibyl at Cumae of Eolides. Sibyls were not known through personal contact but through the Sibylline Books, that is, a collection of oracles, or responses of the past applied to the future. In Rome, the right of appealing to a sibyl was a prerogative of the Roman senate. Yet in the second century A.D., if we are to believe the Christian apologist Justin, it was forbidden in Rome to consult the Sibylline Books. But in the fourth eclogue Virgil was able to quote a non-Roman sibylline oracle without violating Roman law. Virgil refers to a Cumaen prediction of a new golden age ("magnus ab integro saeclorum nascitur ordo—iam redit et Virgo, redeunt Saturnia regna"). These kinds of interpretations of universal history seldom appear in pagan Sibylline Books. The interpretation of single, limited events, and thus limited predictions for the future, were more common. But the characterization of the oracles of pagan sibyls is rendered more difficult by the possibility that in the Jewish-Christian Sibylline Books we may find fragments of pagan oracles. I will soon give an example. Further, it is possible that Virgil was acquainted with Jewish imitations of pagan Sibylline Books, but his reliance on these texts is not demonstrated. The fact that we find a clear allusion to Virgil as predecessor in the eleventh Sibylline Book is more remarkable. A Christian reader such as Constantine shared this opinion.

The first time a Jewish sibyl is mentioned in a non-Jewish text is in Pausanias (second century A.D.) but the oldest sibylline oracles of our collection go back at least to the second century B.C. The third Sibylline Book contains a nucleus from the second century with rather evident allusions to Ptolemy VI Philometor and to the Book of Daniel, which was written around the middle of the same century. The fourth book may be older. It mentions a list of four monarchies and ends with a generation (the tenth) for the Macedonian monarchy. The same text alludes to an earthquake in Rodi, and we learn from Pausanias that the earthquake of 303 B.C. had been prophesied by the Sibylline Books. This part of the fourth book appears to have been written in the third century and may be a fragment of pagan origin. In general we can infer that in the second century B.C. at the latest, a Jew—or various Jews— got the unique idea of imitating pagan Sibylline Books in order to disseminate Jewish representations of history and the future. This idea was truly remarkable. This Jew evidently was convinced that he could communicate messianic, eschatological, or perhaps simply anti-Hellenic or anti-Roman opinions in sibylline terminology. He must have had in mind a pagan public capable of appreciating these Jewish expectations. Perhaps we can define these pagans as latent proselytes. But, in general, one does not write simply to persuade other people; one also writes for oneself and in order to persuade one's coreligionists. Jews who composed sibylline texts perhaps invented their texts for themselves and for their coreligionists.

Here we should consider two points. First, the sibylline format with its pagan presuppositions was likely to be appealing to Jews in itself. Second, Christians collected, examined, assimilated, and imitated forged Jewish texts. Both of these points deserve to be examined more closely. It was not easy to express a universal history from a Jewish point of view. After all, traditional biblical historiography was concerned only with the history of the Jews. Jewish prophets, of course, necessarily had to be concerned with the relationship between Jews and the great Oriental powers, but only the eschatology we find in Daniel has a framework of universal history. I suspect that Daniel borrowed the theory of the four universal kingdoms from Greek historiography and the applied eschatological ideas to it. The universal empires are mentioned, of course, in Herodotus, Ctesias, Polybius, and others. What is new in Daniel is the eschatological dimension. Here the empires of the world are dissolved by the Kingdom of God. The eschatology is intrinsically connected with history. But Daniel has remained a book for Jews, even in its Greek version. The forged Sibylline Books were supposed to enable even non-Jews to understand the historic interpretation and the eschatological ending of the book. This was made possible by a presupposition. A Jewish sibyl or perhaps a pre-Jewish sibyl was invented. This sibyl was not entirely Jewish because she was represented as the daughter of Noah, or more often as Noah's daughter-in-law. Strictly speaking, Noah was not Jewish and as the hero of the Flood he represented a historical figure who might hold some meaning for pagans as well. As a pagan or as a not-yet-Jewish figure, this sibyl could easily produce sibylline prophecies. As we were saying, in non-Jewish sources the Jewish sibyl appears for the first time in Pausanias. Her name was Sabbe, but Pausanias hints at the possibility that there is some confusion with a Babylonian sibyl, because he claims that the Jewish sibyl was the daughter of Berossus.

What is even stranger is that the Christians adopted these forged Jewish texts and perpetuated them. Christians, of course, have received and adopted many elements of the Jewish inheritance in Greek. We should bear in mind that the texts of the Septuagint, of Philo, Flavius Josephus, and the Letter of Aristeas were soon forgotten by the Jews, and that this literature has come down to us only through the Christian tradition. There are also other more problematic cases of possible Christian reelaborations of Jewish texts, such as the story of Joseph and Aseneth and perhaps the Testaments of the Twelve Patriarchs. The sibylline responses that the Christians imported, augmented, and superficially Christianized over the course of many centuries were already known, in part, to Clement of Alexandria at the end of the second century. Other texts were known to Lactanius not much later, but the last texts of this Christian collection which are clearly Jewish appear to allude to the Arab conquest of Alexandria, that is, they were drafted as Jewish texts in the seventh century.

Christians were certainly aware of Jewish interest in sibylline oracles. The evidence is found in a text that so far has not been utilized from this point of view. As is known, Ernst Sackur, in his 1898 book *Sibyllinische Texte und Forschungen,* has proved that the medieval oracles of the Tiburtine Sibyl included texts from the fourth century. In 1949, Silvio Giuseppe Mercati announced the discovery on Mt. Athos of the Greek original of these Latin texts from the fourth century. My old colleague Mercati was unable to publish the original text. Paul Alexander, who edited this text in 1967 under the title *The Oracle of Baalbek: The Tiburtine Sibyl in Greek Dress,* has given a somewhat different interpretation, and in my opinion rightly so. The Greek text is not the original of the Latin Tiburtine texts but an enlargened version, probably written around 502. Mercati, however, was essentially right in considering the Greek texts from Mt. Athos as the model for the Latin texts. This Greek text has two peculiarities that distinguish it from the Greek texts of the Jewish-Christian collection. First, this text, like the Latin Tiburtine texts, explains the circumstances in which the prophecy takes place: in this case, it is stated explicitly that the sibyl is present on the Capitol in order to answer the questions of one hundred Roman judges. The second peculiarity, which is particularly interesting, is the presence of Jewish priests, who respectfully question the sibyl regarding the rumor, spread among the pagans, that God would generate a son; the sibyl obviously confirms the rumor. This is all the Jewish priests have to say, and they do not appear anywhere else in the text. It is evident that the Christian author of this sibylline text presupposes that the Jews have interest in and respect for the sibyl. I will stress, here, that the sibyl who speaks in this text is not a Jewish sibyl.

Jews and Christians clearly agree on one point: their concept of history differed from the pagan one and could be communicated to the pagans only through the expedient of the Sibylline Oracles. But we cannot help imagining that both Jews and Christians were pleased in thinking that a pagan sibyl could confirm the truth of the Jewish or Christian faith.

The essential point of contact between Jews and Christians was their faith in an imminent end of the world, which was expressed in many eschatological books for their edification. The Sibylline Books could bring faith to those pagans who were unable or unwilling to take the Book of Daniel or the Revelation of John seriously. But the literary genre of the Sibylline Books also made it possible to consider historical events more closely and to judge them in the framework of a universal history. Thus, the Sibylline Books are a rich source of information for the appreciation Jews and Christians had for the Roman Empire, but it isn't always easy to distinguish between a Jewish appreciation and a Christian one. It is sufficient to remember that book 13 of the Sybilline Oracles ends with an elogy of Odaenathus of Palmyra, which must have been written before he was murdered in 267. The Greek text published by Paul Alexander, which we have already mentioned, contains a summary of Roman history from Augustus to Anastasius with details we find only here, for example, the news that Constantinople was called Eudocopolis, which can be related to Eudocia, the wife of Theodosius II. The text also alludes to heretic statements by Leo I, which are mentioned only here.

The phenomenon of interpreting history through sibylline oracles relies upon two presuppositions. The first is that the pagan thought of Greeks and Romans did not possess a truly apocalyptic or eschatological dimension. The second is that Jews and Christians did not possess a univocal tradition for interpreting political events of universal history, apart from eschatological points of view. Both of these presuppositions should be examined more closely. A scholar of the caliber of Walter Burkert has recently claimed the opposite opinion in the important essay "Apokalyptik im frühen Griechentum," which is his contribution to the international symposium "Apocalypticism in the Mediterranean

World and the Near East." But I am not sure that Burkert actually has been able to prove that the Greeks, beginning in the archaic and classical age, developed a truly apocalyptic thought. In my opinion, Burkert has not succeeded in establishing a connection between the four ages of Hesiod and the apocalyptic vision of Daniel. The epigraphy of Balaam, which was discovered in 1967 at Deir'Alla in Jordan, is undoubtedly an apocalyptic document that adds something to the tradition of Balaam in the Old Testament, but it has nothing to do with Greek thought. The text of Derveni, which is written in Greek and belongs to the orphic tradition, is more revealing. But, as far as I know, in the papyrus of Derveni, the kingdom of the god Dionysius, who is supposed to introduce a new apocalyptic era, is not mentioned explicitly. We can, of course, establish many connections between the four (or five) ages of Hesiod and the four kingdoms of Daniel. As I have already said, the kingdoms mentioned in Daniel are probably Greek in origin. But what I have not managed to find in Greece is the eschatological solution we find in Daniel. As it now stands, apocalypticism in the classical world remains a Jewish-Christian novelty.

The second presupposition is perhaps more important. At a certain point, Jews developed their own political historiography in Greek. This historiography seems to have disappeared with the destruction of the Second Temple, that is, more or less at the time of Flavius Josephus. For over two centuries Christians had no historiography, but in the fourth century an entirely new type of historiography quickly developed, the history of the Church. It is interesting to note that the process of Christianizing political historiography took place very slowly and vaguely. We know that Christian historians such as Procopius were still using a language of pagan origin. It is not easy to establish exactly when a political historiography with clear Christian features developed. As a matter of fact, it was difficult for a Christian to consider political events from a Christian point of view. Perhaps it is not surprising that Orosius, a disciple of Saint Augustine, is the first historian we know who provides a Christian interpretation of Roman history. It was difficult for Christians to realize that it was they who made up the Roman Empire. A much greater difficulty lies in establishing what political history meant to the Christians in general. The silence of the Jews after the fall of Jerusalem and the very strong effort with which the Christians were able to create their own historiography are events that may stem from similar causes. For both groups the focus of historical considerations lies in religious events and institutions. It was difficult for Jews to write, as Jews, the history of the Jews after the destruction of the Temple; it was difficult for Christians to write, as Christians, about events that did not have to do with the Christian community and the Church. If we consider these difficulties, we can understand more easily why the Sibylline Books were so successful in Jewish and Christian circles. They provided a link between strictly religious thoughts and political judgments both for Jews and for Christians. Eschatological expectations gave political thought a religious dimension. The choice of political events was arbitrary and determined by special circumstances. One wonders why the compilers, in a rapidly changing situation, did not simply erase certain texts, for example, the judgment on Odaenathus that was no longer relevant after his death. It is possible that the compilers no longer understood certain oracular statements. Were they still capable of identifying Odaenathus—who is not mentioned under his own name—in the corresponding passage of book 8?

Sibylline oracles thus provided the possibility of interpreting political and religious events from a Jewish or Christian point of view at a time when neither Jews nor Christians were capable of writing history. For Jews the situation lasted, practically, until the late Renaissance, in fact, until the eighteenth century. Because rabbis controlled apocalyptic tendencies, there was no continuity or replacement for Sibylline Books. In any case, Jews in the Middle Ages did not possess a real historiography. For Christians, the Sibylline Books always played a marginal role. Church history, at least from the fourth century, provided the opportunity for an understanding of Church politics. Later, a syncretism of classical and Christian elements slowly developed. Throughout the Middle Ages, the Sibylline Books were successful if only within political prophecy, that is, within the religious interpretation of given political events. Historiography as such prevails, and some historians, for example, Giraldus Cambrensis, readily introduce prophetic oracles in their writings.

Sibylline texts from antiquity cannot be treated in isolation. In one of his early essays, Arthur Darby Nock draws our attention to what he calls "theological oracles." We know that Porphyry collected and appreciated these texts from a lost work on the philosophy of oracles. Not much later, Lactantius quoted these oracles in support of the Christian faith. We also know of "pagan" oracles in which the gods state their defeat and monotheism is proclaimed victorious. But these texts appear to be characterized negatively because they lack an apocalyptic dimension. Overall, what defines the peculiarity of the Sibylline Books is the combination of historical and apocalyptic elements. Finally, they represent the attempt by Jews and Christians to interpret history at a time when an adequate historical genre had not yet been worked out.

I would like to end this essay by noting that the Sibylline Books deserve to be studied closely if one wishes to understand the problem inherent in the relationship between Christianity and historicity as discussed by scholars of Saint Augustine such as Wilhelm Kamlah. Scholars of the problem "Judaism and historicity" have not yet reached Kamlah's level, but questions have been raised recently that are close to the problem Kamlah raises, for example, by Yosef Hayim Yerushalmi in the book *Zakhor*. Now is the time to include the Sibylline Books in the problem of Judaism and historicity.

## Bibliography

Alexander, Paul J. *The Oracle of Baalbek: The Tiburtine Sibyl in Greek Dress.* Washington, 1967 (Dumbarton Oaks Studies X).

Burkert, Walter. "Apologetik im frühen Griechentum. Impulse und Transformation," in *Apologeticism in the Mediterranean World and in the Near East*, ed. D. Hellholm, pp. 235–54. Tübingen, 1983, Proceedings of the International Colloquium on Apologeticism, Uppsala, 12–17 August 1979.

Nock, Arthur D. "Oracles théologiques," *Revue des Études Anciennes* 30 (1928): 280–90.

Sackur, Ernst. *Sibyllinische Texte und Forschungen. Pseudomethodius, Adso und die tiburtinische Sibylle.* Halle, 1898.

Yerushalmi, Yosef Hayim. *Zakhor: Jewish History and Jewish Memory.* Seattle, 1982. The Samuel and Althea Stroum Lectures in Jewish Studies.

# 11

## A Medieval Jewish Autobiography

Hugh Trevor-Roper and I have for a long time shared interests both in Jewish history and in the history of historiography. An unusual text by a German Jew has attracted my attention on both accounts. I would like to offer some remarks on it to Hugh Trevor-Roper as a token of gratitude for all that I have learned from him.

Medieval autobiographies are a relatively rare commodity, and this one—by a German Jew telling of his conversion to Christianity (and of becoming a White Canon)—is in no danger of being forgotten. The *Opusculum de conversione sua* by Hermannus quondam Judaeus, who lived from c. 1107 to c. 1181, was written about the middle of the twelfth century. The text was re-edited with great care on behalf of the *Monumenta Germaniae Historica* by Gerlinde Niemeyer as recently as 1963. A few years earlier it had been given eighteen pages in the *Geschichte der Autobiographie* by G. Misch (III [2], 1 [1959], 505–22). Even better, it has been placed in its Jewish-Christian context with unique authority by B. Blumenkranz in his paper "Jüdische und christliche Konvertiten im jüdisch-christlichen Religionsgespräch des Mittelalters," which is included in the collective volume *Judentum im Mittelalter* (ed. P. Wilpert, Berlin, 1966).

As the Middle Ages are admittedly terra incognita to me, my readers may well ask what I am doing there. The answer is that one needs help precisely when one is *in* terra incognita. Having read this text on more than one occasion as evidence for the history of Jewish institutions and for the history of biography, I have been left with two or three puzzles, none of which seems to have been solved—or even noticed—by the modern scholars whom I have consulted. In any case the text as a

Originally published in English in *History and Imagination: Essays in Honour of H. R. Trevor-Roper*, London, 1981, pp. 30–37. Reprinted by permission of Giulio Einaudi editore s.p.a.

whole provides food for thought to anyone concerned with the modes and limits of the expression of individuality in autobiography.[1]

The basic facts are well known and easy to summarize. At the age of twenty Judas Levi, son of David, acting as the representative of his father, lent a large sum of money to bishop Ekbert of Münster without asking for security. The father, alarmed, sent Judas back from Cologne to Münster with instructions to remain there until the loan had been repaid. It took Judas twenty weeks to recover the money, and he filled the time in friendly contacts with the bishop's retinue and apparently with the bishop himself. He explored local churches and had the opportunity of accompanying the bishop on a visit to the recent Premonstratensian foundation of Cappenberg. He was not reluctant to dispute with Christians, but above all he was impressed by what he saw. He began to think of the possibility of conversion. Months of doubts and of family tension followed. His inclinations had not escaped notice in his Jewish circle. He tried to postpone marriage with the girl to whom he was engaged. The marriage, however, took place: later it appeared to the writer as the Devil's supreme trick. "Decursis autem tribus mensibus, ex quo letargico hoc anime mee morbo ceperam laborare" (ch. 11), young Judas was again ready to contact Christian priests, monks, and nuns, both in Cologne and in the neighborhood. He soon decided to run away from home and to kidnap a seven-year-old stepbrother, who for unknown reasons lived with his mother in Mainz. Having succeeded in both operations, he took refuge in an Augustinian establishment near Mainz. There he left his stepbrother, who was more or less forcibly baptized and consequently never returned to the family. Judas himself entered another Augustinian foundation at Ravengiersburg as a catechumen. He was solemnly baptized in Cologne in November 1129 under the name of Hermannus, and soon afterward was admitted as a novice at Cappenberg, the Premonstratensian place he had visited and loved not long before. There

1. G. Niemeyer's edition of Hermannus's *Opusculum* was reviewed by F. J. Schmale, *Hist. Zeitsch.* 200 (1965): 114–20. Previous bibliography in P. Browe, S. J., *Die Judenmission im Mittelalter und die Päpste,* Rome, 1973, p. 62. The text, it seems to me, is basically misunderstood by W. P. Eckert, in *Monumenta Judaica. 2000 Jahre Geschichte und Kultur der Juden am Rhein,* ed. K. Schilling, Cologne, 1963, pp. 150–51. For background, in the same *Monumenta Judaica* see the section by E. Roth, pp. 60–130. See furthermore G. Kisch, *The Jews in Medieval Germany,* Chicago, 1949, 2d ed., New York, 1970, and the two papers by H. Liebeschütz, *Journal of Jewish Studies* 10 (1959): 97–111; 16 (1965): 35–46. For medieval biography in general, see K. J. Weintraub, *The Value of the Individual,* Chicago, 1978, pp. 18–114 (on Hermannus and the Premonstratensians, p. 63). See also Pl. F. Lefèvre and W. M. Grawen, *Les statuts de Prémontré au milieu du XIIᵉ siècle,* Averbode, 1978, and W. Goez, *Gestalten des Hochmittelalters,* 1983, pp. 238–53.

he learned Latin. He took holy orders perhaps about 1137, as apparently he had to be thirty years old before he could be ordained. The autobiography ends at this point, but we know from documentary evidence that Hermannus quondam Judaeus was Provost of Scheda in 1170. Two years later he moved to a canonry in the Church of Maria ad Gradus in Cologne. He was still alive in 1181. The title "primus abbas ecclesiae Scheidensis" given to him by some recent manuscripts of the *Opusculum* seems to be due to confusion. What happened to Hermannus's wife after he left her is of course no part of his story: this 'vita nuova' was without a Beatrice.

Hermannus's autobiography, like all autobiographies by converts, raises the problem of the way in which conversion affected the perception of preconversion events. A man who changes his own name because he has become another man has to define the borders between his present and his previous self. Hermannus makes it clear that he writes for Christians, not for Jews. At the same time, he projects back into his Jewish past his activities as a controversialist on behalf both of the Jewish and of the Christian faith. In other words, he recognizes that these activities did not lead to anything. This point—which has already been duly emphasized by B. Blumenkranz—deserves some further clarification because it is central to Hermannus's view of his own conversion. Born in an age of religious controversies, young Judas Levi had obviously been trained to dispute and, as I have already mentioned, had relished open disputations. In that journey to Münster, which proved decisive for his future life, the twenty-year-old moneylender had managed to enter into a (public?) debate with no one less than the redoubtable abbot Rupert of Deutz, whose *Annulus sive Dialogus inter Christianum et Judaeum* was written just in those years between 1126 and 1128. During the following months, while still searching for an answer, Judas had numerous discussions 'opportune importune' with Christian clergymen (ch. 9). On his own showing he had never yielded his ground: in fact, he had come out of these disputations rather well, especially in that with Rupert of Deutz. Seen from the Christian point of view, these controversies had contributed nothing to his conversion. By implication his Christian opponents were involved in the failure: they had been unable to enlighten a man who wanted to be enlightened. What is more remarkable, almost on the eve of his conversion Hermannus attempted a disputation inside a synagogue—this time as the champion of Christianity. But he ended by disavowing what he had said. To be more precise, when he was already on his way to being converted he visited an older brother in Worms and went to synagogue with him. As an opportunity was offered, he produced arguments in support of Christianity. As soon as his brother and other listeners began to be alarmed, he blandly assured them that he had intended only to show the Jews which arguments they should expect from Christian controversialists: "quam illi responsionem gratanter acceperunt" (ch. 16). Perhaps he had no choice but retreat, as he wanted to conceal his intention to become a convert himself. All the same, objectively, he had failed as a champion of Christianity, while before he had succeeded only too well as a Jewish apologist against his Christian opponents.

Hermannus, therefore, pointedly opposes the barrenness of his controversy with Rupert of Deutz (which is also the barrenness of Rupert's controversy with him) to the spiritual fruitfulness of the kind concern shown to him by a domestic of bishop Ekbert. If the bishop had allowed it, that domestic would have submitted himself to an ordeal for the sake of the Jew's soul.

In the sole digression in his story, which he appends to this episode, Hermannus emphasizes that love is the only way to convert the Jews: "Confirment igitur ad illos caritatem eorum, quantum valent, necessitatibus communicando ac totius eis forma pietatis existendo, quatenus quos verbo non possunt, lucrentur exemplo" (ch. 5). Hermannus must have known that his famous older contemporary and fellow-convert Petrus Alfonsi (alias Moses Sephardi from Huesca) had championed a more aggressive controversial style with Jews and exploited his knowledge of rabbinical literature to reinforce traditional Christian arguments against Judaism. Whether Hermannus had Petrus Alfonsi in mind or not, his words declared disagreement by implication. He had been converted not by such arguments but by the benevolence and affection with which he had been received in the bishop's palace, by the discovery of claustral life at Cappenberg, and finally by the prayers of two ascetic women, Berta and Glismut, to whom he had recommended himself (see especially ch. 5 and ch. 12). These women had procured for him that gift of grace which he had been unable to obtain by commending himself to St. Paul and then to the Cross ("frequenter cor meum signo eiusdem crucis consignabam")—no mean steps for a man who was still a Jew (see ch. 6 and 11). Paradoxically, but coherently, the only time in which Hermannus presents himself as successful for the right cause in a dispute is on the very eve of baptism, but this happens in a dream, and his defeated opponents are apparently already dead. He dreams of meeting two relatives in the other world and reproaches them for not having understood that Isaiah 9:6 had alluded to the Cross. The poor relatives can produce no objection. They know by now for themselves that they are damned: "eterne destinati sumus gehenne" (18).

112

In the language of the Psalms with which he had been familiar since his early childhood, Hermannus could claim that God "de stercore pauperem erexit et eum cum princibus populi sui collocavit" (see Ps. 112:7–8). In this perspective a dream he had had in his thirteenth year acquired capital importance in his eyes. It determined the structure of his biography and, in some sense, constitutes the first of my puzzles.

The account of the conversion which I have so far summarized and commented upon is sandwiched between the description of this dream and its true interpretation. In other words, the autobiography is presented as the evidence required to explain the dream. The thirteen-year-old boy dreamt that he received a visit from the Emperor Henry V, who gave him a white horse and a purse with seven coins in it, hanging from a glamorous belt; furthermore, the emperor promised to give him the entire property of a prince who had just died. The boy was then asked to accompany the emperor to his palace and to take part in a banquet. Apparently Jewish dietary rules were observed at the feast, for the emperor shared with him a dish of herbs. The boy had more or less dreamt of himself as a new Mordecai after the death of Haman. A learned relative to whom he turned for the interpretation of the dream confirmed him in his expectations of honors and wealth: he specified that the white horse was the promise of a beautiful and noble wife (see Babylonian Talmud, *Berakot* 56b, *Sanhedrin* 93a). But, to use Dante's language, which is relevant here, "lo verace giudicio del detto sogno non fue veduto allora per alcuno, ma ora è manifestissimo a li più semplici." Reflecting on this dream after his conversion, Hermannus was in a position to give its true explanation: the emperor stood for God; the horse, perhaps less conventionally, for baptism; the seven coins for the seven gifts of the spirit; and so on.

What I do not know—and should like to know—is whether there are other (medieval) autobiographies so neatly constructed to explain a dream. Hermannus places the whole of his autobiographical data between the account of the dream and its interpretation. Dreams, of course, play an important part in autobiographies, though it does not seem to have occurred to any of the commentators of Dante's *Vita Nuova* whom I have consulted that the *Opusculum* by Hermannus Judaeus might be a useful text to compare.[2] Dreams occur prominently in documents of two conversions of Christians to Judaism in the late eleventh and early twelfth centuries, though even these do not offer the exact parallel I am seeking. The Cairo Geniza has preserved at least two auto-

2. See M. Pazzaglia in *Enciclopedia Dantesca*, 1976, 5:1086–96. For medieval theories on dreams, F. X. Newman, *Somnium*, Princeton, 1962. See also A. Löwinger, *Der Traum in der jüdischen Literatur*, Leipzig, 1908.

biographical accounts in Hebrew by converts to Judaism: one is anonymous (but by a former priest); the other is by a Norman aristocrat from Southern Italy (almost certainly also a former priest), Johannes of Oppido, who in 1102 on conversion took the name of Obadiah.[3] The anonymous account has been attributed by B. Blumenkranz to Andreas, the archbishop of Bari, whom we know from Obadiah to have preceded him in the conversion by several decades; but the attribution is not cogent, and the story of Andreas's conversion is a problem in itself into which I do not intend to enter. The anonymous writer, who speaks in the first person, tells in a letter of a dream that persuaded one of his jailers to allow him to escape. More relevant to Hermannus's story is the account by the other convert. Johannes-Obadiah, who speaks in the third person in a fairly lengthy personal memoir, of which several fragments are preserved, states that he was inspired to become a convert not only by the example of Andreas, but also by a dream he had had in his youth, when he was still in the house of his father and in some situation of impurity. He dreamt of being in a cathedral and of receiving some message or warning from a man (angel?) who stood

3. A critical edition is about to be published under the title "Megillat Obadiah hager" with a discussion in Hebrew by N. Golb in *S. D. Goitein Festschrift*, Jerusalem, 1980, making all these fragments available together. The bibliography provided by *Encyclopaedia Judaica*, s.v. "Obadiah the Norman Proselyte," 1971, 12:1306–8, is supplemented by A. Scheiber, "Der Lebenslauf des Johannes-Obadja aus Oppido," in *Antiche Civiltà Lucane*, ed. P. Borraro, Galatina, 1975, pp. 240–44. The most recent contribution, of great importance, is by J. Prawer, *Studies in Medieval Jewish History and Literature*, ed. I. Twersky, Cambridge, Mass., 1979, pp. 110–34. I indicate here only the previous editions of texts and the discussions relevant to my argument. The anonymous text published by S. Assaf in *Zion* 5 (1940): 118–19 (and also in the volume *Meqoroth u-mehqarim*, Jerusalem, 1946, p. 143; corrections to this edition by N. Golb, *Journ. Jewish Studies* 16 [1965]: 71) was attributed to Andreas, archbishop of Bari, by B. Blumenkranz, *Journ. Jewish Studies* 14 (1963): 33–36, whereas S. D. Goitein, *Journ. Jewish Studies* 4 (1953): 74–84 had preferred the identification, already hinted at by Assaf, with Obadiah. Neither suggestion is cogent, as N. Golb remarks, in *Journ. Jewish Studies* 16 (1965): 69–74. The main fragments of Obadiah's autobiographical text in the third person were published by E.-N. Adler, *Rev. Ét. Juives* 69 (1919): 129–34; J. Mann, *Rev. Ét. Juives* 89 (1930): 245–59; S. D. Goitein, *Journ. Jewish Studies* 4 (1953): 74–84 (English trans. only); A. Scheiber, *Acta Orientalia Hungarica* 4 (1954) 271–96 (basically repeated in *Kiryath Sefer* 30 [1954–55]: 73–98 and *Journ. Jewish Studies* 5 [1954]: 32–37); A. Scheiber, *Hebrew Union College Annual* 39 (1968): 168–72 (text already translated by Goitein in *Journ. Jewish Studies* 4 [1953] but Scheiber publishes also a letter in verse concerning another convert to Judaism of about 1100). Relevant also is the paper in Hebrew by N. Golb, "A Study of a Proselyte to Judaism who Fled to Egypt at the Beginning of the Eleventh Century," *Sefer Zikkaron le-I. Ben Zwi*, Jerusalem, 1964, pp. 87–104 (especially pp. 102–4). Essential for the background is S. D. Goitein, *A. Mediterranean Society: The Jewish Communities of the Arab World*, Berkeley, 1971, especially 2:308–11. It is to be hoped that all the evidence about Obadiah will be translated and commented upon with the consideration of the traditions of Norman historiography.

near him by the altar. A probable interpretation of the text is as follows: "Now in the first year in which Johannes was initially defiled in the night in the house of Dreux, his father, in that year he had a dream. He was officiating in the Cathedral of Oppido . . . when he looked up and beheld a man standing to his right, opposite the altar. The man said to him: Johannes." The content of the message is not preserved; and the situation of impurity in which the dream developed is obscurely described and has been variously interpreted (as its meaning is irrelevant to my argument I refrain from comment).[4]

Obadiah wrote his autobiography after 1121; Hermannus, as I said, became a Christian in 1129. The fragments we have of Obadiah's autobiography come from more than one copy of the text; some are vocalized. A Bible quotation from Joel (3:4) is in Latin, though written in Hebrew characters. The text was therefore meant for wide diffusion, even to those who needed vocalized Hebrew and could appreciate a biblical text in the Vulgate. Obadiah was by then in Eastern Islamic countries where he met at least one self-proclaimed Messiah, but he needed to maintain contacts with the West—if for no other reason, at least to produce evidence for his previous life. In any case his text would be in demand among Jews; it was of obvious interest. One wonders whether Hermannus knew Obadiah's text. It contained a decisive dream in a decisive situation, which seems to be the nearest parallel to Hermannus's dream at the age of thirteen. Both converts considered themselves summoned to conversion in a dream they had had in adolescence.

The natural assumption is that Hermannus had his dream at thirteen, when a Bar Mitzvah. The assumption, however natural, is not without difficulties. The age of thirteen is recognized in Talmudic texts as the beginning of full religious duty and responsibility. Though difficult to date, these texts are unambiguous in their contents. A "Saying of the Fathers" (5:21) attributes to either Samuel the Small (first century A.D.), or the perhaps later Rabbi Jehudah ben Tema a definition of the fourteen stages of human life: one of the stages is "at thirteen for the commandments (*Mitzvot*)." A minor Talmudic treatise, *Masseket Soferim*, which is usually dated in the eighth century, is even more definite (18:5): "There was likewise a beautiful custom in Jerusalem to train the young sons and daughters to afflict themselves on a fast day . . . and at the age of thirteen [the boy] was taken round and presented to every elder to bless him and to pray for him that he may be worthy to study

4. For the more probable interpretation, see N. Golb, *Sefer Zikkaron le-I. Ben Zwi*, pp. 102–3 and *Journ. Jewish Studies* 18 (1967): 43–63. For dreams of another convert, A. Scheiber, *Tarbiz* 34 (1964–65): 367.

the Torah and engage in good deeds" (trans. A. Cohen). Furthermore, *Bereshit Rabbah*, a homiletic commentary on Genesis, usually dated in the fifth century, attributes (63:10) to Rabbi Eleazar ben Simeon, the controversial rabbi of the second century A.D., a saying destined to great fortune in later Judaism: "A man is responsible for his son until the age of thirteen; thereafter he must say: 'Blessed is He who has now freed me from the responsibility of this boy' " (trans. H. Freedman). Notwithstanding these and other pieces of evidence (for which see *Jewish Encyclopaedia*, s.v. Bar Mitzvah), specialists, as far as I know, still seem to accept as valid the demonstration given in 1875 by Leopold Löw in his classic book *Die Lebensalter in der jüdischen Literatur* (pp. 210–17) that the Bar Mitzvah ritual as we know it originated in Germany around the fourteenth century. S. B. Freehof ("Ceremonial Creativity among the Ashkenazim," *Jewish Quarterly Review* 75 [1967]: 217–21) substantially confirms this date and origin. Indeed the use of the expression Bar Mitzvah to indicate a boy exactly at the stage of initiation does not seem to occur earlier. According to Löw's account, in the fourteenth century it became a custom among Ashkenazi Jews that a boy should be called for the first time to read at least a chapter from the weekly portion of the Law on the first Sabbath after he has entered his fourteenth year. On that occasion his father recites the blessing attributed to Rabbi Eleazar ben Simeon. The festivity included, and till includes, presents to the Bar Mitzvah, a banquet, and, if the child is gifted, a learned speech by him to the guests. Concurrently he assumes the duty of wearing phylacteries, *tefillin*, at least during morning prayers except on Sabbaths and holy days.

Now if we go back to the dream Hermannus had at the age of thirteen we find the banquet, the presents, and maybe even the speech ("tum ego regali munificentiae debitas rependens gratias"), though admittedly before the banquet. The boy's age and the nature of the dream invite the conclusion that as early as 1120 the Ashkenazim of Cologne already had something like a Bar Mitzvah ceremony. The Mordecai pattern of the dream as a whole would not represent an objection. But how legitimate is the conclusion itself?

Whether the *Opusculum de conversione sua* by Hermannus quondam Judaeus offers a unique example of autobiography inserted between the account of a dream and its explanation; whether the *Opusculum* was written with some knowledge of Obadiah's autobiography; and whether this initial dream is the earliest evidence for the Bar Mitzvah ceremony in Germany—these are the questions I ask but cannot answer. The text remains a very telling document of conversion in an age of controversy, because the man who loved controversies before conversion virtually recognized their inanity after it. The relation between this autobiography and the spirituality of the Premonstratensian order to which Hermannus belonged would deserve special study. But if we want to know too much about Hermannus's identity we shall of course end by knowing nothing.[5]

5. I am deeply indebted to my colleague Professor N. Golb of the University of Chicago, who allowed me to use his critical text of Obadiah's fragments before publication and discussed their interpretation with me. I owe further information to Dr. B. Smalley, to my daughter A. L. Lepschy, to Rabbi L. Jacobs, and to Joanna Weinberg.

# Part Two

# *12*

# The Jews of Italy

## I

Italian history is always a difficult subject. Behind it and inside it there is the extraordinary variety of regional and urban units: the history of Florence is not the history of Pisa, or even that of Arezzo or Siena or Volterra. Where the Jews are involved, the differences in local traditions are increased by substantial local differences in the past treatment of Jews. Much of Southern Italy and Sicily—splendid Jewish centers in the Middle Ages—lost their Jews in the sixteenth century during the Spanish rule. It is sometimes forgotten that Jews were kept out of most of Lombardy for more than a century until the Austrians replaced the Spaniards in 1714.

In addition, there are the differences of origins of the Jews themselves. Some of us are descendants of the Jews who lived in Italy during the Roman Empire. Some are Ashkenazi Jews who, especially in the fourteenth century, left Germany and came to Italy. French Jews had to leave France in the same century, and there was the Sephardi immigration and the return of Marranos of Spanish origin to Judaism at the end of the fifteenth and during the sixteenth century. Contacts with the East always existed, especially in Venice and Southern Italy, as long as Jews were allowed to remain there. Other Jews from Muslim coun-

Originally published in English in *The New York Review of Books*, 32, 16, 24 October 1985, pp. 22–26. Reprinted by permission of Giulio Einaudi editore s.p.a. This essay was prepared for a meeting at Brandeis University in 1984 in honor of Vito Volterra, the great Italian mathematician who died in 1940. Volterra had been a professor at three Italian universities—Turin, Pisa, and Rome—where I also taught. He was elected by the king to the Italian senate in 1905. Two distinguished mathematicians of my own family, Eugenio Elia and Beppo Levi, were inspired in their work by him. My friendship with his sons, especially with Edoardo, a student of Roman law, goes back to 1929, when I had just moved to Rome from Turin.

tries were attracted by the new *porto franco* of Leghorn (Livorno) after the middle of the sixteenth century.

Leghorn remained the easiest Italian town for Jews to live in during at least two centuries and developed that Jewish style of its own which is preserved in the books of Elia Benamozegh and of which perhaps the paintings of Amedeo Modigliani show traces. The differences of origins were of course reflected in the differences of rituals and melodies, and in their turn the differences of rituals were preserved by separate synagogues. Three synagogues—*la scola italiana, la scola tedesca, la scola spagnola*—were frequently to be found in the same town; in Rome not long ago, there were still five synagogues preserving an interesting distinction between *scola catalano-aragonese* and *scola spagnola.*

We in Piedmont, together with Italian, Sephardi, and Ashkenazi synagogues, had that curious *minhag apam*—the three rather small congregations of Asti, Fossano, and Moncalvo—which preserved the fossil of a French medieval ritual with its peculiar *mahzor,* or prayer book. That the Jews were tolerated in one of the states of Italy, however, did not mean that they were tolerated in all parts of the same state. That the popes allowed the Jews to live in Rome and Ancona, where we find the Volterras, does not imply that they were allowed to live in Bologna. It fell to one of my grandfather's brothers, the rabbi Marco Mordechai Momigliano, to be sent in 1866 to rebuild the Jewish community of Bologna. This community, where Obadiah Sforno, Azaria di Rossi, and Samuel Archevolti had worked and thought, had been closed down in 1593 and had not existed, at least officially, for more than 250 years. On the other hand, the Jews prospered at Ferrara under the same papal rule and preserved some of the brilliance characteristic of their culture under the house of Este, which ended in 1597. The explanation is partly in the agrarian situation of the region, which helped to form the pro-Fascist attitudes of the Jews of Ferrara centuries later.

Differing in rituals and often with conflicting interests among themselves, the Jews of Italy were not, however, beset by more linguistic differences than their Christian counterparts. The linguistic situation of Italy was already complicated enough in itself. What we call Italian remained basically a written language to the end of the nineteenth century. Ordinary people spoke what we call dialects, and the Jews spoke the same dialect as the other inhabitants of the place. Venetian Jews spoke and speak Venetian, and we Piedmontese Jews spoke Piedmontese. My parents spoke Piedmontese between themselves and Italian with us children. So my sisters and I were the only native Italian speakers of our little Piedmontese town and much admired for our lin-

guistic accomplishments. When I grew up I returned to the Piedmontese dialect in conversations at home with my parents—though not
with my sisters.

No doubt, ghetto life favored some peculiarity. The dialect of the Roman Jews is known to have remained considerably more archaic than
that of the Roman Christians, and of course Hebrew words and sen-
tences were inserted into the local dialect. In the Piedmontese jargon of
the Jews there were some Yiddish words imported into Piedmont by
Jews of Ashkenazi provenance—the Ottolenghi, Treves, and Diena,
who were destined to play such an important part in recent Italian history. So it was usual to speak of the *Becher* for kiddush, or of the *Orzai*
for *Jahrzeit*, the anniversary of a death.

The other element that has to be kept in mind concerning the Italian
Jews is that we have been so few—so few especially in the last centuries. There were at most perhaps 30,000 Jews at the beginning of the
nineteenth century, including the Jews of Trieste, which was technically in Austria, and those of Nice, which became French in 1859. This
represented about one per thousand in the population of Italy. Before
the last war there were about 50,000. Ten thousand of us were murdered by the Fascists and the Nazis in alliance, and this included eleven
members of my family, among whom were my father and mother.
About six thousand emigrated, never to return. Others were lost during the period of the persecution when the rate of conversion was
higher than average. Among the converts, as is well known, was the
chief rabbi of Rome, Israel Zoller, baptized in Santa Maria degli Angeli
at Rome on February 13, 1945. If there are now between 30,000 and
35,000 Jews, it is because emigration from Libya, and to a lesser extent
from Eastern countries, has swollen the native Jewish population. This
figure represents one person for each two thousand of the entire population of Italy. Most of the Jews are now concentrated in a few large
towns. Most of the old synagogues are empty, if they still exist.

## II

Every time I am in an Italian town, I try to figure out whether and how
Jews fared in it. Some of these cities I know well enough. I have passed
many summers in the peace of the beautiful town of Spoleto in Umbria.
Going around the city, I can easily reconstruct the history of Spoleto
since the time of Hannibal. But when I enter the little medieval street
which is at present called Via San Gregorio della Sinagoga I am baffled.
When did the synagogue there stop being a synagogue? Does the

name of the street imply that the San Gregorio church was superimposed on the synagogue? And where are the descendants of the famous Renaissance Jewish doctors of Spoleto, one of whom was David De' Pomis, the author of the Hebrew-Latin-Italian dictionary *Zemah David*, "the offshoot of David," which I used daily as a child? At the moment there is in Spoleto one Jewish family that moved from Rome. Perhaps I ought to add that two or three years ago I discovered that a couple of American Jewish artists were trying to make a living by opening a sandwich bar in Spoleto. I hope they are successful.

The disappearance of the small Jewish communities makes it difficult to follow up family histories and, even more, local cultural traditions. I wish I could explain how the Volterra family left Tuscany, where they were well established in the Renaissance, to go to Ancona. There is, as we know, more than one version of the transfer of Disraeli's grandfather to England in 1748: some have him depart from the small but learned community of Cento, others from Venice. Research now in progress at Tel Aviv by Shelomo Simonsohn and his colleagues will no doubt clarify many details; and the Jerusalem volume by Robert Bonfil has already told us much that we did not know about the Italian rabbis of the Renaissance. Research on Jews has become fashionable in Italy, too.

It still remains difficult to say something precise even about one's own family. I envy my colleague Vittore Colorni, the remarkable professor of the history of Italian law at the University of Ferrara, who has been able to produce a neat genealogical tree of his family from 1477 to 1977 in a book dedicated to the memory of Umberto Nahon and published in Jerusalem in 1978. His success was made possible by the unusual fact that his family, the Colorni, remained for more than four centuries in the same place, Mantua. As for my family, I can at least say that about the beginning of the fourteenth century an ancestor of mine had the prudence to leave the little Jewish community of Montmélian in Savoy for the capital of Savoy, Chambéry, where he was duly registered as Lionel—or, if you prefer, Jehudah—de Montmélian. The *juiverie* of Montmélian virtually disappeared about fifty years later when Jews were thrown into the wells as responsible for the black plague.

The descendants of Lionel de Montmélian, following up the expansion of the dukedom of Savoy into Piedmont, went into trade, moneylending, and rabbinical positions in the small Jewish communities of Piedmont: Busca, Cuneo, Mondovì, Asti, Chieri, Ivrea. There they remained for centuries, terribly poor, pious, and scholarly, until Napoleon brought new ideas, new hopes, and—as my grandfather, the last traditional zaddik, or "just man," of Italy, was never tired of repeating—new delusions to the Italian Jews.[1]

How are we to explain the sudden explosion of initiative, creativity, intellectual and political responsibility that characterize the history of Italian Jews after Napoleon and above all after 1848? That was the year in which the king of Piedmont and Sardinia gave to the Jews the equality later to be extended to the other regions of Italy in what ultimately became the unification of Italy; the process took more than twenty years.

No doubt the irrational factor—patriotism—had a decisive influence. I shall only indicate what may seem an absurd fact: the sudden enthusiasm of a basically conservative Jewish scholar. Samuel David Luzzatto—Sadal—in 1848. It is not by chance that the *Giudaismo illustrato* by Luzzatto appeared in 1848. It is self-explanatory in its appeal to the tradition of Italian Jews from the days of Shabbatai Donnolo and of the various members of the Kalonymus family of Lucca and Rome to the present day. It is even more characteristic that Luzzatto was moved by seeing a man of Jewish origin, although baptized, Daniele Manin, become the president of the revolutionary republic of Venice in 1848–49. Daniele Manin's ancestors had been called Medina until the end of the eighteenth century.

This patriotism, this devotion to the new Italy of the Risorgimento, has been in our blood since the days of our great-grandfathers and fathers, whatever reservations they and we may have about what was happening and is happening in Italy. It explains why my grandmother used to cry every time she listened to the "Marcia Reale"—the royal hymn of the Italian monarchy—and if you can cry at such atrocious music, you can cry at anything. More seriously, it explains why during the First World War the three university professors who died in battle were all Jews, and at least two of them were volunteers. One of the best-known heroes of the First World War remains Roberto Sarfatti, the eighteen-year-old student who happened to be the son of Margherita

1. Although I am not the first trained historian of my family to be interested in our history—I have been preceded by a better man than myself, my late cousin and friend Arturo Carlo Jemolo, a Momigliano on his mother's side, a Sicilian Catholic on his father's side—there are too many facts we do not know. I wish I knew more of Giuseppe Vita Momigliano of Ivrea, who was one of the representatives of the Piedmontese Jews in the Napoleonic Sanhedrin of 1806. Another Piedmontese Jew of the Segre (my wife's) family, Salvatore Segre, was the *av-bet-din*, the chairman of the same Sanhedrin. I wish I knew more also of Isacco Momigliano, who pestered eminent men with his questions on religions and literature; it was to him that Sadal—Samuel David Luzzatto—wrote his famous letter on Judaism and Christianity, arguing, of course, for the right to exist of the former.

Sarfatti, who was later the mistress and the biographer of Mussolini. Even in the disgraceful Abyssinian and Spanish wars of 1936, the young hero was one of our Jewish students in the University of Turin, Bruno Jesi, who soon found himself confronted by the racial laws.

Interestingly enough, it was not the change in economic conditions that gave a new direction to the lives of Italian Jews. No doubt, there was a new opening of opportunities, and they were taken. The most important was the possibility of becoming farmers and landowners. Italian Jews, especially of Piedmont, Veneto, Emilia, and Tuscany, were indeed strongly inclined to buy land and settle on it or near it. This, incidentally, explains the strong conservative bias of many Italian Jews. But Italian Jews never became leading capitalists and industrialists. None of the few great Italian industries, such as Fiat, has been in the hands of Jews; there was an attempt to import a branch of the Rothschild bank into Italy—in Naples, of all places—but it did not last long. The nearest approximation to Jewish ownership of great industry is to be found in the Olivetti firm, with its peculiar tradition of technical sophistication and attention to social problems. Many Jews prospered in the medium-sized industries and in the insurance business; others, like my people, stuck to the traditional Italo-Jewish combination of banking and silk mills (*filande*) to which first Japanese competition and later artificial silk dealt mortal blows.

But the explanation for the high contribution of the Jews, both in quantity and quality, to the Italian social and intellectual life of the last 150 years is to be found elsewhere. First of all, even before 1848, they had managed to get for themselves a very good modern education, all the legal obstacles notwithstanding. Some Piedmontese Jews like the future secretary of Cavour, Isacco Artom, were sent to study in Milan where, under Austrian rule, Jews were allowed to go to a public school. A banker, who was a member of the Todros family, emigrated from Turin to Paris in about 1835 in order to give a good education to his children. The future mother of Cesare Lombroso put only one condition to her father, a Piedmontese Jew, when he was going to arrange her marriage: the husband should be a subject of Austria where education for Jewish children was better. So it happened that Cesare Lombroso, the erratic genius who revolutionized psychiatry and much else, was born in Verona and there he has his monument. But normally it was by reorganization of the traditional school, the Talmud Torah, that Italian Jews acquired knowledge of modern culture before they were admitted to the state schools. As for the Italian universities, there was limited entry for Jews to some, such as Padua and Ferrara, especially in medicine. Later Italian Jews studied hard both in Italian and foreign schools and were known to go gladly abroad to improve themselves. I believe that Leone Sinigaglia, the exquisite musician who collected the Piedmontese songs, was the only Italian pupil of Mahler in Vienna; Sinigaglia died when the Nazi-Fascists knocked at his door in Turin to capture him.

## III

What the contribution of traditional Jewish instruction was to this renovation of Italian-Jewish culture is more difficult to say. One fact is obvious. Both traditional Jewish studies and modern research and education prospered in the places where there was greater liberty and prosperity. In certain cases, the continuity from traditional, rabbinical education to ordinary modern humanistic and scientific formation is clearly recognizable. Jewish traditional learning was strongest in places like Trieste, Gorizia, Venice, Padua, and Mantua, especially under Austrian rule, then in Leghorn and in Ferrara. During the eighteenth century, Isacco Lampronti, the Talmudic encyclopedist of *Pahad Yizhak*, came from Ferrara; new sections of his *Encyclopaedia* are still being published in Israel. One of the founders of modern Hebrew literature, Moshe Luzzatto, came from Padua. In the nineteenth century, Isacco Reggio lived in Gorizia; Sadal, the greatest of all, was born in Trieste and taught in Padua. Elia Benamozegh, the mystically minded adversary of Sadal, lived in Leghorn, where at the beginning of the century David Azulai had ended his legendary life as *"Wunderrabbi."*

Rome, which had the largest Jewish community, was not conspicuous for intellectual activity: there Jews were the most miserable and the most oppressed. It must be generally emphasized that there was in Italy more traditional learning and more use of Hebrew as a learned language than is usually believed, at least among modern-day Italian Jews. We even exported a member of the Artom tribe to become the *Haham,* or rabbi, of the London Sephardi community (1866). He was a poet in Hebrew and in Italian. And of course Sabato Morais came to the United States and became, perhaps to his surprise, one of the founders of the Jewish Theological Seminary of New York.

It is also worth reminding ourselves that the last Italian poet in Hebrew was a woman, Rachele Morpurgo, the cousin and friend of Sadal and a member of that Morpurgo tribe which has contributed so many professors to the Italian universities and several members to the Italian Parliament, and in recent years has produced the first woman professor of comparative philology at Oxford University, Anna Morpurgo.

If one looks, then, at the map of the provenance of learned professors, the correspondence between the older Jewish and the newer
Italian culture is fairly obvious. The greatest comparative philologist
and, in the absolute sense, the greatest Italian philologist in the nineteenth century, Graziadio Isaia Ascoli, came from Gorizia where he
had been a pupil of Rabbi Reggio. He remained a close friend, even in
his Milan days, of Sadal and of Sadal's son Filosseno Luzzatto, the
promising Assyriologist who died prematurely. The great master of
Italian studies, Alessandro D'Ancona, who was a director of the Scuola
Normale of Pisa, grew up in Tuscany. From Venice and Trieste came the
families Venezian, Pincherle, and Polacco, to fill the Italian universities
and Parliament. The learned rabbi of Mantua, Marco Mortara, whose
library was famous, was destined to be the father and grandfather of a
dazzling family, the greatest member of which is indisputably
Lodovico Mortara (1855–1937), first-class jurist, head of the Supreme
Court of Cassazione, minister of justice in 1919, and vice-prime minister.

Examples could easily be multiplied of this continuity of secular and
religious Jewish tradition. I shall add only one case which has always
seemed to me the most bizarre. The name Mussafia is connected in the
seventeenth, eighteenth, and early nineteenth centuries with a series
of distinguished rabbinical scholars. The best known is Benjamin ben
Immanuel Mussafia, who in the late seventeenth century published in
Holland a supplement to what remains the most important Italian contribution to Talmudic studies, the Lexicon *Arukh*. Two other Mussafias,
father and son, followed each other as rabbis and Talmudic scholars at
Spalato (Split) in Dalmatia at the beginning of the nineteenth century.
Their linguistic and hermeneutic abilities were suddenly transferred
by their respective grandson and son, Adolfo Mussafia, to the study of
the romance languages. Adolfo Mussafia, the son and grandson of
rabbis, became a convert to Catholicism and a professor in Vienna in
about 1855, and was later even a member of the upper house of the
Vienna Parliament. He introduced into romance philology incompar-
able rigor and subtlety. In later life he felt more and more that he was an
Italian, not an Austrian, and towards the end of the century he left
Vienna to live and die in Florence. The only devoted pupil he ever had
was Elise Richter, a Jewish woman who lived long enough to die in a
Nazi torture camp.

This transition from Jewish to secular culture with all its vagaries is
striking enough, but what is perhaps characteristic of the Italian Jews is
that during the twentieth century they came to play a very important
part in the state administration as civil servants, judges, and above all

soldiers. Italy must have been the only country in Europe where Jews were welcomed in the army and navy and could reach the highest rank without any difficulty. The Piedmontese Jews became famous at that. General Giuseppe Ottolenghi, as a minister of war, did much to reorganize the Italian Army at the beginning of the century after the African disasters. General Roberto Segre, as a commander of artillery in the battle of the Piave in June 1918, was the mind behind the strategy that saved Italy. The military profession passed from father to son, as was the case with Roberto Segre and even more conspicuously with two eminent generals, Guido Liuzzi and his son Giorgio.

In 1939, when the Jews were thrown out of the army, the navy, and all other governmental positions, the Italian fleet, which had been rebuilt by the Jewish naval architect General Umberto Pugliese, was commanded by two Jewish admirals, Ascoli and Capon, the latter being the father-in-law of Enrico Fermi. In 1940 the Italian fleet was virtually destroyed by English bombing in the harbor of Taranto, and General Pugliese was called back to save what could be saved of the fleet he had built and the Fascists had lost. Admiral Capon, if I remember correctly, was allowed to fall into Nazi hands.

One should of course dwell on all the branches of the Italian civil service, including the Foreign Office, to give a correct picture. I shall only mention *pietatis causa* the name of Giacomo Malvano, who as an authoritative permanent secretary at the Foreign Office controlled Italian foreign affairs for about thirty years at the turn of the century. Given the close connection between civil service, universities, and politics in Italy, access to the civil service made the entry into universities and politics easier, and vice versa. My impression is that the transition from the ghetto to the upper class happened more frequently in Jewish families through entry into the civil service and the universities than through prospering economic activities.

University professors have made up a very high proportion of the people prominent in Italian politics since at least 1870. During the last decades of the nineteenth century attempts were even made, ultimately to no purpose, to limit the number of university professors who could be members of the House of Deputies at any given time. University professors often became ministers of the crown and even prime ministers. In this sense Luigi Luzzatti, the only Jewish prime minister, conformed to pattern in 1910. He had been both a high civil servant and a university professor of law.

But other factors contributed to the prestige of Jews in politics. One was the advantage some of them had of foreign, especially British, connections. Sidney Sonnino, technically a Protestant but the son of a Jewish landowner from Tuscany, derived advantage from the connections represented by his English mother. He was twice for a short time a prime minister, but above all he is known as the foreign secretary during the entire First World War. He will forever remain associated with the name of his Jewish friend, Senator Leopoldo Franchetti, with whom he undertook some of the most penetrating research yet made into Italian social problems. English connections also counted for Ernesto Nathan, a mayor of Rome at the beginning of this century and the head of the Freemasons: the British branch of his family had been the friends of Giuseppe Mazzini during his exile in England.

A second element to be considered is the decisive importance of the Jews of Trieste in the so-called *irredentismo,* the claim of Trieste to be Italian. To the cultural side of the problem I shall return briefly in a moment. As for the political side, Trieste's political *irredentismo* was personified by three Jews: Felice Venezian, Salvatore Barzilai, and Teodoro Mayer. The Italian character of Trieste was and is due to a great extent to Jews who were often of German and Eastern origins but chose Italy—the Italy beyond the border, which seemed to offer an equality for Jews that did not exist in the Austrian Empire.

And finally came socialism. In Italy very few Jewish socialists studied Karl Marx deeply. One exception—the professional economist Achille Loria of the University of Turin—was attacked by Engels and had a bad reputation with the left. He was destined to make a lasting impression in America on Frederick Jackson Turner and his frontier hypothesis. But socialism as a messianic movement appealed to Jews in Italy as elsewhere. It gave them an alternative faith. Emanuele Modigliani, Claudio Treves, and Rodolfo Mondolfo are perhaps the most important of the early Italian Jewish socialists.

As a member of a family that has a permanent place in the history of the Italian socialist movement, I have always had the feeling that somehow the messianism did not quite fit. In fact the most original thinker among my socialist relatives, Felice Momigliano, a professor of philosophy in the University of Rome, tried to combine socialism, Mazzini, and the Hebrew prophets, but found himself thrown out of the Socialist party when the war came in 1915. About the enigmatic and tragic character of this religious thinker, who was basically a reformed Jew like his friend Claude Montefiore—in a country where there has never been any organized reform Judaism—there is much to be said, if we want to understand why the Jews were less a part of Italian life than they thought they were. I felt the same even about the other conspicuous name in my family, Attilio Momigliano, the interpreter of Dante, Ariosto, and Manzoni, of the last of whom he profoundly understood the Catholic inspiration. Though he had many devoted pupils in the Universities of Pisa and Florence, Attilio was deeply alone.

It will be enough here to say that this is in effect the question lying behind those Jewish Italian writers whom Stuart Hughes has recently put together under the suggestive title, *Prisoners of Hope*. What perhaps my friend Stuart Hughes ought to have made clearer is that writers of Jewish origin existed, of course, and were respected in the nineteenth century. Tullo Massarani and Giuseppe Revere, two friends who did the most to introduce Heine into Italy, were widely read and respected. They were consciously and explicitly Jewish; so were other, less-read writers—such as David Levi, the author of poems on Jewish themes, or Enrico Castelnuovo, the author of a novel on Italian Jews, *I Moncalvo*, and, incidentally, the father of the mathematician Guido Castelnuovo.

Younger generations of writers, for example, the half-English Jewish poet Annie Vivanti—whom Carducci loved—never explicitly admitted their Jewishness until 1939. Three of the greatest writers came from Trieste or nearby, Italo Svevo, Umberto Saba, and Carlo Michelstaedter, the last an extraordinary thinker who committed suicide at the age of twenty-three. A fourth, Alberto Moravia, lives in Rome but is of Venetian origin.

Characteristically, Svevo, Saba, and Moravia used pseudonyms, but while Italo Svevo and Alberto Moravia were concealing the non-Italian names of Schmitz and Pincherle, Saba, whose real family name was Poli, was trying to convey cryptically his allegiance to his Jewish mother rather than to his Christian father. Even when the persecution of Jews made it absurd to deny the Jewish experience—and Carlo Levi, Giorgio Bassani, and Natalia Levi Ginzburg did not deny it—a deeper problem remained: what could Judaism mean for these writers? Primo Levi is, of course, the exception: he really has a sense of Jewish tradition, but he had to acquire it by surviving in a Nazi extermination camp.

## IV

Jewish Italian society developed on its own lines—realistic, connected with business, comparatively open to foreign ideas, but fundamentally introspective, concerned with social justice and yet suspicious of too much novelty. Music, painting, literature, socialism, and science became intense preoccupations of the Italian Jews. Profane music had been one of their interests since at least the Renaissance. Now we had composers such as Vittorio Rieti, Alberto Franchetti, Mario Castelnuovo-Tedesco, and Leone Sinigaglia. Painting was more of a novelty. Perhaps it is no chance that the socialist leader Emanuele

Modigliani and the painter Amedeo Modigliani were brothers. Jewish scientists showed uncommon methodological preoccupations: two Jews, Eugenio Rignano and Federico Enriquez, created that important international forum for scientific methodology, the periodical *Scientia.*

How much this brooding, introspective mood contributed to the greatness of Italian mathematicians, physicists, and chemists I can only guess, thinking as I do of some who were my relatives and friends. Where were the roots of the legendary mathematical imagination of Tullio Levi-Civita? Fascism was bound to exclude most of those Jews who had solid liberal or socialist traditions behind them, while economic interests led some Jews to direct involvement with Fascism. One of the most honest Fascists was Gino Olivetti, the representative of industrial interests inside Fascism. Fascist ideological sympathies were also to be found among jurists like Gino Arias and Giorgio del Vecchio, who wanted a reform of the Italian state on corporate lines. I have already mentioned the special situation of Ferrara, where the Fascist mayor was a Jew with a prestigious Jewish name, Ravenna.

But most of the Jews were clearly out. And men like Vito Volterra, a teacher and a senator of immense prestige, spoke clearly and fearlessly for the majority of Jews. To the name of Vito Volterra I would like to add at least the name of my Roman teacher, Giorgio Levi della Vida, the Orientalist of rare distinction, who was for some years during the war a professor at the University of Pennsylvania. Max Ascoli, who in 1924 had published a book on Judaism and Christianity (*Le Vie dalla Croce*), came to the United States in 1931; Piero Sraffa, the economist, left Italy for England (Cambridge) even earlier. Active opposition was personified by the two brothers Carlo and Nello Rosselli, in whose ancestral house at Pisa Mazzini had died. They were both assassinated on Mussolini's order. The repugnance towards Fascism was repugnance towards Mussolini. During his career he had been helped by Jews, both men and women. He had exploited them ruthlessly, above all the women—and he had betrayed them. He betrayed his Jewish mistress Margherita Sarfatti and his old comrade Angelica Balabanoff and innumerable friends from the early years. When the hour of rebellion came, Jews went into the resistance movement, led it, died for it.

Umberto Terracini, the Jewish Communist leader who had survived about twenty years of confinement in a Fascist prison, was the president of the constituent assembly following the referendum in 1946. Guido Castelnuovo emerged from persecution to become the first president of the revived Accademia dei Lincei in 1946. But a whole generation had been deprived of its best members: men like Eugenio

132

Colorni, the philosopher, Leone Ginzburg, the critic, Emanuele Artom, the young historian of Judaism, and Sergio Diena, a smiling hero full of intelligence and determination. The deaths in the Nazi-Fascist torture camps created an empty space that has not yet been filled. It made more questionable the existence of a Jewish variety of Italians.

The problem had existed before. It is obvious in a great writer like Italo Svevo, so charged with Jewish Central European culture, and yet so ignorant of traditional Jewish culture and so reluctant to admit his Jewish past. For a few Jews there was a straight choice in favor of a return to Judaism via Zionism and immigration to Palestine. But those who, like myself, have still been fortunate enough to know the older generation of the Italian Zionists—Dante Lattes, Alfonso Pacifici—and to be friends of Enzo Sereni, know also that their choice was not so simple. It was not by chance that Enzo Sereni came back to Italy during the 1940s to fight and die for what he, in private conversation, had always recognized as indissociable ideals, Zionism and anti-Fascism.

Talmudism had practically ceased to interest Italian Jews at the end of the eighteenth century. Even Sadal was no longer interested in the Talmud. Reform Judaism, as I said, had no roots in Italy. Mystical and Kabbalistic trends persisted longer, well after Moshe Luzzatto had removed his *Maggid*—the "angel" who accompanied him—from Padua to Amsterdam. My grandfather found consolation in his old age in reading the Zohar every evening and sang Simeon Labi's Hebrew hymn, "Happy are you, Bar Yohai! He anointed you," on Lag b'Omer, the anniversary of the death of Simeon bar Yohai, who is believed by Kabbalists to be the author of the Zohar. But in fact Jewish culture was seldom transmitted in the sense we Jews intend it to be transmitted. If the Jews themselves know so little about their own Judaism, they can hardly complain that their neighbors understand it even less. Even Benedetto Croce, who was so near to us during the years of persecution, could only recommend that the Jews try to eliminate their peculiarities. It would be foolish to close on a note of optimism when a Jewish child can be assassinated in the synagogue of Rome, as one was in 1982, without an outcry of public opinion. The lines of Nahman Bialik on the murder of children come back to my mind, but I shall not repeat them. And unlike Immanuel of Rome, our old friend who, if not the friend of Dante, was at least the friend of Cino da Pistoia, I do not intend to give any advice to the Messiah. I shall therefore *not* say: "But if you mean to ride on an ass, my Lord, go back to sleep."

I shall rather seek some consolation in the words of my earliest predecessor, the chronicler Ahimaaz of Oria in southern Italy, who wrote his book of genealogies in the year 4814 of the creation of the world (1054 C.E.)—the first Jewish historian of the Jews of Italy:

> I will set down in order the traditions of my fathers, who were brought on a ship over the Pishon, the first river of Eden, with the captives that Tirus took from the Holy City, crowned with beauty. They came to Oria; they settled there and prospered through remarkable achievements; they grew in number and in strength and continued to thrive. Among their descendants there arose a man eminent in learning . . . master of the knowledge of God's Law, distinguished for wisdom among his people. His name was . . . .[2]

Ahimaaz says "Rabbi Amittai." But he might as well have put another name, "Vito Volterra."

2. *The Chronicle of Ahimaaz*, trans. M. Salzman (Columbia University Press, 1924).

# *13*

# Jewish Stories and Memoirs of Our Times

## I

The Jewish slaughter, which the Nazis deliberately organized as a precondition of their hegemony in Europe, remains politically one of the most significant facts, and morally perhaps the most significant, from the decade 1933–43. The same can be said of the reactions of those countries where the plan of the slaughter was applied, or against whom it was applied. As regards the Nazis, despite the great number of documents that have been made public, many facts remain to be told, all the more so since some continue to conceal the facts or even to deny their existence.

Among the recent books we find the series of testimonies and judicial documents about the torture and extermination camp Treblinka, which deserves special attention: *The Death Camp Treblinka: A Documentary*, edited by A. Donat (New York: Holocaust Library, 1979). As is known, according to the official communication of the SS Sturmbannführer Hermann Hoefle, beginning on July 22, 1942, it was possible for the camp to exterminate by asphyxia as many as 6000 Jews per day. It appears, however, that in the course of the 400 days in which the camp remained active, the number of Jews exterminated does not exceed 1,200,000; 700,000 is the minimal figure, acknowledged as being too low by the Court of Dusseldorf in 1965. The relative inefficiency of the operation was partly due to a deficiency in the gas chambers, which was later remedied; partly due to the delay in turning in Jews to be eliminated; and partly due to the practice of employing Jews for domestic chores, such as the stripping of the dead, as well as for the various forms of entertainment (for example, outdoor concerts of Polish and Yiddish songs) the butchers required. The camp activity was interrupted further for some time on August 2, 1943 by the action of three hundred Jews who were able to arm themselves and rebel against the Nazis. They were almost all killed after one day of battle. Shalom Kohn (who is supposedly still alive in Israel) and a few others who managed to escape pay tribute to these events in the above-mentioned book.

On the reactions various countries had to Nazi politics around 1939–40, when the Nazis were clearly opting in favor of a "final solution," we have two recent books, one on Italy and the other on England. These books have been immediately welcomed as being especially committed and competent. The author of the first book, the Israeli Meir Michaelis, has been a contributor to our review (the *Rivista Storica Italiana*) and has already published in Italy a series of preparatory articles on the current theme, *Mussolini and the Jews: German-Italian Relations and the Jewish Question in Italy 1922–45* (London: Institute of Jewish Affairs; Oxford: Clarendon Press, 1978). The book on England, *Britain and the Jews of Europe, 1939–1945"* (the same publishing houses, 1979), is by a young British academician, Bernard Wasserstein, who has had complete access to Israeli and American archives and a wide access to English archives. It appears that Michaelis was unable to make wide use of Italian archives, but he has made the most of Italian documents taken from English and German archive collections.

On the whole, Michaelis documents events that those who have lived through the period 1936–40 know from personal experience, that is, that direct German pressure on the Italians for the adoption of an anti-Semitic policy was weak. It was not necessary. The Fascist government, short of ideas and lacking an effective military force, was ready to imitate the Germans with the goose step and all the rest. By persecuting the Jews, the Fascists knew they were tapping into instincts rooted in tradition. On the other hand, Michaelis insists on the Italian army's sense of repugnance at becoming an accomplice in this politics and on the disapproval by the public and the clergy, which Mussolini probably had not expected. The Resistenza and the Allied occupation occurred shortly thereafter, putting an end to this situation; nonetheless, one-fourth of Italy's Jewish population was slaughtered.

Wasserstein's depiction of Britain contains greater elements of surprise. England was a place of refuge, protection, and salvation for German, French, and Italian Jews (among whom was myself). However, during the war, English political authorities were reluctant to make known what they knew: that the German policy envisaged the exploitation, torture, and ultimate elimination of the greatest possible number of Jews. The fear of Jewish mass emigration both in Britain and in the United States was a reason to conceal reality. A concern about Arab reaction in the delicate and controversial issue of Palestine, which was under a mandate, prevailed. Particularly surprising, as Wasserstein reveals, is the deep dislike for Jews at the administrative level. While Britain was prepared to accept 300,000 refugees from Belgium and Holland (who ended up not going) in 1940, a few hundred Jews from Luxembourg were denied entrance to Tanganyika because they were not war refugees "but simply racial refugees." As Richard Crossman, a British politician and academician, and a deeply learned man, observed in his diary after having visited the camp at Dachau, which had just been occupied by the Allied troops: "The chasm that separates the outside world from the camp influences both parts equally. These 32,000 pariahs are so remote from civilization as we know it, that we are content to leave them as they are, by improving their standard of living slightly" (*Palestine Mission*, 1946, p. 21).

This leads us back to the essential point that it is impossible to understand the events concerning the Jews of Europe (and particularly concerning the Jews in Germany and Poland, who were forever uprooted from the countries to whose civilizations they had contributed for centuries) without considering those elements of religious and social tension that resulted in the long tradition of anti-Semitism. Some theologians, who are less reluctant than us historians in calling such things by their name, recently have produced various instructive and especially courageous books: for example, Charlotte Klein, *Theologie und Anti-Judaismus* (Munich: Kaiser, 1975; in English with a new appendix, *Anti-Judaism in Christian Theology*, London, 1978); Rosemary Ruether, *Faith and Fratricide: The Theological Roots of Antisemitism* (New York: Seabury Press, 1979). But in the Italian case, which concerns us more directly, it is also impossible to avoid the opposite aspect—Mussolini's personal situation with regard to the Jews. Mussolini had been in close contact with men and women of Jewish origin, and in each case, the relationship had turned sour. These relationships were mostly with women: Angelica Balabanoff, Margherita Sarfatti, and, *a contrario*, Anna Kuliscioff (Ronzenstein), of whom Mussolini apparently lamented to the end that he had not managed to win her trust (Carlo Silvestri, *Turati l'ha detto*, Milan, 1943, p. 351). Among the men were Claudio Treves, Mussolini's most tenacious opponent at the time of his ascent in the Socialist party and with whom he had a duel, and the Rosselli brothers. At least three members of my family—Felice, Riccardo, and Eucardio Momigliano—had personal contacts with Mussolini that later turned sour (with the first two, Felice and Riccardo, in the Socialist period; with Eucardio, who was considerably more flexible, in the first Fascist period, whence Mussolini's poisonous attack on him in *Popolo d'Italia* in 1924, now in *Opera Omnia*, 20:223). As I have had the opportunity to note in my review of Michaelis's book in the *Journal of Modern History* (1979), for Mussolini, the so-called racial campaign also provided him with the opportunity to liquidate his own past.

## II

The insufficiency of diplomatic history, even if conducted with the expertise of Michaelis and Wasserstein, causes us to attach special importance to the books of personal memoirs of Jews, which are being published in various countries. The above-mentioned book on Treblinka is, in a way, a collection of personal memoirs, imbued with the horror of persecution in its most inhumane aspects. Two books of memoirs, the first by Augusto Segre (*Memorie di vita ebraica*, Rome, Bonacci, 1979), who has played a modest but honorable role in our history, and the second by the greatest Jewish historian of our times, Gershom Scholem, offer us a more relaxed atmosphere. But at least one more book should be mentioned briefly: *Quand vient le souvenir* by the famous historian Saul Friedländer (Paris, Ed. du Seuil, 1979; there is also an English translation entitled *When Memory Comes*). Born in Czechoslovakia to parents who ended up in Auschwitz, Friedländer was baptized as a child and apparently destined to become a priest. Later in life he decided to return to Judaism, and at the age of sixteen, in 1948, he went to fight for the nascent state of Israel. He spent the rest of his life as a professor in France and Israel, facing many difficulties.

Augusto Segre, born in 1915, is the son of a rabbi from the old community of Casale Monferrato, which still maintains its "German" rite. Segre thinks as a Piedmontese with the interpolations of traditional Hebrew expressions he has learned in his paternal home; from his mother he has inherited a touch of Venetian. The first part of his book is a nostalgic reconstruction of a provincial family atmosphere so rare that it is bound to acquire a historical significance for Italian Jews. But it was the racial campaign, when he was twenty and a student at the rabbinic college of Rome, that caused him to confront two little-known aspects of reality: the ever-increasing persecution of Jews, and the Piedmontese peasants who saved him as a Jew and helped him as a partisan ("I learned that the Piedmontese dialect, through a typical and unmistakable inflection, lends itself . . . to express ideas with extraordinary subtlety and biblical simplicity, to narrate facts," p. 321). In just a few words, Segre leads us to understand that his commitment for life to the Judaism of Italy and Israel, as a journalist, teacher, and representative of institutions, was indeed a difficult one. A woman friend from his youth died in a Nazi camp; his wife is a survivor of Auschwitz (I recommend that the reader meditate on pages 429–34, which describe this event).

It is also evident that this man of great courage and noble faith is incapable of expressing in Italian (or Piedmontese!) the Hebrew culture he derives from his rabbinic education and from his work as the translator of Scholem's greatest book on Jewish mysticism. This inability is common to other Italian Jews and is curiously confirmed by the fact that among them (or, to be more exact, among us) those who are more inclined to speak of Jewish things in general, and of Israeli things in particular, are those who know the least about them. To this corresponds the surprising inability of non-Jewish intellectuals to acknowledge the Hebrew tradition, which has been a component of Italian culture since the beginning of Christianity. Augusto Segre himself quotes an Croce's recommendation to Italian Jews in 1947: "to mingle more and more with other Italians, taking care to eliminate those elements of distinction and division in which they have persisted for centuries and that, as they have provided in the past a pretext for persecution, it is to be feared they will provide other reasons for persecution in the future" (*Scritti e discorsi politici*, 1963, 325; see *Terze Pagine Sparse*, 1955, 2:249–51). Few eminent men have been sympathetic to the Jews, Italian or German, who were victims of racial persecution. Benedetto Croce and I can testify to this personally. Hence Croce's statement stems from his affection and sympathy for the Jews. As Dante Lattes quickly observed, "Croce's statement is a recommendation he would not make for any other religious group, for any other ethnic or national group . . . not even for the liberals." Only a complete lack of contact with Jewish culture can explain the fact that not even Benedetto Croce managed to understand that Italian Jews have the right (which subjectively can be a duty) to remain Jewish.

In this context we can understand better how a strange book, *The Parnas*, can take us closer to the reality of the life of an Italian Jew. The author, Silvano Arieti, is an Italian Jewish psychiatrist who emigrated to New York in 1939. His book was recently published in English (New York, Basic Books, 1979), arousing considerable interest. The book talks about the last years and death of Giuseppe Pardo Roques, a well-known figure in Pisa in the period between the two wars. An aristocrat, the moral head of a local Jewish community ("Parnas"), Pardo Roques, as the tombstone placed in his home reveals, was assassinated in his Via Sant'Andrea home by German soldiers in 1944, together with seven Jewish guests and five loyal Christian relatives. Arieti, the son of a Pisan doctor who was an intimate friend of Pardo Roques, reconstructs the event out of a personal inquiry. The episode of Pardo

Roques's death is rendered more tragic by the fact that he was afflicted by an obsessive fear of being attacked by animals and had decided not to leave his ancestral home during the war. An excellent psychiatrist and an excellent writer, Arieti understands Pardo's personality—a conscious heir of a long Sephardic cultural tradition and well informed of contemporary thought (I can confirm this with some personal memories). Unfortunately, Arieti is not a rigorous historian and does not draw a line between what is ascertained as true and what is conjectural, perhaps fictional. But the appendix to the book, where the speaker is no longer the historian but the psychiatrist who knows how to measure the human implications of that which was or was bound to become the final solution of the Jewish issue, should be recommended as true history.

## III

The creator of, or at least the author who has perfected with unquestionable originality, a new line of interpretation of Jewish history and life, G. Scholem does not run the risk of being too nostalgic or domestic. His breach with Germany was clamorous: a flat refusal to fight for the country in World War I. Even more sensational and persistent was his breach with his own family, especially with his father, a good German bourgeois. Scholem condemned all German Jewish effort to live and die as Germans. He proclaims loud and clear that there never was any dialogue between Jews and Germans. On the other hand, he readily acknowledges his debt to the German romantic movement, which revalued the mystic elements in Judaism, especially Joseph Franz Molitor (1779–1860). Earlier, Scholem had assumed Reuchlin, one of the humanists who discovered the Kabbalah in his search for a common basis for all religions. Thus, in Scholem we have the awareness of a debt to the German tradition of philological and religious thought and at the same time a complete aversion to bourgeois Germany and those Jews who are ready to accept with a false conscience impossible conditions of coexistence. Had not Mommsen, a liberal and enemy of anti-Semitism, recommended conversion to those Jews who no longer practiced ancestral orthodoxy?

*Von Berlin nach Jerusalem* (Frankfurt, Suhrkamp Verlag, 1977), Scholem's memories of his youth, range from his birth in Berlin in 1897 to his appointment as a teacher at the Hebrew University of Jerusalem in 1925. Written at the age of eighty-one, the book recounts in the simple German prose of which he is a master the main events of his revolt against assimilation, from which stemmed the decision to leave

Germany and mathematics for Jerusalem and the history of Jewish mysticism. For those who wish to know more about explicit and argumented stances on teachers and friends from the German period (especially on Martin Buber and Walter Benjamin) as well as more general reflections on his themes of historic research, see *Jews and Judaism in Crisis: Selected Essays* (New York, Schocken, 1976; paperback 1978), which is more representative even if in English translation; the translator, W. J. Dannhauser, has had the benefit of Scholem's personal cooperation. Here we find the important essays on Martin Buber and Walter Benjamin. Buber inspired Scholem's studies of the Kabbalah and Benjamin was his more influential friend from the German period (his ensuing separation from Benjamin is described with equal clarity). Here, too, we find the essays on the relations between Jews and Germans, Diaspora and the state of Israel, tradition and heterodoxy in Judaism. There is now available an essential monograph on Scholem the historian by David Biale, a young American researcher, *Gershom Scholem, Kabbalah and Counter-History* (Harvard University Press, 1979), which appears to determine with substantial fairness Scholem's historiographic position within the German-speaking "Science of Judaism."

An anarchist by instinct, Scholem did not react to assimilation in order to return to orthodoxy. For him the study of the Kabbalah represented an opening, rigorously controlled by philology, to the experience of an anomalous of even anomic Judaism, capable of leaps into the void. The basis of Scholem's research is the conviction that legalism has kept Jews together while mysticism has inspired them to accomplish unpredictable events (especially in the modern age). After some uncertainty, he has ascribed the main Kabbalistic text, the Zohar, to Moses de Leon (around 1270–90), thus turning it into a document of reaction to Maimonides' rationalism and eliminating from it any alleged pretense of antiquity. On the other hand, he has traced back to the second or third century A.D. certain texts of Hebrew gnosticism, such as the *Shi'ur Komah* ("a measure of the dimensions" of God), which are usually dated five or six centuries later. Hence, medieval mysticism is connected to ancient gnosticism and to ancient apocalyptics. There is a continuity that extends to the messianic movement of Sabbatai Zevi in the seventeenth century. According to Scholem, the failure of Sabbatai Zevi drove Jews to apostasy (as in the Frankist movement, which led to the Polish nationalism of Mickiewicz), or to rationalism (Haskalah),[1] or

1. The Haskalah is the Jewish Enlightenment. The term designates a reform movement that originated in Berlin and spread throughout Jewish society beginning in the 1770s; it became widespread and influential for about a century. Its founder was Moses Mendelssohn. The Haskalah developed from the European Enlightenment. Among the

to the mystic quietism of the Hasidim,[2] or finally to Zionism. According to Scholem, Zionism, because it is a lay solution to a religious problem, is also a solution filled with intrinsic contradictions. Scholem does
not conceal the difficulties. While in recent decades he has kept away
from active politics in Israel, in distant years (before 1933) Scholem was
a supporter of a binational Arab-Jewish state in Palestine. But there
is one point on which Scholem has no doubts. Being open to all currents of Jewish thought, Zionism makes it possible to reevaluate them
all and to accept them all—be they legalistic or mystical, anomic or
rationalist—within Judaism. It is precisely in this sense that Scholem's
interest in the Kabbalah is inseparable from his Zionism, even if he re-
pudiates all messianic interpretations of Zionism. For Scholem, the
state of Israel is an earthly city where the ambiguous events of Germany cannot take place.

It is hardly necessary to add that in all of its aspects, including that of
the relationship between Jews and Germans, Scholem's use of language is exceptional. It is enough to compare the writings of Adorno,
Horkheimer, H. J. Schoeps, and E. Bloch—or the tiny book by E. Kahler,
*The Jews among the Nations* (New York, 1967) with its chapter on Jews
and Germans (pp. 95–119)—to realize that all of these writers tend to
stress the positive aspects of the long German-Jewish symbiosis. If anything, despite the differences that emerged violently at the Eichmann
trial, there is more substantial affinity between Scholem and Hannah
Arendt (at least the Arendt who published a biography of Rahel
Varnhagen in 1957 with chapter titles that speak for themselves: "Jewess and Shlemihl," "Between Pariah and Parvenu," "One Does Not
Escape Jewishness"; compare also the essays that for the most part precede the book on Varnhagen, now collected under the title *The Jew as
Pariah* by R. H. Feldman, New York, Grove Press, 1978). One wonders
whether a position such as that of Scholem, who fundamentally ig-
nores the dilemma of the state of Israel (whether it should opt for a sec-

---

movement's objectives, we find the development of lay studies in the context of a traditional Jewish religious education and a tendency toward assimilation as a necessary condition for emancipation. In the rationalism of the Haskalah there is only one truth:
reason. Mendelssohn gave a Jewish interpretation of deistic themes and claimed that in
Judaism there is nothing contrary to reason.—Ed.

2. The Hasidim ("pious men") are particularly orthodox and meticulous in the observance of the Law. Hasidism is a popular Jewish religious movement that developed in
the second part of the eighteenth century in Lithuania and Galicia. Its charismatic leader
was Israel ben Eliezer Ba'al Shem Tov (around 1700–1760). Ba'al Shem Tov's followers
believed that he had the power to work miracles and perform healings, to dominate natural law because of his special union with God, and they followed him with ecstasy and
joy.—Ed.

ular or an ecclesiastical form of government), can ever become something more than a personal attitude. Among the interpreters of Scholem we also find those who have inquired to what extent he considers himself the heir of Kabbalists in the interpretation of Kabbalists. It is no wonder that Kafka's writings took on "canonical value" for Scholem, at least during one period of his life. But, after all, a historian can only speak the truth that stems from his interpretive effort. After breaking away from Germany, Scholem finds himself speaking to Germans with authority in their own language. Not only by referring to Reuchlin, but by taking part independently in the debate of the Jung circle, Scholem has suggested, in his own way, where the dialogue between Jews and Germans could not continue but must take off.

The Italian situation is completely different. In Italy, racial policy offended the very principle on which the country was founded, and both Jews and non-Jews were involved in the Resistenza. But it is to be hoped that a better-informed generation, one less inclined to shut its eyes, consider the problem of debits and credits between Jews and Christians in a land where we have coexisted since the beginning of Christianity and even earlier.

# 14

## Felice Momigliano (1866–1924)

### I

As a young boy, Felice Momigliano lived the life of a traditional Piedmontese Israelite family, disciplined by the fear of God, filled with tender and quiet domestic affection, intellectually divided between traditional Jewish culture and enlightened ideas. General emancipation from the French period, which ended in 1848, had aroused new emotions and suggested new responsibilities. Italy had finally become a reality, and Felice was proud that his father had fought with courage in the battles of the Risorgimento. But in his paternal home (rendered more conservative by poverty, a poverty that compelled Felice to make incredible sacrifices in order to study) religious exclusivism and Italian sentiment went hand in hand. Uncle Marco, rabbi major in Bologna was a model for both of these feelings, while more resolute and brave relatives and friends (among them the Sinigaglias, Artoms, Malvanos, Dienas, and Ottolenghis) were contributing to the economy and the political regime of the Kingdom of Italy. Felice soon became convinced that for the Israelites emancipation implied the responsibility of freeing Judaism from narrow-mindedness and from what was no longer historically valid in order to bring it back to its prophetic sources and to accept the moral preaching of Jesus as the final speaker of Israel's prophetism. It is not easy to understand today how difficult it must have been for Felice, then a young man, to abandon Talmudic Judaism while he was opening up his heart to philosophy and poetry in the lyceum of Mondovi and in the department of literature of the University of Turin and University of Pisa. Felice later taught his nephews to recite the Pater Noster in his own Hebrew translation; he also translated into Italian the book on Jesus by the English liberal Claude Montefiori. Felice's Jesus was essentially the one described by Renan,

144

to whom Felice felt close because of his personal involvement with analogous spiritual battles.

Felice never forgot the prayers and ceremonies from his youth. He had a musician friend collect some of the chants he remembered hearing in the small synagogue of Mondovi (if I remember correctly). He died reciting a prayer of the fathers, "Hear O Israel."[1] Felice had never questioned his religious beliefs. His strife stemmed from his poverty and from not managing to find an emotional center after his mother's death when he was still a boy; his suffering was not related to religious beliefs. The Italian Risorgimento had led him to the preaching of justice and purity as is found in the prophets; among the figures of the Italian Risorgimento, it was in Giuseppe Mazzini that he found the continuation of that prophetic inspiration. The religion of the prophets was revived by the ideal of a Young Europe. Socialism was to embody this ideal.

For Felice, prophetism, Mazzini, and socialism were hardly separable. The purification of Judaism, the spiritual rebirth of Italy, and the establishment of social justice in Europe were to him three aspects of the same reality. Felice preached socialism in the years when socialists were persecuted; between 1894 and 1900 he faced arrest and was confined. He became a candidate to Parliament for the constituency of Mondovi, and he remained a member of the Socialist party until the socialist opposition to the war of 1915 appeared to him to be incompatible with the Mazzinian interpretation he attributed to Italy's intervention in the war. But well before leaving the Socialist party, Felice had already grown uncomfortable with the prevailing materialism of the official socialist conception. In 1907 he wrote: "For me the social question is a question of human dignity. The criticism and sarcasm of Karl Marx and the ethical imperatives of Immanuel Kant stem from the same source." Felice felt much closer to certain small groups, such as the pacifists of the *Vita Internazionale*, the mystics of the *Coenobium*, and the supporters of a critical Christianity hosted by *Bilychnis*. In his search for sympathetic souls he would turn to Tolstoy, about whom he wrote a profile, or—the contradiction is only apparent—to some unusual figures of the Risorgimento, such as Cattaneo and Ferrari. After having abandoned the Socialist party entirely, Felice devoted himself to the preaching of Mazzini through a series of publications and through

---

1. "Although I have professed and upheld in my writings and in propaganda a personal kind of Judaism that adopts the ethical values of the teachings of Jesus as the ultimate result of the prophets of Israel, I intend to die in the religion of my Fathers" (quoted from his will).

the so-called Università Mazziniana di Roma, of which he became the head. In 1922, shortly before the advent of Fascism, Felice summed up his program of Mazzinian socialism in a pamphlet entitled *Il Messaggio di Mazzini*, where we find the following admonishment: "Italian socialism must free itself from the remains of the stingy materialism to which the false prophets have debased it. . . . For every social class that is raised to power, the declaration of rights must be a function of the assumption of duties."

## II

Felice Momigliano realized that the three elements—prophetism, Mazzini, and socialism—which his experience merged into one stemmed from three different historic circumstances, but between his intellectual acknowledgment (complex) and his faith (simple) it was his faith that prevailed. He was never the kind of scholar who would subject the articles of his faith to scientific inquiry. Nor did he ever engage deeply in research that did not involve subjects he considered vital. His books on Mazzini and on other figures of the Italian Risorgimento naturally have their place in Italian culture as representative of the Mazzinian left, where the message of Cattaneo is reintegrated; they are not, however, in the opinion of the writer, important contributions to the understanding of that historical period. At times Felice appeared to be doing a good job with some of his research on the history of philosophy. Particularly significant is the beginning of a study on late scholasticism, the life of Paolo Veneto, which is rich in archival research (1907). Giovanni Gentile has acknowledged the importance of this work in a review in *Critica*. But the monograph on the life of Paolo Veneto was never completed.

Felice's culture blended with his faith in a special way. His longing for a freedom of the spirit and for a religious austerity of life also involved his desire to live the most different experiences in life. And because he was endowed with an exceptional memory and was naturally eloquent, he was able to communicate his knowledge and his states of mind to others without effort. Students from various lyceums in Italy, where he had spent the best years of his life, and students from the Magistero of Rome, where he taught from 1912 until his death (and where he exercised considerable influence on his colleague and friend L. Pirandello) preferred him to all other teachers.

Felice also possessed those qualities that characterize a solidly acquired spiritual freedom: he was generous, delicate in personal relationships, simple in his customs to the point of neglect. It is very doubtful that his friend Alfredo Panzini described him faithfully as Felix, a tormented philosopher in *Viaggio con la giovane ebrea* (to a certain extent Panzini had already described Felice in *Mondo è rotondo*). At school and during his long walks with friends in the Piedmontese countryside, which he loved, his soul would free itself from any form of ill-being and torment. His language combined jest and meditation, nostalgia and ideals, poetry and rare learning. All those who happened to know him were inspired by a higher moral and intellectual life. And to those who have known him, Felice has recommended a meditation on the ethical experience of the Old Testament and on the contribution of Mazzini to the idea of social reform in Europe.

# 15

## Jacob Bernays

### I

In 1839, at the age of twenty-four, Jacob Bachofen came to England to study medieval law. Fifteen years later, the time he had spent in England still seemed to him the best of his life. The only unpleasant experience was a visit to Oxford: "Oxford entsprach meinen Erwartungen nicht."[1] But he escaped from Oxford to Cambridge, and there he found what he wanted. There he indulged in his favorite hunt for medieval "Prozessualisten." The good Cambridge dons did not quite understand what he was after, but apparently Magdalene College offered him a fellowship. Before the end of 1840 Bachofen was back in his native Basel where he settled down for the rest of his life.

His different reactions to Oxford and Cambridge are not surprising. Oxford was then in the middle of the Anglo-Catholic revival led by Newman. Mark Pattison, who was born two years before Bachofen in 1813, was busy transcribing medieval lives of saints, not medieval "Prozessualisten." At Cambridge, the Apostles were studying Niebuhr and Savigny, and even G. B. Vico. Connop Thirlwall, soon to become the Bishop of St. David's (1840), had translated Niebuhr and was writing a *History of Greece* according to Niebuhr's method.[2] Bachofen, a pupil of Savigny, was sure of a good reception in that group. Nobody could guess that within a few years Bachofen would

Originally published in English in *Mededelingen der Koninklijke Nederlandse Akademie van Wetenschappen, Afd. Letterkunde*, Nieuwe Reeks, Deel 32, No. 5, 1969, pp. 151–78. Reprinted by permission of Giulio Einaudi editore s.p.a. [A biography of J. Bernays by H. Bach, Tübingen, 1974, has now appeared.]

1. J. Bachofen, *Selbstbiographie und Antrittsrede*, ed. A. Baeumler, Halle, 1927, p. 18ff.
2. K. Dockhorn, *Der deutsche Historismus in England*, Göttingen, 1950; D. Forbes, *The Liberal Anglican Idea of History*, Cambridge, 1952.

have developed into the most fiery opponent of Niebuhr and would have disagreed with Savigny—affection notwithstanding.

Oxford went German when the Oxford Movement was defeated. In 1845 Newman left Oxford; in 1850 the Royal Commission was set up. The first to change, though gradually, was Mark Pattison himself, who emerged from the Oxford Movement as a free thinker in holy orders with a strong bias towards German "Wissenschaft." His revulsion from Newman is best expressed by a passage in his *Memoirs:* "A. P. Stanley once said to me 'How different the fortunes of the Church of England might have been if Newman had been able to read German.' That puts the matter in a nut-shell."[3] The failure to become the Rector of Lincoln in 1851 gave Pattison ten years of sadness and of leisure, which he exploited not only for solitary fishing in Yorkshire and Scotland but also for visits to Germany. In 1859 he was there in his official capacity as an inspector appointed by the Education Committee of the Privy Council to report on elementary education in Prussia and other German states. More frequently he went to German universities to learn. When at last in 1861 he became the very influential head of his own college, he made it his business to encourage Oxford dons to go to Germany to complete their studies.

John Sparrow, who knows more than anybody else about Mark Pattison, has recently devoted an absorbing little book to the difficulties in which Pattison involved himself by advocating in Oxford the Humboldtian idea of a university.[4] Pattison had started with the assumption that, in Oxford, colleges had to be developed as independent units and that the college tutors, not the university professors, were the potential scholars in a German sense. He recognized at the end that the Royal Commission had transformed Oxford into a "cramming-shop." Examinations—not "Kultur"—had become the main preoccupation of tutors and undergraduates. Thus in 1868 Pattison wrote his suggestions for academic organization to reverse this trend. He now championed professors against tutors. He proposed the abolition of the colleges and of the fellowships and the transfer of their endowments to the university. Those colleges that did not become headquarters of faculties might be used as noncompulsory halls of residence. In Pattison's dream students would flock to Oxford for the mere love of learning. If any of this was really meant as a practical suggestion, he lived long enough, until 1884, to be disabused.

3. M. Pattison, *Memoirs*, London, 1885, p. 210.
4. J. Sparrow, *Mark Pattison and the Idea of a University*, Cambridge, 1967. See V. H. H. Green, *Oxford Common Room*, London, 1957; W. R. Ward, *Victorian Oxford*, London, 1965.

PART TWO

The Warden of All Souls is not the man to miss the relevance of Pattison's experience to our 1965 or 1968 university problems. Old Pattison had to admit what young Pattison had not needed to know: that a vocational training and a liberal education are not interchangeable. But the warden's account of Pattison is deliberately unilateral. He does not examine Pattison's scholarly work, nor does he examine the nature of his relations with German scholars. Something is therefore inevitably lacking in his interpretation of Pattison's idea of a university.

## II

The type of research which Pattison made his own and for which he remained famous was common neither in England nor in Germany.[5] This was the history of classical scholarship. Pattison also did other things after giving up the study of saints which Pusey and Newman had encouraged. His editions of Milton's sonnets and some of Pope's poems are described as first rate by John Sparrow, who should know, but they did not take much of his time and appear to have been mostly "Parerga" of his old age.[6] He started his work on Casaubon in 1853 and published his biography of him in 1875. His biography of Scaliger dragged on from about 1855 to his death and was never completed.

In writing the lives of great scholars Pattison naturally wanted to advance the cause of pure, disinterested research, but he also tried to express some of his religious and social beliefs. In his view Casaubon had been sidetracked and then killed off by theology. All those years spent in refuting Baronius and helping King James to compile his theological tracts! Pattison is even impatient with Casaubon for filling pages of his *Ephemerides* with mere religious emotions. In one of his earliest biographical studies, on Bishop Huet, which he published in the *Quarterly Review* in 1855,[7] Pattison dramatized the conflict between Huet the scholar and Huet the philosopher. The latter belonged to "that class of philosophers who have taken up philosophy not as an end, but as a means—not for its own sake, but for the support of religion." To such philosophers Pattison attributed "the desperate design of first ruining the territory they were preparing to evacuate."

There was only one scholar in Pattison's time who had a similar interest in the history of classical scholarship: Jacob Bernays. This name is

5. *Isaac Casaubon*, London, 1875 (2d ed., 1892); *Essays*, ed. H. Nettleship, 2 vols., Oxford, 1889. One must compare the curious volume of *Sermons*, London, 1885.
6. A bibliography of M. Pattison was compiled by J. M. Hoare in an unpublished thesis of University College London, School of Librarianship, 1953.
7. *Essays*, 1:244.

not to be found in John Sparrow's book on Pattison and is not often mentioned in Pattison's own *Memoirs,* but one mention in the *Memoirs* is of great importance. When Bernays's book on Scaliger appeared in 1855, Pattison undertook to translate it into English. A letter from Max Müller to Bernays, dated February 5, 1856, makes it certain that by that time Pattison was firmly committed to the translation of Bernays's *Scaliger.* Max Müller remarked about Pattison: "Seine Kenntniss der deutschen Sprache ist vielleicht nicht ganz gut, er kennt aber die Sache, die damalige Zeit, und ist eine ehrliche, obwohl etwas trockene Seele."[8] Pattison indeed summarized Bernays's book in two lengthy papers in the *Quarterly Review* in 1860.[9] What the *Memoirs* reveal is that Pattison was persuaded by Christian Carl Josias von Bunsen, a former Prussian envoy to the Court of St. James, to improve upon Bernays and to write another book about Scaliger: "I soon came to view in Scaliger something more than the first scholar of the modern age. The hint was given me in a conversation I had with Chevalier Bunsen at Charlottenburg in 1856. Speaking of Bernays' masterly monograph on Scaliger, just published, he pointed out that Bernays' creed had interfered with his seeing in Scaliger 'the Protestant hero.'"[10]

By linking Pattison with Bernays and Bunsen, this passage provides a key to the understanding of the three persons involved. To see the Protestant hero in Scaliger proved to be more difficult than Bunsen had anticipated. Pattison never translated Bernays and never wrote his own book. One of his difficulties was that he himself was more anti-Catholic than Protestant. On the other hand, Bunsen was perhaps less certain of his Lutheranism than he cared to admit. In the twenty years, 1818–38, in which he was a diplomat and a scholar in Rome, he was suspected of Catholic sympathies. His later work on the early Church and on Oriental religions is, at least to one reader, not conspicuous for clarity of theological notions.[11] Both Pattison and Bunsen admired Scaliger for qualities that were beyond their reach. They also knew that J. Bernays was intellectually and morally closer to Scaliger than they were ever likely to be. It is a sign of their nobility that this awareness was the foundation of their long friendship with J. Bernays. Bernays returned their friendship with his characteristic warmth and devotion,

---

8. M. Fraenkel, *Jacob Bernays. Ein Lebensbild in Briefen,* Breslau, 1932, p. 91, further quotations from letters in the text are taken from this book.

9. *Essays,* 1:132.

10. *Memoirs,* p. 321.

11. *Aegyptens Stelle in der Weltgeschichte,* 1845–57; *Christianity and Mankind,* 1854; *Die Zeichen der Zeit,* 1855; *Gott in der Geschichte,* 1857–58, etc. Bibl. in Bussmann, *Neue Deutsche Biographie,* 1957, 3:17–19.

but he had decided to remain alone. A Jew of unshakable faith, he sacrificed his scholarly career and much else in obedience to the law of his Fathers.[12]

## III

Jacob Bernays was born in Hamburg in 1824 as the eldest son of Isaak Bernays. The father was an almost unique combination of orthodox Talmudic scholar and follower of Schelling. Something more must be said about him, because it is essential for the understanding of his son. Isaak ben Ja'akov Bernays was born in 1792 and died in 1849. In Würzburg he had been a pupil of Rabbi Abraham Bing and a close friend of Rabbi Jacob Ettlinger, but he had also been able to study at the University of Würzburg, thanks to the short-lived Napoleonic liberalization. In 1821 he published anonymously two installments of *Der Bibel'sche Orient*, which created a sensation. It was inspired by Schelling. Isaak Bernays never explicitly admitted that he was the author. In the same year, 1821, he came to Hamburg as Chief Rabbi with the task of creating a bridge between the Orthodox and the Reformed Jews of the city. The latter had set up their Tempel-Verein in 1817. The Jewish community of Hamburg was then mainly made up of moderately affluent shopkeepers, who fought for their civic rights and wanted a modernization of their educational institutions.[13] The destitute and the very rich were on the fringe of the congregation, and among the very rich the dominant figure was the banker Solomon Heine. His nephew and protégé Heinrich had abandoned Hamburg two years before, in 1819, after failing both in business and in love, but the shadow of Heinrich Heine—the poet and the apostate—lingered on in Hamburg and, especially, in the Bernays family, which was somehow related to him.

Isaak Bernays wanted to be known not as a rabbi but as a *Haham* in

---

12. On Bernays in general: C. Schaarschmidt, *Bursians Biographisches Jahrbuch* 4 (1881): 65–83; Th. Gomperz, *Essays und Erinnerungen*, Stuttgart, 1905, pp. 106–25 (originally published in 1881); H. Usener in *Deutsche Allgemeine Biographie* 46 (1902): 393–404 and in the introduction to Bernays, *Gesammelte Abhandlungen*, 2 vols. Berlin, 1885; S. Frankfurter in *B. B. Mitteilungen für Oesterreich* 5 (1933): 173–83; W. Schmidt in *Bonner Gelehrte* (Philosophie und Altertumswissenschaften), Bonn, 1968, pp. 137–43. M. Fraenkel's selection of letters (quoted above) was reviewed by R. Harder, *Gnomon* 8 (1932): 668. Some information is also in works by and on Max Müller (for instance, *The Life and Letters of Friedrich Max Müller*, vol. 1, London, 1902) and on Chr. J. von Bunsen.

13. H. Krohn, *Die Juden in Hamburg 1800–1850*, Hamburg, 1967. On Isaak Bernays (apart from usual reference books): H. Graetz, *Geschichte der Juden*, 2d ed., 1900, 9:387 and 506; E. Duckesz in *Jahrb. d. Jüdisch-Literarischen Gesellschaft* 5 (1907): 297–322. G. Scholem in *Leo Baeck Institute Yearbook* 7 (1962): 249 (on Isaak Bernays as the author of *Der Bibel'sche Orient*, Munich, 1821).

the Sephardic tradition. He did not succeed in reuniting the Temple of the Reformed with the Synagogue of the Orthodox, but at least in the first twenty years of his office he managed to keep them together for political, legal, and charitable purposes and was obviously respected by both sides. He reformed the Jewish school system—the Talmud Torah—by including a great deal of ordinary German education. He lived long enough to see the de facto emancipation of the Hamburg Jews in 1848, but full legal equality was granted only in 1860. In June 1863 the Warburgs, just emerging to prominence, changed the name of their business from "Geldwechsler" to "Bankiers."

Isaak gave Jacob all the Jewish education he needed. Jacob became a master of the Hebrew language, was thoroughly acquainted with the Talmud, and was later able to teach Hebrew medieval philosophy. Isaak seems also to have been Jacob's first teacher in Latin and Greek. Jacob perfected his classical education in the local Johanneum. One special feature of the Hamburg situation was that the great classical school had been opened to Jews in 1802. Both Jacob and his younger brother Michael, later an eminent student of German literature, went to the Johanneum. Niebuhr's approach to classical scholarship permeated the school. Niebuhr's influence was also felt in Bernays's home because of the friendship between Haham Isaak and Meyer Isler, a Jew who was a librarian in the municipal library and made his reputation by editing Niebuhr's lectures at Bonn. After a spell in the local academy— "das Akademische Gymnasium"—Jacob Bernays went to Niebuhr's university, Bonn, in 1844.

## IV

In Bonn Bernays studied with F. G. Welcker, Christian Brandis, and F. Ritschl. It is difficult to say what he owed to Welcker, though his interests in religion and religious poetry—such as tragedy—were related to Welcker's thought. Christian Brandis, the friend and biographer of Niebuhr, taught Bernays how to study the pre-Socratics and Aristotle, including the fragments of the lost dialogues, and opened to him the world of the scholiasts. But the beloved master—to Bernays, as to many others—was F. Ritschl. Though he did not succeed in interesting Bernays in what he himself was interested in at the time— Dionysius of Halicarnassus—Ritschl understood and helped Bernays in every way.[14] It soon became evident that Bernays, even as an under-

---

14. O. Ribbeck, *F. W. Ritschl*, Leipzig, 1881, 2:95–98. Bernays helped Ritschl for some time in his ill-fated edition of Dionysius's *Roman Antiquities*. The details are given by Ribbeck.

graduate, had developed critical methods of his own in the study of Greek philosophy as well as of textual criticism.

In 1846 Bernays won the prize for a study on the manuscript tradition of Lucretius. His paper, which was published by Ritschl in *Rheinisches Museum* in 1847, solved in all its essential elements the question of the relations between the four branches of the tradition of Lucretius—the *Quadratus*, the *Oblungus*, the *Schedae*, and the *Italici*. Lachmann's edition of Lucretius, which appeared in 1850, inevitably obscured the merits of Bernays's essay. Bernays himself, in his own edition of Lucretius published by Tuebner in 1852, had nothing but admiration for Lachmann and minimized his own contribution. Though Lucretian scholars such as Usener and Monro were aware of the importance of Bernays's paper, the true state of affairs was first reestablished by S. Timpanaro in his little volume *La Genesi del Metodo del Lachmann* (1963). "Il metodo del Lachmann" was really to a great extent "il metodo del Bernays."

Meanwhile, Bernays had obtained his doctorate in 1848 with a dissertation, *Heraclitea pars I*,[15] which indicated a new way toward the study of the pre-Socratics. Following up a suggestion he had characteristically found in a paper by Johann Matthias Gesner (1752), Bernays discovered the influence of Heraclitus on (ps.) Hippocrates' *De diaeta*. In the second part of his research on Heraclitus published in *Rheinisches Museum* in 1850, he used the same method to find Heraclitean material in Plutarch. Two years later the discovery of the so-called *Philosophoumena*, first attributed to Origen, then to Hippolytus of Rome, confirmed the validity of his method and gave him new scope for the recovery of the lost Heraclitus. Th. Gomperz tells us that Otto Jahn called his attention to Bernays's *Heraclitea*, "eine kleine Schrift, die meinen Altertumsstudien eine neue Wendung gab."[16]

In the warm political atmosphere of 1848 all seemed easy. Immediately after his doctorate, Bernays became a Privatdozent in Bonn. His "Habilitationsvorlesung," *De Philologiae Historia*, confirmed the interest in the history of classical scholarship he had inherited from his father. Under the auspices of Ritschl he published two brief but original florilegia of humanistic texts in the Bonn yearly program for the birthday of the King of Prussia in 1849 and 1850. He also became an assis-

---

15. Reprinted in *Gesammelte Abhandlungen*, 1:1–36. Bernays was in the Akademisches Gymnasium of Hamburg for one year before going to Bonn in 1844. See C. H. W. Sillem, *Die Matrikel des Akademischen Gymnasiums in Hamburg*, 1891, p. 189.

16. *Essays und Erinnerungen*, Stuttgart, 1905, p. 38 (the text is not unambiguous in its reference to Bernays). See H. Gomperz, *T. Gomperz. Briefe und Aufzeichnungen*, Vienna, 1936, pp. 146, 160.

tant editor of the *Rheinisches Museum* and contributed a chapter on Spinoza's Hebrew grammar to a book *Descartes und Spinoza* by his friend C. Schaarschmidt (1850), which showed his command of Spinoza's philosophy.

Though very poor, Bernays found himself in a circle of friends that included poets, aristocrats, and even near-royalties. One of his close friends was Georg Bunsen, the son of the Prussian envoy to London. The friendship with Paul Heyse was to last until the end of his life. It was his only emotional friendship and was born out of the common interest in modern literatures. Paul Heyse, in his *Jugenderinnerungen und Bekenntnisse*, admitted that meeting Bernays had introduced a new element of seriousness into his own intellectual life.[17] To Bernays he later dedicated his translation of Leopardi (1878). Bernays's letters to Heyse have only been partially published. Even so they touch upon a variety of subjects and of emotional experiences on which he was usually silent. The fact that Heyse had a Jewish mother, but was ignorant of both Judaism and Christianity, allowed Bernays to speak to him about Jewish matters with irony and tenderness: "Wie traurig, dass Goethe nicht so gut hebräisch gewusst hat, wie ich . . ." (1856); "Gehörte ich nicht zum Volk des Spinoza, dem eine Portion hilaritas zum Erbtheil gegeben ist . . ." (1858).

Through Georg Bunsen, Bernays became a frequent visitor to the house of the Fürst zu Wied, whose wife, Marie Prinzessin von Nassau, hung on his lips. Their daughter Carmen Sylva—or Elizabeth, Queen of Rumania—devoted a whole chapter of her memoirs to Bernays, who had puzzled her so much in her childhood because he refused to take food in her house and knew the New Testament much better than her parents.[18]

With the political reaction of the early 1850s, it was soon clear that there was little hope for a Jew of getting a chair in a Prussian university. Christian Josias von Bunsen must have assessed the predicament of his son's friend realistically when he invited him to London in 1851 with the intention of introducing him to English scholars. Bunsen had had some part in transplanting Max Müller, but Max Müller was not a Jew, and the East India Company was interested in his services. Bernays ate nothing and drank only tea at the Prussian embassy where he was a guest for about three months. He helped Bunsen in his work on Hippo-

17. *Jugenderinnerungen und Bekenntnisse*, 3d ed., Berlin, 1900, pp. 104–7.
18. *Mein Penatenwinkel*, 2d ed., Frankfurt a.M., 1908, 1:57–71. It was probably through his friendship with the Wied family that Bernays became a member of a committee to improve the situation of Balkan Jews in 1878; N. M. Gelber, *Leo Baeck Inst. Yearbook* 5 (1960): 235.

lytus, and as a parting gift he sent him that *Epistola critica ad Bunsenium* in which he showed how one could use book 10 of the *Philosophoumena* to emend books 5–9. During a visit to Oxford Bernays apparently signed a contract for a Latin commentary on Lucretius and established his friendship with Max Müller and Mark Pattison. If more was expected from Oxford, the times were unpropitious. Less than two months after Bernays's visit, Pattison was defeated in the Lincoln election and retreated from Oxford affairs. Max Müller himself had to wait until 1868 for the Chair of Comparative Philology.

Documents on the early relations between Bernays and Pattison, if they existed, do not seem to have survived. The unpublished letters between them, which are preserved in the Bodleian, belong to the period after 1859. Later on, Pattison regularly sent the most promising Oxford dons to Bernays. In 1865 he introduced Henry Nettleship, a fellow of Merton; in 1868 he introduced Ingram Bywater as "a serious student of ancient philosophy." Bywater, as we know, became Bernays's English pupil and under his guidance put together the edition of Heraclitus (1877). In 1870 Pattison introduced D. B. Monro as a man "who takes a leading place in directing philological studies in this University." The correspondence, as we have it, contains some important letters from Bernays. There is a letter of 1865 in which Bernays gives his opinion on the authenticity of Plato's Seventh Letter and also an interesting judgment on F. A. Wolf (see appendix A).

We should like to know more about the relation between Bernays and Pattison in the 1850s when Bernays needed an academic position and Pattison was far from being firmly established in his own. What we know is enough to show that Pattison's *Memoirs* are no safe guide to the importance of Bernays for his early development. I do not believe that Pattison's interest in the history of classical scholarship was originally suggested by Bernays, though chronology would not be against this hypothesis; but if Pattison started independently, he soon had to take into account the standards of criticism and research set up by Bernays in his *Scaliger* of 1855.

What is more curious is that through Pattison and Bywater Bernays came to exercise a very deep influence on the reform of classical studies in Oxford. Even Oxford's special interest in Aristotelian research, as we shall soon see, cannot be separated from Bernays's example. But this poses two questions to which I shall not try to give an answer: 1) whether anyone in Oxford, Pattison or Bywater or Nettleship or W. L. Newman, had any suspicion that what they learnt from Bernays was by no means typical of German scholarship; 2) whether any of them had at least a notion of what Bernays meant by his research.

# V

The journey to England ended in failure. A few years later Bernays obtained the consent of the Clarendon Press to discontinue his work on the commentary on Lucretius, which had reached line 689 of the first book. In a letter of November 7, 1852, Christian von Bunsen made it clear to Bernays that England was the only alternative to conversion. This letter, to which a second part was added on November 14, was far from being a cool analysis of the situation. Bunsen was a mystic and expected much from his friend's conversion. He quoted the Gospel of St. John. Evidently he himself felt that his invitation did not stand much of a chance. He was ready to welcome Bernays to his house again, "als Jude wie als Christ." Bernays's answer has rightly become a classic in Jewish-German literature.[19] The matter, as far as he was personally concerned, could not even be discussed.

The question of conversion was essential to German Jews from the beginning of the nineteenth century to the end of the First World War. Bunsen was a believer in Christianity. He was entitled to hope for the conversion of the Jews. But even liberals and atheists among the Germans asked the Jews to become converts as a demonstration of their loyalty to German institutions. Mommsen himself, the champion of the Jews against Treitschke, invited the Jews to conversion— apparently to make things easier for their defenders.[20] As men are better than their doctrines, Mommsen remained surrounded by unrepentant Jews to the end of his life: we shall find Bernays among them. "Taufjuden"—Jews who had chosen conversion not because they believed in Christianity, but as a concession to social pressure—became a demoralizing factor in German life, both on its Jewish and on its Christian side. As Bernays said in his reply to Bunsen: "Er selbst, Jesus von Nazareth selbst, jetzt als Jude geboren, würde es nicht können"— namely to accept conversion under those conditions.

Bernays was soon to have a "Taufjude" in his own family. His brother Michael became a convert in 1856. He lived through another twenty difficult years before his outstanding contributions to the study of Goethe were recognized by the creation for him of a chair of German literature in the University of Munich. It is said that Jacob mourned his

---

19. M. Fraenkel, *Jacob Bernays*, pp. 50–60, reprinted in F. Kobler, *Juden und Judentum in deutschen Briefen aus drei Jahrhunderten*, Vienna, 1935, pp. 290–93. See Frances Baroness Bunsen, *A Memoir of Baron Bunsen*, London, 1868, 2:270 on the London visit.

20. Mommsen, *Reden und Aufsätze*, 3d ed., Berlin, 1912, pp. 410–26, especially pp. 423–24. The main texts of the controversy are now collected in W. Boehlich, *Der Berliner Antisemitismusstreit*, 2d ed., Frankfurt a.M., 1965.

brother as dead. This would have been in keeping with the tradition of the Fathers, who had preferred death to apostasy. But after Jacob's death the main part of his library passed to Michael. Jacob certainly made a will, because he bequeathed his manuscripts to the Bonn Library and his Hebrew books to the Jewish Theological Seminary of Breslau. What his testament said about his brother I do not know, but we must assume, until the contrary is proved, that Jacob did nothing to prevent the rest of his library from going to Michael. He certainly was intensely grieved by his brother's conversion. Fifty years later Carmen Sylva still remembered that sorrow and commented: "Ich muss sagen: er hatte Recht."

By the time of his brother's conversion Bernays had found an intellectual home as a teacher of classics and of Jewish philosophy in the newly created Jüdisch-Theologisches Seminar of Breslau. It is not possible to evaluate here the importance of the Breslau seminary from the moment in which it was opened by Zacharias Frankel in 1854 to its destruction in 1938. The seminary's object was to train rabbis and teachers of the Jewish religion in up-to-date scientific methods. It also hoped to reinterpret the Jewish orthodox heritage through scholarly research. Heinrich Hirsch Graetz, the great historian, was, together with Zacharias Frankel, the dominant inspiration of the seminary from its inception. The *Monatsschrift für Geschichte und Wissenschaft des Judenthums* reflected their ideas. The thirteen years during which Bernays taught at the seminary between 1854 and 1866 were the most creative of his life. The friendship with Heyse was, no doubt, a primary factor in his profound concern for Aristotle's theory of tragedy. In one of the very few letters to Bernays that have been preserved, Heyse expresses his full appreciation of the contribution Bernays had made to his own ideas on art. Bernays acquired a new lifelong friend in Theodor Mommsen, who was professor in Breslau from 1854 to 1858. At Breslau the newly married Mommsen completed his *Römische Geschichte* and began to organize the *Corpus Inscriptionum Latinarum*. Bernays shared in the domestic happiness and in the intellectual vigor of his older friend Mommsen. He translated the Book of Job for Mommsen; he and Mommsen revised Heyse's translations from the Italian. They both contributed emendations to the *editio princeps* of Granius Licinianus by K. Pertz (1857). Bernays was able to follow Mommsen's intellectual development when the latter passed from Breslau to Berlin and from Roman political history to the Roman constitution. The essay Bernays wrote in 1874 on Mommsen's *Römisches Staatsrecht* was a revelation to Mommsen himself. It determined his place in the history of classical scholarship. With all his contempt for reviewers Mommsen had to make an exception: "Gott helfe mir, oder Jahwe, wenn Sie das lieber hören, ich weiss keinen, der Ausnahme macht als Sie oder wenigstens wie Sie." The friendship between Bernays and Mommsen, as we can see from a detailed study by L. Wickert, was more generous and delicate on Bernays's side than on Mommsen's.[21] Bernays helped Mommsen ungrudgingly. He contributed an important paper on the *metuens* (Gottesfürchtige) in Juvenal for the *Commentationes in honorem Theodori Mommseni* in 1877. It is a famous academic anecdote that the next year Mommsen asked Bernays's opinion on the meaning of *metuens*. Bernays answered in a tone few would have permitted themselves with Mommsen: "Ich kann mich nicht enthalten gleich nach Empfang Ihres Briefes . . . zu danken für den eben so schlagenden wie schmeichelhaften Beweis, dass Sie meine Abhandlung des Gottesfürchtigen bei Juvenal, enthalten in dem grossen Band commentationes in honorem Theodori Mommseni, nicht gelesen haben." Mommsen admitted defeat for once: "Ja, lieber Bernays, auslachen können Sie mich immer, aber übel nehmen dürfen Sie das nicht. Es ist Ihnen ja auch nichts Neues von mir."[22]

But even in the Breslau days Bernays remained aloof. He had an excellent pupil for Hellenistic literature, Jacob Freudenthal, but he antagonized other students such as Hermann Cohen.[23] He continued to advise Bunsen and to contribute scholarly appendices (for instance on Sanchuniathon) to Bunsen's not very serious big works, until Bunsen died in 1860. He never quite identified himself with the religious opinions of the leaders of the Jewish Theological Seminary. As far as I know, he took no part in the polemics provoked by the appearance of the *Darke ha-Mishnah* by Frankel in 1859. An increasing detachment from the surrounding world, a feeling of limited possibilities within the contemporary situation, were to characterize Bernays's activity.

In 1866 he consented to go back to Bonn. A full chair was still out of the question, though by that time he was recognized as one of the

21. *Historische Zeitschrift* 205 (1967): 265–94. See also Th. Mommsen and O. Jahn, *Briefwechsel*, ed. L. Wickert, Frankfurt a.M., 1962, p. 201 and elsewhere (index s.v. Bernays). Bernays's essay on Mommsen in *Gesamm. Abhandlungen* 2:255–75.

22. M. Fraenkel, *Jacob Bernays*, p. 163.

23. Some information in M. Brann, *Geschichte des jüdisch-theologischen Seminars in Breslau*, Breslau, 1904, pp. 54–60, 124–26 (important for Bernays's Jewish interests). H. Cohen as a student left the seminary after disagreements with Bernays. Even later he disliked his memory. See H. Cohen, *Jüdische Schriften*, Berlin, 1924, 2:420–21 (1904): "Es war kein lebendiges, schaffendes, aufbauendes Denken, welches in dieser gewaltigen Maschine arbeitete. . . . Daher empfand er den Trieb nicht in sich, die Idcen des Judentums, das fortwirkende Wesen desselben seinen christlichen Freunden bckannt und deutlich zu machen."

greatest classical scholars of Germany (chairs in Breslau and Heidelberg had been denied to him by the relevant ministries). As is well known, in 1865 the violent quarrel between F. Ritschl and O. Jahn shook German academic life. Ritschl left Bonn for Leipzig and took with him his pupils E. Rohde and F. Nietzsche. O. Jahn died in 1869 after years of physical illness and mental anguish. Bonn's classical school had to be reconstructed from its foundations. Bernays was offered the direction of the University Library and a chair as Extra-ordinarius, which he accepted. He was fortunate in the two successors of Ritschl and Jahn. H. Usener, who came with him to Bonn in 1866, understood Bernays's mind as probably nobody else could. After Bernays's death in 1881, he made himself the editor of his *Nachlass* and his biographer. Bernays's *Gesammelte Abhandlungen*, published by Usener, are a monument both to the author and to the editor, as Wilamowitz realized. F. Bücheler, who returned to Bonn in 1870, in his more extrovert way loved the man who (as he wrote immediately after Bernays's death) "der Einsamkeit ergeben, las und bedachte unendlich viel, sinnend und ratend über Politik und Judentum, Philosophie und gelehrte Welt, den Geist spannend ohne Nachlass, bis das Hirn tödlich geschlagen ward."[24]

Bernays was also fortunate in his pupils of the Bonn years—Ingram Bywater and U. Wilamowitz-Moellendorff. Two of the best pages of the not very inspired *Erinnerungen* by the eighty-year-old Wilamowitz are an affectionate tribute to the master of his youth. This says much for a man who, already a professor, had had to apologize to Usener for his arrogant behavior as a student: "Er war nicht nur strenger Jude . . . sondern trug den Stolz auf sein Judentum zur Schau. . . . Es war eine sonderbare Sorte von Adelsstolz, der die meisten abstiess; mir hat er imponiert, denn da war alles echt hatte alles Stil."[25]

After 1870 Bernays became very interested in politics. He disliked the new world of mass movements. He had no faith in democracy but even less faith in Bismarck. His letter to Max Müller, dated December 16, 1870, is eloquent enough. His translation with commentary of the first three books of Aristotle's *Politics,* though—needless to say—a work of exquisite craftsmanship, was suggested by the political situation and appeared relevant to it when it was published in 1872. Bernays never moved from Bonn after his return there in 1866. One of the few

24. *Kleine Schriften,* 1927, 2:424 (from *Rh. Museum* 36 [1881]: 480). On Bernays in Bonn, see also P. E. Hübinger, *Hist. Jahrb.* 83 (1964): 162. In 1869 I. Bywater spoke of "the critical tact and poetical insight into the mind of antiquity by virtue of which he (B.) stands so completely alone among living scholars" (*Journ. of Philology* 2, 55).

25. *Erinnerungen,* 1928, pp. 87–88.

glimpses into his private life of that period is provided by Berthold Auerbach, who tells of his Passover night, the seder, with Bernays in 1867. Bernays was no good at singing and enjoyed the performance of Auerbach who, before becoming the favorite writer of the German upper bourgeoisie, had been trained as a rabbi.[26]

In 1880 Treitschke initiated his anti-Semitic campaign. Graetz and Mommsen were involved, and naturally Graetz resented Mommsen's defense almost as much as Treitschke's attack on the Jews. In a remarkable letter (December 15, 1880), Graetz invited Bernays to answer Mommsen: "Dieser Bewunderer der Staatsstreiche scheint kein Gefühl für die Immoralität zu haben, die darin liegt, die Lüge eines Glaubensbekenntnisses, das man vielleicht gar verabscheut, öffentlich auszusprechen."[27] We do not know what Bernays replied to Graetz. He was probably aware that Graetz had made some unwise remarks in his courageous public answer to Treitschke. Nor would he easily have taken up his pen against his friend Mommsen. But there is little room for speculation. In that very winter 1880–81 he began to feel ill. In May 1881 he suffered a stroke, and on May 26 he rejoined his Fathers. The anti-Semitic crisis, one suspects, had killed him (see appendix B).

## VI

From 1854 to 1881 the lines of Bernays's intellectual activity are firmly drawn. He stated his credo in his monograph on Scaliger, which appeared in 1855 and was dedicated to F. Ritschl. Scaliger was no Protestant hero to Bernays for the simple reason that Scaliger was not a Protestant hero in any case. He was a man who had applied the same type of philological research to the classical and to the Oriental worlds and had consequently unified the two fields of research. Bernays emphasized this unity of method and vision. He progressively acquired a formidable knowledge in the history of classical scholarship from the sixteenth century onward, as the appendices of his own works show and the admirable "Quellennachweise zu Politianus und Georgius Valla" in *Hermes* (1876) confirm. He also studied the political and historical thought of the eighteenth century in general, gave lectures on Gibbon, which Wilamowitz admired,[28] and hoped to publish a mono-

26. B. Auerbach, *Briefe an seinen Freund Jacob Auerbach*, Frankfurt a.M., 1884, 1:328; see 2:459 where Bernays's dictum is quoted: "man habe kein Recht die Tradition aufzulösen."

27. The letter is reprinted in the Tel Aviv *Leo Baeck Institute Bulletin* 4 (1961): 321 by M. Reuwen. It was originally published in *Der Morgen* II (1935–36): 365 by M. Fraenkel.

28. H. Usener and U. Wilamowitz, *Ein Briefwechsel*, Berlin, 1934, p. 36.

graph on him. The notes he left on Gibbon have not lost their value after one hundred years, but his book on Scaliger was not merely a contribution to the history of classical scholarship; it was a declaration of method, and to it we shall have to return to our concluding remarks.

Aristotle was another constant interest. His first important contribution was an article in *Rheinisches Museum* (1853) in which he reconstructed Aristotle's lost theory of comedy from the Anonymus Coislinianus. In 1857 he published the *Grundzüge der verlorenen Abhandlung des Aristoteles über Wirkung der Tragödie*, which created a sensation and provoked innumerable replies and discussions.[29] Bernays started from the simple observation that *Katharsis* is a medical term and indicates the removal of impurity, the purge of excess: it does not denote moral purification, as Lessing believed. The remark was not entirely new, though neither Bernays nor his immediate critics were aware of the fact that Heinrich Weil—a German Jew like Bernays, and like him unable to get a position in a German university—had propounded the same medical interpretation of *Katharsis* in a paper published in the *Verhandlungen der zehnten Versammlung deutscher Philologen*, Basel, 1848 (pp. 131ff.). What was really new in Bernays was the development of the implications of the medical interpretation for the understanding of Greek tragedy. Bernays connected the cathartic process with the ecstatic practices of the Dionysiac rites. The way was open for Nietzsche.

In 1872, after the publication of *Die Geburt der Tragödie*, Nietzsche wrote to Rohde: "Das Neueste ist, dass Jacob Bernays erklärt hat, es seien *seine* Anschauungen, nur stark übertrieben." Nietzsche went on to comment: "Die Juden sind überall und auch hier voran, während der gute teutsche Usener . . . dahinten, im Nebel bleibt." Rohde answered in a suitable tone: "vergleiche den Juden Bernays, der alles schon lange selbst sich so gedacht hat."[30]

What exactly Bernays thought and said about Nietzsche's book is another matter, but he was certainly entitled to see in this book an ex-

29. See for instance, S. H. Butcher, *Aristotle's Theory of Poetry and Fine Art*, 2d ed., London, 1898, p. 236; G. Finsler, *Platon und die Aristotelische Poetik*, Leipzig, 1900, p. 96; I. Bywater's commentary on the *Poetics*, Oxford, 1909, ad l. (pp. 152–61); L. Golden, *Trans. Am. Phil. Ass.* 93 (1962): 51–60; D. W. Lucas, commentary on the *Poetics*, Oxford, 1968, pp. 273–90. F. Ueberweg and K. Praechter, *Philosophie des Altertums*, 1926, pp. 120–21 gives a bibliography until 1925. See also L. Cooper and A. Gudeman, *A Bibliography of the Poetics of Aristotle*, New Haven, 1928; M. T. Herrick, *Am. Journ. Phil.* 52 (1931): 168. The fortunes of Bernays's interpretation of *Katharsis* deserve a special investigation (see K. Gründer's introduction to the reprint of the *Grundzüge*, Hildesheim, 1970).

30. *F. N's. Briefwechsel mit Erwin Rohde*, Leipzig, 1923, pp. 273–80.

treme development of his interpretation of *Katharsis*. The link between Bernays and Nietzsche—both, as we know, pupils of Ritschl—is obvious, but to us Bernays's analysis of *Katharsis* suggests the name of Freud even more than the name of Nietzsche. It is interesting that in 1931, after having said that "das Wesentliche [on *Katharsis*] hat Jakob Bernays gesehen," Max Pohlenz added that through his theory of *Katharsis* "Aristoteles erwidert 'psychoanalytisch' " to Plato's criticism.[31] The discoverer of the Oedipus complex, who throughout his life had an insatiable curiosity for the classical world, became a nephew of Jacob Bernays by marrying Martha Bernays, a daughter of Berman Bernays, one of Jacob's brothers.

There is no doubt about what Haham Isaak Bernays meant to Freud when he became engaged to Martha. In a letter he tells his fiancée how he entered into conversation with a little Jewish shopkeeper who turned out to have been a pupil of Isaak and to have known the whole Bernays family in his Hamburg days. The figure of the wise rabbi suddenly became archetypal for Freud, and he concludes his letter by a sui generis profession of faith: "Wenn die Form, in der die alten Juden sich wohl fühlten, auch für uns kein Obdach mehr bietet, etwas vom Kern, das Wesen des sinnvollen und lebensfrohen Judentums, wird unser Haus nicht verlassen."[32]

I have no evidence that Freud studied Jacob Bernays's works. Freud's biographer, Ernest Jones, is unhelpful on such matters,[33] and Ernst Kris, who went professionally into the question of Aristotelian *Katharsis*, is no better.[34] But I am not acquainted with the historical research on the development of Freud's thought. Michael Fraenkel, however, must have had some good reasons for dedicating his selection of Jacob Bernays's letters to Sigmund Freud. I should be surprised if Bernays's famous memoir on Aristotle's *Katharsis* was unknown to Freud in his formative years.

To go back to Bernays's Aristotelian studies, in 1863 he published and dedicated to Mark Pattison his book on the lost dialogues of Aristotle. Not much comment is needed here. We all know that Bernays was the man who effectively resurrected the exoteric Aristotle, that is, the only Aristotle who was known outside his school in the Hellenistic age. He was the first to show how much one could learn about the lost Aristotle

31. *Griechische Tragödie*, Leipzig, 1930, 1:529–33.

32. S. Freud, *Briefe 1873–1939*, Frankfurt a.M., 1960, pp. 19–24. See D. W. Lucas, commentary on Aristotle's *Poetics*, 1968, p. 289.

33. E. Jones, *Sigmund Freud: Life and Work*, London, 1953, 1:112.

34. E. Kris, *Psychoanalytic Explorations in Art*, London, 1953, pp. 62–63.

from Neoplatonic writings. His pupil Bywater followed him in discovering slices of Aristotle's *Protrepticus* in Iamblichus.[35] W. Jaeger and E. Bignone built on Bernays's foundations, and not everyone is certain that their building has the solidity of its foundations. The main disagreement between Bernays and Jaeger—on the existence of a "Platonic" stage in Aristotle's development—is still a controversial subject.

The third direction of Bernays's research was the study of texts bearing on the position of Judaism in the Greco-Roman world. He was not particularly fond of Jewish-Hellenistic literature as such, and explained why in the study he dedicated to Theodor Mommsen in 1856, *Ueber das Phokylideische Gedicht.*[36] Bernays recognized a Jew, or rather a Jewish proselyte, writing about the beginning of the Christian era, in the author of a poem transmitted to us under the name of Phocylides. The author, who wanted to appeal to the pagans, expressed himself ambiguously. He avoided a clear statement of Jewish beliefs. Bernays's comment is that the ambiguity explains why Jewish-Hellenistic literature was doomed to oblivion. Any attempt "das Concrete durch Compromiss oder Abstraction zu verflachen," is bound to be contemptible.

What Bernays liked best was to discover in pagan literature new pieces of evidence either for Jewish history or for the slow conversion of pagan minds to Jewish and Christian beliefs. In 1861 he published what may well be his masterpiece in historical interpretation: *Ueber die Chronik des Sulpicius Severus.* Bernays was exceptionally well acquainted with the political and religious situation at the end of the fourth century A.D. and subtly presented Sulpicius Severus's view of his own time. But the most sensational conjecture was that Sulpicius Severus's account of the destruction of Jerusalem summarized the now lost section of Tacitus's *Histories.* There is no doubt that Sulpicius Severus agrees with Valerius Flaccus (1.13) against Flavius Josephus (64.3) in stating that the destruction of the Temple was decided by Titus. As Bernays saw, Josephus's version must be treated as an attempt to whitewash Titus in the eyes of the surviving Jews. Sulpicius Severus used Tacitus elsewhere, and this particular passage shows traces of Tacitean style under the early fifth-century veneer. It is therefore reasonable to conclude with Bernays that Sulpicius Severus depended on Tacitus. His conjecture has indeed been generally accepted.

35. *Journ. Philology* 2 (1869): 55–69. See W. Jaeger, *Aristotle,* English trans., 2d ed., Oxford, 1948, p. 60; A.-H. Chroust, *Symb. Osloenses* 42 (1968): 7–43.

36. Now in *Ges. Abhandlungen,* 1:192–261. F. Dornseiff amusingly tried to save this poem for Phocylides in *Echtheitsfragen antik-griechischer Literatur,* Berlin, 1939, pp. 37–51. See also Bernays's note "Zur vergleichenden Mythologie" (*Rh. Mus.* [1860]), now in *Ges. Abhandlungen,* 2:294–96, with its characteristic conclusion in the style of Heine.

Jacob Bernays

A recent attempt by Canon Hugh Montefiore to refute it is not convincing. Montefiore simply replaces the name of Tacitus as the source of Sulpicius with the name of the man who was probably the source of Tacitus, Antonius Iulianus: no gain and greater obscurity.[37]

I should like to include the book *Theophrastos' Schrift über Frömmigkeit* (1866) in the series of Jewish studies rather than in the Aristotelian series, though the method is that of the Aristotelian essays. Bernays proves beyond doubt that Porphyry's *De abstinentia* is largely based on Theophrastus's περὶ εὐσεβείας. The analysis is subtle and cautious. What interests Bernays most is that, approached in this way, Theophrastus becomes the first of the Greek writers directly available to us to have dealt with the Jewish religion. Furthermore, Bernays shows that Theophrastus developed a criticism of traditional Greek practices about sacrifices which implied a rapprochement to Judaism. Bernays's demonstration has since been refined and perhaps corrected in detail. Jaeger, for instance, has indicated in Hecataeus of Abdera a possible (but to my mind not probable) source of Theophrastus about the Jews.[38]

The little book on the letters attributed to Heraclitus appeared in 1869. As a lifelong student of this philosopher, Bernays had originally been interested in them as a source for Heraclitus's thought. He rightly suspected that the forger used Heraclitus's writings to lend plausibility to his products. During the progress of his research it became obvious that the letters were by several hands. Bernays tried to prove that some of the authors were either Jews or Christians in disguise. His demonstration was accepted for a long time. It now appears more probable that the letters in question (4, 7, and 9) are by a cynic. But his analysis of the letters remains of basic importance. What Bernays gets out of these texts is truly astonishing. He was the first, as far as I know, to pose the problem of the relations between cynicism and Jewish-Hellenistic literature.[39]

The study of Philo's *De aeternitate mundi* accompanied Bernays for many years. In 1863 he published his discovery that the text had been

37. J. Bernays, *Ges. Abhandlungen*, 2:81–200 (dedicated to Max Müller); H. Montefiore, *Historia*, 1962, 2:156–70.

38. W. Jaeger, *Diokles von Karystos*, Berlin, 1938, pp. 134–53; *Scripta Minora*, Rome, 1960, 2:169–83. For later research the ed. by W. Pötscher, *Theophrastus, περὶ εὐσεβείας*, Leiden, 1964.

39. See E. Norden, *Jahrb. f. class. Phil.*, suppl. 19 (1893): 386, and the very different opinion in *Agnostos Theos*, reprint 1923, pp. 389–90; I. Heinemann, *Pauly-Wissowa*, suppl. V (1931): 228–32. See E. Schürer, *Geschichte des jüd. Volkes*, 4th ed., 1909, 3:624–25, also for Diogenes ep. 28 studied by Bernays.

165

transmitted with chapters in the wrong order. This was a capital contribution to the understanding of the difficult text. In 1876 Bernays published an edition with translation in the *Abhandlungen* of the Berlin
Academy, of which he had become a member in 1865. In 1882 Usener
edited from the *Nachlass* the introduction to the text and an unfinished
commentary—"Bernaysium nusquam magis Bernaysium videris," as
he wrote to Wilamowitz.[40] According to Bernays, who knew he had
predecessors as illustrious as G. Budé, the text cannot be by Philo. It
maintains that the world is eternal and uncreated, which is not Philo's
opinion in other works. It is hardly necessary to say that Bernays, as a
constant student of Maimonides and Spinoza, lived in full awareness
of the problem about the eternity of the world in Jewish thought. The
solution adopted by Bernays was one of three possibilities, all of which
he had considered. The second possibility was that Philo had changed
his mind. The third was that he intended to refute the thesis of the eternity of the world in a lost section of the treatise.

F. Cumont defended the second solution in his edition (1891); other
scholars (H. Leisegang among them) have opted for the third, which is
indeed preferable. Nobody has ever denied that all the problems were
first formulated by Bernays and that Bernays contributed enormously
to the emendation and understanding of the controversial text.

We come now to the two works of Bernays's last years, in which a
mysterious element of deep detachment from the world and even of
revolt against it underlies the philological research. The book *Lucian
und die Kyniker* appeared in 1879, two years before his death. Lucian's
*Peregrinus* had traditionally been interpreted as an anti-Christian pamphlet. With the help of a hitherto unnoticed passage from Galen,
Bernays clarified the background and showed that Lucian attacked
Peregrinus not as a Christian (which he had been for a short time) but
as a cynic. Two elements emerge from Bernays's demonstration, which
is followed, as usual, by a careful translation and annotation of the text.
Lucian was no Voltaire. His irony and satire lacked the support of the
serious and noble convictions that characterize Voltaire. Lucian hated
the cynics because the cynics, in their contempt for ordinary social con-
ventions, joined Jews and Christians in the protest against the world as
it was. Even those who do not accept this interpretation admit, in
Jacques Schwartz's words, that Bernays "a écrit la première étude sé-
rieuse sur Peregrinos."[41] It was more than that.

40. Usener and Wilamowitz, *Briefwechsel*, p. 26.
41. Lucien de Samosate, *Philopseudès et De Morte Peregrini*, Paris, 1951, p. 63.

Protest against political life—withdrawal from the city—was what characterized Greek philosophers in general, according to Bernays's last work, *Phokion und seine neueren Beurtheiler* (1881). Greek philosophers were normally émigrés or political rebels. With Alexander, and after him, they supported Macedonia because they hated the ways of the polis. Phocion, who had been educated in the Platonic school, shared their dislike and was ultimately the victim of the democracy he disliked. Bernays's starting point was the difference of opinion on Phocion, which began to emerge in the second part of the eighteenth century. Previously, admiration for Phocion had been almost as general as the admiration for his biographer Plutarch. Bernays saw that hostility to Phocion reflected the new democratic trend: it was to prevail in the nineteenth century. Bernays, who did not like democracy, reacted by returning to unconditional admiration for Phocion. He presented an analysis of the situation of the philosophers under Macedonian rule, which for the first time focused attention on the political commitments of the philosophers and is still the starting point of any research on the subject. Wilamowitz, who had listened to Bernays's lectures on this topic in Bonn, declared his debt to Bernays even before the book on Phocion was published.[42] The whole volume on *Antigonos von Karystos* is hardly separable from Bernays's teaching, but the section on "Die Philosophenschulen und die Politik," the most important of the book, is literally unthinkable without Bernays. When in 1959 I tried to give a picture of the cultural situation in Athens at the time of the historian Timaeus, I had to return to Bernays. It was a shock to discover how little I had understood of his book when I first read it almost thirty years earlier during my study of Demosthenes and Philip of Macedon. Bernays's hostility to Grote, his sympathy with reactionary currents, were not what we expected in 1930 from a great master who had lived in the happy year 1880. In 1959 it was at least clear that Bernays was not one of the many who idealized Macedonia in order to justify Prussia. He had Treitschke in mind when he spoke of the inevitable opposition "zwischen dem selbständigen Hochsinn philosophischer Charaktere und der bald platten, bald wilden Politik demokratischer Stadtgemeinden."[43] We know that in his last years Bernays was working on a commentary on the prophet Jeremiah, the first work on a biblical text he had ever undertaken. This perhaps indicates better than anything else where his thoughts were going.

42. *Antigonos von Karystos*, Berlin, 1881, pp. 182 n. 4, 339.
43. *Phokion*, p. 97.

## VII

One does not have the immediate sense of a premature death in the case of Jacob Bernays because every piece he wrote was a self-contained masterpiece. His control of philological techniques had been exceptional since his youth. Few have ever had a similar command of the language of Greek philosophy. He was good at emending texts, but above all an interpreter of rare thoroughness and acumen. He expressed himself in a lucid and minutely polished style and created a new type of philological treatise—short, closely argued, confined to the essentials, never deriving his assumptions from the work of another. He never worked on a subject he did not consider intrinsically important. To his treatises he appended notes or excursuses, each of which was a little dissertation in its own right about points of the history of classical scholarship, of lexicography, of philosophy. His articles in learned journals were relatively few and in certain cases supplemented someone else's contributions, but even these articles were, as a rule, self-contained pieces of the highest distinction. I mention as an example his paper "Philon's Hypothetika und die Verwünschungen des Buzyges in Athen" (1876), which begins by clarifying the title of a lost work by Philo and ends by throwing much light on an Athenian rite. But if I had to choose a few pages for an anthology I would probably choose the little note published in *Rheinisches Museum* (1862) with the title "Ein nabatäischer Schriftsteller." Bernays emends an unintelligible sentence of Ammonius, the commentator of Aristotle, by identifying in it the name of a Nabataean god which he had read in Hesychius. By successive steps he conjures up a whole group of Greek writers in the Arabian city of Petra—a new paragraph in the history of Hellenism.[44]

Many of his emendations are no longer to our taste. None of us would eliminate an inconvenient θεοί in Pseudo-Phocylides by emending it into νέοι (l. 104). But I know of only one serious error made by Bernays. It is to be found in his last work on Phocion, which shows signs of strain. Here Bernays undoubtedly misunderstood the political standing of Xenocrates, the leader of the Academy. He seems to have overlooked the evidence provided by the *Index Academicorum Philosophorum Herculanensis*, though the text had been revised by F. Bücheler

---

44. *Ges. Abhandlungen*, 2:291–93 with an important addition to the original text in *Rh. Museum*. Another admirable piece of research discovered interpolations in Ps.-Apuleius, *Asclepius*, which were suggested by antipagan laws of the fourth century A.D.: see *Ges. Abhandl.*, 1:328, and A. D. Nock and A. J. Festugière, *Corpus Hermeticum*, 1945, 2:288 n. 2.

in 1869. Theodor Gomperz, who admired Bernays but admired George Grote and Athenian democrats even more, made this mistake an occasion for an unjustified attack against the whole book on Phocion in *Wiener Studien* 4 (1882): 102–20.[45]

Bernays had certainly intended to do more work on the history of classical scholarship which he knew so well, but he did not share the interest in the continuity of classical forms or in the transmission of classical texts which was to become typical of Jewish scholars of the next generation, such as Eduard Norden, Ludwig Traube, Ernst Kantorowicz, and of course Aby Warburg. To him Scaliger was not a link in the chain, but an absolute. Like any other Jewish boy Bernays carried in his mind—and almost in his blood—the rule of Rabbi Gamliel: "make thee a master." Even more than Ritschl, Scaliger was the master he gave himself. Scaliger was his master because he had kept out of theological controversies and had worked out a philological method that applied equally to Hebrew and classical writers and was beyond sectarian doubts. What Bernays wanted was an uncontroversial philological interpretation of what Greeks and Romans, Jews and Christians had thought and done. Having received a faith, he did not have to look to history for one, as many of his contemporaries did, including perhaps his friend von Bunsen.

When he formulated his program in 1855 in his *Scaliger,* he was in fact propounding a via media between the wild Orientalizing speculations of Creuzer and the sound classical distrust of Lobeck. When he died in 1881 there was perhaps general agreement that he had been right. But the general agreement concealed a basic misunderstanding, a misunderstanding far more serious than the quasi-theological disagreements of thirty or forty years before.

In the 1880s Wilamowitz and Wellhausen dedicated books to each other and proclaimed that the method of dealing with the *Iliad* was the same as the method of dealing with Genesis. Even more significantly, Eduard Meyer, a product of the Hamburg Johanneum, was just embarking on his history of antiquity, where Amos and Hesiod, the Book of Samuel and Herodotus were taken to be fragments of the same archaic world. Yet the Jews whom Wilamowitz, Wellhausen, and Meyer were prepared to admit into their own picture of civilization had all been dead before Cyrus King of Persia allowed their descendants to go back to Jerusalem. It was the age of the prophets that belonged to the West—not what we call normative Judaism, which was Bernays's Juda-

45. See G. Maddoli, "Senocrate nel clima politico del suo tempo," *Dialoghi di Archeologia* 1 (1967): 304–27.

ism. Hans Liebeschütz, in his admirable recent book *Das Judentum im deutschen Geschichtsbild* (1967), has shown to what lengths German historians and theologians went in trying to eliminate Judaism from civilization.

Mohammedans, and, to a lesser extent, Catholics received analogous treatment. This explains why Jewish and Catholic scholars were particularly committed to establishing standards of objective interpretation of unpopular beliefs, doctrines, historical periods. Bishop Karl Josef Hefele, Père Delehaye, Cardinal Ehrle are obvious names in this connection; so is the name of Ignaz (Isaak Iehuda) Goldziher, the secretary of the Jewish community of Budapest, who introduced new understanding into the study of Mohammedan law and theology. Bernays is not quite in the same category. He neither needed nor wanted polemical attitudes: he never argued about his faith in public, and perhaps not even in private.[46] But he worked in the same direction. It is not by chance that he met with sympathy, especially from Usener, who among the free thinkers was most aware of the problems of free thinking. In his mild way Usener had told Wilamowitz of their radical difference: "Sie suchen die Schöpfungen des Willens in der Geschichte, ich das unwillkürliche, unbewusste Werden."[47]

46. H. Cohen, *Jüdische Schriften*, 2:421 spoke of the "Schellingscher Mystizismus" which J. Bernays inherited from his father. This is not apparent in his writings, though a letter to Heyse after Schelling's death in 1854 (M. Fraenkel, p. 75) implies admiration for, and perhaps personal acquaintance with, Schelling. Bernays's interest in Neoplatonic thought, even if it was originally inspired by Schelling and Creuzer, was later independent of their influence. Bernays's sympathy with Voltaire and Gibbon is not easily reconcilable with the alleged "Schellingian mysticism," but, as I have said, Bernays never made public his deepest beliefs.

47. Usener and Wilamowitz, *Briefwechsel*, p. 7. [Additional note (April 1969). My colleague Professor G. J. Weiss has drawn my attention to a letter from Sigmund Freud to Arnold Zweig in their recently published *Briefwechsel* (Frankfurt a.M. 1968, p. 59) which shows that Freud took a direct part in the publication of M. Fraenkel's book *Jacob Bernays. Ein Lebensbild in Briefen*, 1932. Furthermore, I should like to refer to N. Rubinstein, "Il Poliziano e la questione delle origini di Firenze," in *Il Poliziano e il suo tempo*, Florence, 1957, p. 108 for the importance of Bernays's discovery that Politianus read Johannes Lydus. Finally, I should like to mention Louis Robert's "De Delphes à l'Oxus. Inscriptions nouvelles de la Bactriane," *Comptes Rendus Acad. Inscriptions*, 1968, p. 451 on the question of Clearchus's reference to the Jews which had interested Bernays in connection with Theophrastus.

# *16*

# A Note on Max Weber's Definition
# of Judaism
# as a Pariah Religion

## I

References to Jews as pariahs can be found early in the nineteenth century. In 1823, Michael Beer, the brother of the composer Giacomo Meyerbeer, wrote and produced a tragedy, *Der Paria*, about a Hindu outcast who is not permitted to fight for his country: a transparent allegory of the modern German Jew.[1] Towards the end of the century, Theodor Herzl and Bernard Lazare used the word *pariah* in reference to modern Jews.[2] More recently, Hannah Arendt has given wider circulation to this word in America.[3] Though she used it in her own sense, she specifically borrowed it from Max Weber, who first introduced the term *pariah* into the scientific study of Judaism.[4]

Originally published in English in *History and Theory* 19, no. 3 (1980): 313–18. Reprinted by permission of Giulio Einaudi editore s.p.a.

1. Efr. Shmueli, "The 'Pariah-People' and Its 'Charismatic Leadership'. A Revaluation of Max Weber's *Ancient Judaism*," *Proceedings of the American Academy of Jewish Research* 36 (1968): 167–247 at 170.

2. See Hannah Arendt, *The Jew as Pariah*, ed. R. H. Feldman, New York, 1978, p. 126.

3. Ibid., p. 68; but for her special usage of the term compare more especially her biography *Rahel Varnhagen* [1957], New York, 1974, pp. 199–215, "Between Pariah and Parvenu." For German terminology about the Jews, see A. Bein, "The Jewish Parasite," *Year Book of the Leo Baeck Institute* 9 (1964): 3–40.

4. See Max Weber, *Ancient Judaism*, trans. and ed. H. H. Gerth and Don Martindale, New York, 1967, and Weber, *The Sociology of Religion*, trans. Ephraim Fischoff and intr. Talcott Parsons, Boston, 1963. "Das antike Judentum" appeared first in the *Archiv für Sozialwissenschaft und Sozialforschung*, 1917–19, and was reprinted with the addition of a supplement on the Pharisees in *Gesammelte Aufsätze zur Religionssoziologie*, vol. 3, Tübingen, 1921. *The Sociology of Religion* is a section of *Wirtschaft und Gesellschaft*, first published in Tübingen in 1922; the English translation follows the revised edition by J. Winckelmann, vol. 1, no. 2, Tübingen, 1956, pp. 245–381.

Among discussions of Weber's texts on Judaism I shall mention only W. Caspari, *Die Gottesgemeinde vom Sinai und das nachmalige Volk Israel. Auseinandersetzungen mit Max*

For Arendt the pariah is one Jewish type, incarnated by Heine, Kafka, Shalom Aleichem, and Charlie Chaplin, to be opposed (and preferred) to another Jewish type, the parvenu. According to Arendt the pariah self-consciously brings his Jewish existence into the unsympathetic Gentile world in which he lives; he neither denies nor idealizes his Jewish heritage while the parvenu does either.

Weber had something else in mind. He starts his monograph on Judaism by stating that "sociologically speaking the Jews were a pariah people, which means, as we know from India, that they were a guest people, who were ritually separated, formally or de facto, from their surroundinges."[5] His question, therefore, is: "how did Jewry develop into a pariah people with highly specific peculiarities?"[6] Weber, of course, knows that the Jews were never inserted into a system of castes and never shared the religion of those who avoided them. The accent is therefore on the quality of "guest people" (*Gastvolk*), of Jews living on foreign soil. He emphasizes that the Jews deliberately chose to become pariahs—a choice arising from definite religious and moral beliefs and expressed by voluntary ritual segregation. As Weber says, the Jews segregated "voluntarily and not under pressure of external rejection."[7]

---

*Weber*, Gütersloh, 1992; I. Schiper, "Max Weber on the Sociological Basis of the Jewish Religion," *Jewish Journal of Sociology* 1 (1959): 250–60 (originally published in Polish in 1924); J. Guttman, "Max Weber's Soziologie des antiken Judentums," *Monatsschrift für Geschichte und Wissenschaft des Judentums* 69 (1925): 195–223; J. Taubes, "Die Entstehung des jüdischen Pariavolkes," in *Max Weber, Gedächtnisschrift*, ed. K. Engisch et al., Berlin, 1966, pp. 185–94; J. Freund, "L'éthique économique et les religions mondiales selon Max Weber," *Arch. Sociol. des Religions* 26 (1968): 3–25; Fr. Raphaël, "Max Weber et le Judaïsme antique," *Arch. Européennes de Sociologie* 11 (1970): 297–336; F. Parente, "Max Weber e la storia dell'antico Israele," *Annali Scuola Normale Superiore di Pisa* 3 (1978): 1365–96. But the most important work is H. Liebeschütz, *Das Judentum im deutschen Geschichtsbild von Hegel bis Max Weber*, Tübingen, 1967; see his previous essay, "Max Weber's Historical Interpretation of Judaism," *Year Book of the Leo Baeck Institute* 9 (1964): 41–68. A critique of Weber from points of view ultimately going back to Durkheim is in A. Causse, *Du Groupe ethnique à la communauté religieuse*, Paris, 1937. For other criticism: J. A. Holstein, "Max Weber and Biblical Scholarship," *Hebrew Union College Annual* 46 (1975): 159–79. See also P. Bourdieu, "Une interprétation de la théorie de la religion selon Max Weber," *Arch. Europ. Sociol.* 12 (1971): 3–21.

5. Weber, *Ancient Judaism*, p. 3. "Das antike Judentum," p. 2: "Denn was waren soziologisch angesehen, die Juden? Ein Pariavolk. Das heisst, wie wir aus Indien wissen: ein rituell, formell oder faktisch, von der sozialen Umwelt geschiedenes Gastvolk."

6. Ibid., p. 8: "Das Problem ist also: wie sind die Juden zu einem Pariavolk mit dieser höchst spezifischen Eigenart geworden?"

7. Weber, *Ancient Judaism*, p. 417. "Das antike Judentum," p. 434: "Und zwar freiwillig von sich aus, nicht etwa unter dem Zwang äusserer Ablehnung."

## II

Clarity, however, ceases at this point. What Weber means by "guest people" is not self-evident. In the section on the sociology of religion in *Economics and Society (Wirtschaft und Gesellschaft)*, he seems to clarify the issue by giving a slightly different version of his definition of the Jews as pariahs. He writes:

> In our usage, "pariah people" denotes a distinctive hereditary social group lacking autonomous political organization and characterized by prohibitions against commensality and inter-marriage originally founded upon magical, tabooistic, and ritual injunctions. Two additional traits of a pariah people are political and social disprivilege and a far-reaching distinctiveness in economic functioning.[8]

Weber does not make here any explicit mention of "guest people"; instead he refers to a "group lacking autonomous political organization." This is certainly clearer than the formulation in *Ancient Judaism*, but does not yet explain why and in what sense a guest people necessarily lacks an autonomous political organization or vice versa.

Second, Weber seems to suggest that an ethic of resentment (*Ressentiment*) is characteristic of the Jews as pariahs. Always a student and admirer of Nietzsche, he uses in both *Ancient Judaism* and the pertinent section of *Economics and Society* the notion of resentment to characterize Jewish ethics. The trouble is that, following Nietzsche, he extends the term to Christian ethics. In *Ancient Judaism* he even suggests that resentment meant less to the Jews than to the early Christians: the rabbis fought against the religious internalization of revenge while "the less sophisticated early Christians" ("das durch Reflexion ungebrochenere alte Christentum") indulged more openly in it.[9] As, according to Weber himself, Paul freed the Christians from the pariah status of the Jews, the unavoidable conclusion is that there is no necessary connection between pariah status and ethics of resentment.[10]

8. Weber, *Sociology of Religion*, pp. 108–9. *Wirtschaft und Gesellschaft*, 2d ed., 1925, 1:282 = 4th ed., 1956, 2.2:300; "eine, durch (ursprünglich) magische, tabuistische und rituelle Schranken der Tisch- und Konnubialvergemeinschaftung nach aussen einerseits, durch politische und sozial negative Privilegierung, verbunden mit weitgehender ökonomischer Sondergebarung andererseits, zu einer erblichen Sondergemeinschaft zusammengeschlossene Gruppe ohne autonomen politischen Verband."

9. Weber says more precisely (*Ancient Judaism*, p. 404): "the struggle of the rabbis against the religious internationalization [*sic*] of revenge is ethically impressive and indicates, indeed, a strong sublimation of ethical feeling." See "Das antike Judentum," p. 422: "der Kampf der Rabbiner gegen die religiöse Verinnerlichung der Rache."

10. Weber, *Sociology of Religion*, p. 260.

The connotations of the pariah status are made still more obscure by uncertainties about the time and circumstances in which, according to Weber, the Jews became pariahs. At one point he seems to imply that even the Patriarchs had been pariahs; at another point he connects the pariah status with the combination of prophecy and traditional ritualism which he describes as characteristic of Judaea at the end of the seventh century B.C. before the destruction of the first Temple.[11] More precisely he states: "This place as a guest people was established through ritualistic closure which, in Deuteronomic times, as we saw, was diffused, and during the time of the Exile, was carried through by Ezra's and Nehemiah's enactments."[12] At other points Weber seems to connect generically the transformation of the Jews into pariahs with their exile and dispersion—though, again, it is not clear whether he means the first exile or the destruction of the second Temple.[13]

These and similar difficulties of interpretation would not be lessened by the hypothesis that Weber's thinking on the matter evolved. The sections on religion of *Economics and Society,* though published after his death in 1920, are said to have been written about 1911–13. The monograph on Judaism was published in Weber's lifetime, 1917–19 (with the exception of the appendix on Pharisaism). Both works belong substantially to the same period of his activity. The differences in formulation between the texts under consideration are more likely to be due to his feverish style of composition than to the evolution of his ideas.

### III

Given these elements of obscurity, the best we can do is to outline the attitude of the Jews towards political power, remaining as it does fairly constant throughout the centuries. We want to see whether it is compatible with that feature of a pariah nation which emerges more clearly from Weber's pages, namely the voluntary segregation and renunciation of political power with its implication of an ethic of resentment.

11. Weber, *Ancient Judaism,* pp. 51, 336ff.

12. Ibid., p. 345. "Das antike Judentum," p. 360: "Diese Gastvolksstellung nun wurde durch die rituelle Abschliessung begründet, welche, in der deuteronomischen Zeit wie wir sahen, verbreitet, in der Exilszeit und durch die Gesetzgebung des Esra and Nehemia durchgeführt wurde."

13. In *Sociology of Religion,* p. 108: "Since the Exile, as a matter of actual fact, and formally since the destruction of the Temple, the Jews became a pariah people." See *Wirtschaft und Gesellschaft* 1:282 = 1.2:300: "Seit dem Exil tatsächlich und auch formell seit der Zerstörung des Tempels waren die Juden ein 'Pariavolk.'" Weber's allusion to the pariah status of the Jews in the conclusion of *Politik als Beruf* belongs to another context.

I shall leave out the Patriarchs. Hebrew historical tradition (as distinct from certain rabbinic speculation) has always maintained that the Patriarchs lived before the Hebrews received their God-given law and God-given land. The status of the Patriarchs cannot be used to define the status which the Jews subjectively attributed to themselves as a consequence of the revelation on Sinai and of the conquest of the Promised Land. The whole Jewish religious tradition from the older strata of the Bible to the present day presupposes that the Jews are committed by pact to obey a divine law and are entitled under certain conditions to own a territory granted to them by God. The loss of political independence and dispersion have never changed this situation in the eyes of believing Jews. The restoration of the land has merely been deferred to a messianic age. Believing Jews have never concealed from themselves that there are serious questions about the ways of reconciling their religious views on legislation and territorial claims with the obligations imposed by foreign rule and dispersion. But, interestingly enough, they themselves have legislated (or interpreted divine law) about these conflicts of obligation. The presupposition of Talmudic reasoning and of the later legal developments culminating in the system of Maimonides is that loss of political independence does not entail renunciation of self-government—or, rather, that the interpretation of the Law given by God must go on under any circumstances. Indeed Talmudic and post-Talmudic legal thought is notorious for not taking any notice of faits accomplis. Maimonides goes on talking about the constitution of the Sanhedrin, the supreme court of law, as if the king and the high priest were still walking on the hills of Judaea. Believing Jews never gave up their sovereign rights and never admitted to being without political institutions of their own. This excludes that subjective acceptance of an inferior, nonpolitical status, which seems to be essential to Weber's definition of the Jews as pariahs.

The only way of saving Weber's identification of the Jews with a pariah nation would be to argue that although they never considered themselves a landless nation without rights, they were treated as such by the political powers under which they successively lived. Lack of "territoriality" would thus become the reason for the pariah status of the Jews. This interpretation, however, would involve a complete transformation of Weber's thesis—and not one to be commended, either. Weber's primary contention is that the Jews themselves chose to be pariahs because of their religious attitude. In the new interpretation the position of pariah would be imposed on the Jews, not developed by the Jews themselves. It would not throw any light on their religious orientation and its consequences for social life. It would not, therefore, explain what after all Weber wanted to explain when he labeled the Jews as pariahs: their inability to contribute to the modern forms of advanced capitalism, as the Calvinists did. It would also involve us in awkward comparative questions. Would Weber ever have referred to the Germans settled on Roman territory in the Late Empire as pariahs?

One could, of course, develop compromise interpretations trying to combine voluntary and involuntary factors of the pariah status of the Jews. For instance, one could argue that the Jews remained permanent foreigners in the countries in which they settled by refusing to give up their original land; or one could argue (with some support from Weber himself) that they were reduced to the status of pariahs by a mixture of subjective decisions about commensality and intermarriage and objective deprivations of territory and political rights. These compromise interpretations would certainly be nearer (almost by definition!) to the realities of Jewish "exile." But would they bring us nearer to the Indian model that was Weber's starting point? What would *we* mean if we called the Jews pariahs?

In commonsense terms, one does not see how the different legal statutes under which the Jews have lived since Hellenistic times could be unified by this definition. The Roman period would have to be excluded in any case. The status of the Jews in Islamic law would again not be amenable to a reduction to the pariah type. The "regimen Iudaeorum" in Christian countries up to the emancipation would, no doubt, be nearer to this description of Jews as guest people. But the definitions formulated by Christian lawyers and theologians at different times characterize far more precisely the status of the Jews at any given moment and place. The term *pariah* has neither law nor theology in its favor.

There is an obvious problem about what discrimination against the Jews meant to the Jews themselves and what it made of them. But this problem is not to be confused with Weber's problem, which was dictated by the conviction that the Jews organized their own ghetto and went into it of their own choice. If the word "pariah" indicates a people who accept their position as inferiors in an alien social system, and work out their own salvation through this acceptance, the Jews were not pariahs. The Jews went on giving laws to themselves and treated their pact with God as their own legal title to the future recovery of their own land in the messianic age. Their morality encompassed rebellion against injustice and martyrdom—attitudes one does not normally associate with pariahs.

## IV

It seems possible that Weber confused ritual separation as willed by a sovereign nation (which is what we find in the Bible, in the Talmud and in later legal treatises) with pariah status. The ritual separation, presupposing sovereign rights, is no indication of statelessness or of guest status. It is not equivalent to segregation and ghetto life. It may not be reasonable, but it is not intrinsically hostile to ordinary human relations. It goes together with proselytism.

Much of what Weber said on ancient Judaism remains valid even if we eliminate his definition of it as a pariah religion. He saw that the biblical writers (whether priests or prophets) and their rabbinic successors had a rational, nonmagic approach to social relations, which identified injustice and oppression as such. He duly appreciated the whole messianic dimension as a promise of future rectification of present injustice: an effort to save the rationality of this world by finding a complement to it in a world to come. The sympathetic understanding of the rabbis, against the entire tradition of German scholarship, is perhaps the most remarkable feature of Weber's interpretation of Judaism. Even his interpretation of the Jewish attitude towards capitalism contains valid elements, though it pays too little attention to the legal constraints on the Jews during the decisive stage of the industrialization of Europe. Proclivity to messianic hopes may indeed encourage anticapitalistic trends.

There remains a curious basic contradiction in Weber's analysis of Judaism. More perhaps than anybody else he gave importance to its juridical structure—the pact between God and the Jewish nation. On the other hand, he did not appreciate the consequence. Throughout the centuries this pact remained the foundation of the self-regulation of the Jewish communities and therefore saved the Jews from whatever self-abasement can be associated with the word *pariah*.[14]

14. I am much indebted to Professor E. Shils for discussing the topic of this paper in our joint seminar on Weber's *Judaism* at the University of Chicago in the autumn of 1979. I owe other critical remarks to Professor J. Ben-David, to S. C. Humphreys, and to Rabbi L. Jacobs. [See F. Raphaël, "Die Juden als Gastvolk im Werk Max Webers" in *Max Webers Studie über das antike Judentum*, ed. W. Schluchter, Frankfurt a.M., 1981, pp. 224–62.]

# 17

# Hermeneutics and Classical Political Thought in Leo Strauss

## I

Leo Strauss is known to us as the defender of the natural law of the ancients against the natural law of the moderns, as the utmost adversary of historicists and political scientists, and, finally, as the author of one of the most elaborated and detailed criticisms of the atheism of Machiavelli.[1] All of this is enough to make Leo Strauss an exceptional figure in the non-Catholic American culture of our times. Scholars of political doctrines who oppose the same way and for the same reasons sociology and historicism, Machiavellianism and liberalism, are not common in the United States. But what is most interesting in Leo Strauss is the special point of view from which his polemic against historicism and sociology is conducted, a point of view drawn both from his criteria as an interpreter of texts and from his moral and perhaps religious presuppositions. A bibliography of his many scattered writings, contained in a book in his honor, *Ancients and Moderns: Essays on the Tradition of Political Philosophy in Honor of L. Strauss* (New York, 1964), will help us to understand the most original aspects of his personality.[2]

Throughout his life, L. Strauss has been above all an interpreter of texts—and of difficult ones. He began by interpreting Spinoza (1930), Maimonides (1935), and Moses Mendelssohn (introduction to the Jubiläumsausgabe, 1929) at a time when he still was permitted to live in his

1. As far as I know, the only book by Strauss that has been translated into Italian is *Diritto naturale e storia*, N. Pierri, Venice, 1957, which is not included in the bibliography below. Among the Italian reviews, see the one to the French translation of the first edition of the book *On Tyranny* by E. Giancotti in *Rassegna di Filosofia* (1954): 383. To my knowledge, the discussion alluded to by G. Sasso in *Giornale Critico della Filosofia Italiana* (1961): 51, n. 2, has not been published.

2. The essays are edited by J. Cropsey, with whom L. Strauss edited the anthology *History of Political Philosophy*, Chicago, 1963.

own country and to publish in his own language. Later, when he was an exile in England, he interpreted Hobbes (although his book was written in German, it could only be published in an English translation). From 1938 on, after he settled in the United States, first at the New School for Social Research in New York City and later (1949) at the Department of Political Science of the University of Chicago, he has interpreted a considerable number of difficult texts. He has returned repeatedly to his beloved Maimonides, for example, in the introduction to *The Guide of the Perplexed* translated by S. Pines. His work on Arab and Jewish thinkers, whom he studied in the original, includes the interpretation of *Kuzari* by Judas Levita and the *Philosophy of Plato* by Farabi. Among the moderns he has interpreted Machiavelli, Locke, and, once again, Hobbes. But in the past decades he has devoted himself to the study of the Greeks: Thucydides, Plato, Xenophon, Aristotle, and finally, not at all unexpectedly, Aristophanes.[3]

The most rigorous formulation of Leo Strauss's antihistoricism is found in his discussion of *The Idea of History* by R. G. Collingwood in the *Review of Metaphysics* 5 (1952): 559–86. As is generally known, in these posthumously published lectures, Collingwood claimed that every historical period is matched by a corresponding historical thought that is absolutely valid for that period of time. He also believed that every historic research is relative to the present time, that is, to something which, by definition, was foreign to the interests of men of the past. Strauss objects that there is no reason to question a thinker of the past unless his problems are our problems and unless we are ready to admit the possibility that, for example, Plato was right. This implies that we should subject our research, at least temporarily, to the research of thinkers from the past, who may be right. This subordination of our research to the thinkers from the past implies in turn that we should follow Plato in his way of thinking, accept, at least temporarily, the limits he gives himself, his way of presenting arguments. Thus, for Leo Strauss, the history of thought is an attempt to regain a level of thought that has been lost. A history of thought would not be necessary unless we had "good reasons for believing that we can learn something of the

3. Main works: *Die Religionskritik Spinozas*, Berlin, 1930, of which *Spinoza's Critique of Religion*, New York, 1965, is a second edition with a rather important new introduction; *Philosophie und Gesetz. Beiträge zum Verstandnis Maimunis und seiner Vorlaufer*, Berlin, 1935; *The Political Philosophy of Hobbes*, Oxford, 1936, reprinted Chicago, 1952; *Persecution and the Art of Writing*, Glencoe, 1952; *Natural Right and History*, Chicago, 1953; *Thoughts on Machiavelli*, Glencoe, 1958; *What Is Political Philosophy and Other Studies*, Glencoe, 1959; *On Tyranny, A Study of Xenophon's Hieron*, Glencoe, 1963; introduction to M. Maimonides, *The Guide of the Perplexed*, trans. S. Pines, Chicago, 1963; *The City and Man*, Chicago 1964; *Socrates and Aristophanes*, New York, 1966.

utmost importance from the thought of the past which we cannot learn from our contemporaries. History takes on philosophic significance for men living in an age of intellectual decline. Studying the thinkers of the past becomes essential for men living in an age of intellectual decline because it is the only practicable way in which they can recover a proper understanding of the fundamental problems."[4] It follows that interpreting Plato is different from criticizing Plato: to interpret Plato means to remain within the guidelines of Plato whereas to criticize Plato means to exceed those guidelines. To expect to judge the past from the point of view of the present means to presume that the present offers a better point of view than the past. The real thinker must keep open the possibility that he is living in an age that is inferior to the past: "one must be swayed by a sincere longing for the past."[5]

This attitude with respect to the past implies on the one hand a certain way of reading books from the past and also supports a certain consideration of the classics of the past. As to how we should read books from the past, two principles emerge from Strauss's books. One is that in order to understand a writer one must follow him, not guide him, trying to bear in mind all of the meanders and apparent contradictions of his thought. For Strauss, the possible danger lies in the fact that a reader might superimpose his own notions of the past onto the past even before he discovers what the ancients thought of a particular issue. Hence, Strauss's lengthy discussion of the book by E. A. Havelock, *The Liberal Temper in Greek Politics* (1957) in the *Review of Metaphysics* 12 (1959): 390–439. Strauss does not like liberals in the modern sense; thus he does not like the attempt (indeed a weak one) by Havelock to single out a liberal tradition in Greek thought. Strauss's indignation is directed against the modern interpreter who replaces the thought of the author he is interpreting with his own personal thought: "Havelock takes it for granted that the modern social scientist, but not Hesiod, understood what happened in Hesiod or to Hesiod."[6]

The second principle of Strauss's hermeneutics is that it is possible for a thinker consciously to leave something implicit, or to become entirely silent as to the most important point of his thought. The most common cases of a thought that intentionally has been expressed tacitly involve writers who find themselves in situations of censorship or persecution. Leo Strauss discusses such cases in a series of essays, *Persecution and the Art of Writing* (Glencoe, 1952). We cannot expect Spinoza

4. Review of R. G. Collingwood, *The Idea of History,* in *Review of Metaphysics* 5 (1952): 585.

5. Ibid., p. 576.

6. *Review of Metaphysics* 12 (1959): 404.

to tell us all that he thinks and only what he thinks in the *Tractatus Theologico-Politicus*. But for Strauss, the cases in which a writer may not tell us everything he thinks are many and varied: these include the cases where an author accepts the distinction between esoteric and exoteric thought. In fact it is difficult to shake off the impression that for Strauss all political and religious thought up to the eighteenth century is by its nature rooted in the distinction between esoteric and exoteric, and thus requires of the interpreter an effort of exegesis at two levels, one for the layman and one for the initiated. Hence the great care—and we should say the great amount of writing—that Strauss devotes to the interpretation of texts he believes possess these double layers.

In my opinion, Strauss's originality consists in having raised a question of principle and of having stuck with it in each of his interpretive essays. The question of principle is that the aristocratic notion of fundamental truths that "no decent person would say in public"[7] has been and continues to be accepted by too many people for it to be neglected when interpreting a text. As against a sociology of knowledge, Strauss notes that this notion developed in a period of relative freedom in Germany when it made sense to wonder if and to what extent a given philosophy expresses a given society. But more often, he adds, the issue is not whether a philosophy expresses a given society but whether a given society makes it possible for a given philosophy to express itself. In the past, philosophers were not the expression of a given society; they protected the interests of philosophy against or notwithstanding society. In the Jewish and Arab culture of the Middle Ages, philosophy was in an even more precarious state than in the contemporary Christian world: philosophy was not necessary for the interpretation of Hebrew or Muslim Law, whereas for the Christians it was the handmaid of theology. According to Strauss, the precarious position of philosophy among Jews and Muslims in the Middle Ages was similar to that of philosophy in Greek cities, where the philosopher disrupted public order instead of justifying it. This explains Strauss's special concern with the interpretation of medieval Arab and Jewish philosophers and of Greek philosophers, especially his constant return to the enigmatic philosopher Maimonides.

According to Strauss, the first problem with Maimonides is that, as a devoted believer in Judaism, he should have stayed away from philosophy, for it is an ancient Jewish premise that to be Jewish and to be a philosopher are two incompatible things.[8] Moreover, Maimonides is

7. *Persecution and the Art of Writing* p. 36. [Y. Belaval, *Critique*, 1953, pp. 852–66.]
8. *The Guide of the Perplexed*, p. liv.

not simply a philosopher: he is a philosopher who intends to give an esoteric interpretation of a book, the Bible, which he holds to be esoteric. Finally, Maimonides does not exclude the layman from his book. Indeed, he organizes his interpretation of the Bible (especially the problems of the incorporeity of God and the creation of the world) in a way that satisfies the doubts of the layman and at the same time suggest questions for the competent or the initiated.[9]

According to Strauss, problems with the interpretation of Greek thinkers and poets are different but no less difficult. In Xenophon's *Hyeron* we have the illusion of finding a series of reasonable recommendations for a tyrant—let us say, for one of the Dionysiuses of Syracuse—written at a time when Socratic philosophers were known to woo tyrants. But with careful reading, a problem arises. Gerone is represented as a tyrant despite himself, aware only of the disadvantages of being a tyrant. But given that he remains a tyrant, the representation of Gerone cannot be considered entirely sincere, or at least simple. On the other hand, Simonides, who encourages Gerone to seek popularity by becoming a virtuous tyrant, is placed in the ambiguous position of a wise man who gives advice to someone who could punish him if the advice were not welcome. The situation presented by Xenophon is such that neither the tyrant nor the wise man can be entirely sincere. A wise man who advises a tyrant is ipso facto caught up in a false situation.

With the more recent book *Socrates and Aristophanes* (New York, 1966), the exegesis of Strauss's Socratic thought tends to become highly complex. The obvious intention of the book is to establish what Aristophanes thought of Socrates and whether Aristophanes' representation of Socrates deserves credit as against the Platonic interpretation: these are old issues. But Strauss is gradually convinced that Aristophanes and Plato come quite close to each other, that they think in a similar way, although they interpret Socrates differently. Aristophanes' Socrates is different from Plato's Socrates primarily in that he is nonpolitical Socrates. But unlike Nietzsche (always present in Leo Strauss), it would appear that Aristophanes' caricature of Socrates, instead of dealing a blow to the entire Socratic tradition, indeed reaffirms the interpretation of political life as we find it in Plato. Aristophanes is a utopian; his representation of the best political order is comical because he realizes that utopia is at the limit of impossibility and thus is an object of laughter. But Plato, too, is a utopian; indeed, as we shall see,

9. Ibid.

according to Strauss, all classical thought represents a noble attempt to come close to this impossibility. And because Plato is aware of the utopian character of his thought, he smiles at himself and indulges in comedy, as the readers of his dialogues know.

In the book *Socrates and Aristophanes,* we do not find any reference to Strauss's previous book, *The City and Man* (Chicago, 1964), as being supplementary to the first. But in my opinion *The City and Man* seems indispensable for an understanding of Strauss's book on Aristophanes. In *The City and Man,* the affinity between Aristophanes and Plato, to the extent that they are both utopians, is even more explicit: "We may . . . say that the Socratic conversation and hence the Platonic dialogue is slightly more akin to comedy than to tragedy. . . . The Platonic dialogue brings to its completion what could be thought to have been completed by Aristophanes."[10] In another work, Strauss has also claimed that the classical philosopher "is driven to adopt a view that is no longer generally held, a truly paradoxical view, one that is generally considered 'absurd' or 'ridiculous.'"[11] And in his major work on natural law, Strauss has stated clearly that for classical thought the best regime is "utopia."[12]

## II

Thus, the hermeneutics of Leo Strauss are strictly connected with the trend of his political philosophy. For Strauss the esoteric nature of philosophy is not only a contingent characteristic of classical thought that is to be kept in mind in the act of interpreting a text; it is the mark of superiority of classical thought with respect to the modern. It is possible that Strauss claims for himself the right to be esoteric, at least to the extent that a follower of classical thought is expected to be esoteric; and thus he reserves for himself the right to make life difficult for his interpreters, just as Maimonides made life difficult for him.

The connection between a hermeneutics of reticence and antihistoricism is stated by Strauss himself in an important discussion with G. H. Sabine, reproduced in *What Is Political Philosophy and Other Studies,* p. 221. The essential reason for this connection is the one we have already mentioned concerning the sociology of knowledge, which for Strauss is only a manifestation of historicism. Almost all of the great thinkers of the past, far from accepting more or less consciously the po-

10. *The City and Man,* pp. 61–62.   11. *What Is Political Philosophy,* p. 91.
12. *Natural Right and History,* p. 139.

litical or religious presuppositions of their time, were opposed to them—and either for reasons of caution or of method they expressed their opposition in cautious terms.

But the connection between Strauss's hermeneutics and his anti-historicism is evident from another point of view as well. In this case the connection does not appear to have been stated by Strauss himself, but it is implied in his concept of utopia. Strauss claims the superiority of classical political thought over the modern (which begins with Machiavelli) because classical thought originates from the notion of the nobility of human nature to which action must try to conform itself; in other words, the classical philosopher asks himself, "what is virtue?" But this does not mean that the classical philosopher expects to provide a sure or probable way of achieving virtue and consequently the good society. The classical philosopher acknowledges that, given the limited power of man, the achievement of the best society depends on chance. Thus, as we have seen, "the classical solution is utopian in the sense that its actualization is impossible."[13] In another context Strauss appears to claim that its achievement is indeed impossible: "Socrates makes clear in the *Republic* of what character the city would have to be in order to satisfy the highest need of man. By letting us see that the city constructed in accordance with this requirement is not possible, he lets us see the essential limits, the nature, of the city."[14] Thucydides is the counterpart of Plato for the very reason that by showing the omni-presence of war in the real city, he reaffirms the utopian character of the city built by the philosophers.[15] No classical philosopher explicitly acknowledges the intrinsic improbability of his discourse; no ancient philosopher explicitly acknowledges that the extent of Plato's feasability lies in the truth described by Thucydides. Hence, we can conclude that reticence is intrinsic to the classical point of view because the classical point of view is utopistic.

It is not my intention to dwell upon the details of the antihistoricist thought of L. Strauss, which is well known.[16] But we should be re-

13. *On Tyranny*, p. 225. For a different interpretation, see G. Lichtheim, *The Concept of Ideology and Other Essays*, New York, 1967, pp. 159–65.
14. *The City and Man*, p. 138.
15. Ibid., p. 239.
16. Two recent reaffirmations: *Relativism and the Study of Man*, ed. H. Schoeck and J. W. Wiggins, Princeton, 1961, pp. 135–57, where L. Strauss criticizes I. Berlin; *The Predicament of Modern Politics*, ed. H. J. Spaeth, Detroit, 1964, pp. 41–54 and 91–103, where we find interesting contacts between L. Strauss and American scholars of St. Thomas Aquinas.

minded that for Strauss the understanding of natural law implies the question *quid sit deus*, which is the open question at the end of *The City and Man*. Hence, according to Strauss, it is only natural that Machiavelli should break the classical tradition by proposing an antireligious code of action: "The only element of Christianity which Machiavelli took over was the idea of propaganda. This idea is the only link between his thought and Christianity. He attempted to destroy Christianity by the same means by which Christianity was originally established."[17] According to Strauss, Spinoza and Hobbes are also atheists. The question *quid sit deus* cannot be conceived by Strauss in generic terms. Between 1925 and 1932, while a member of the Akademie für die Wissenschaft des Judentums in Berlin, Strauss worked on his books on Spinoza and Maimonides as well as on his contributions to the edition of M. Mendelssohn. Strauss belongs to that movement of rebirth of Jewish philosophical and historical thought in Germany, a movement headed with different approaches by M. Lazarus and H. Cohen respectively, which led, among other things, to the foundation of the Academy for the Science of Judaism.

The story of this rebirth in Germany is short-lived because Hitler put an end to it in 1933. Franz Rosenzweig, the major German-Jewish thinker from this period, the author of *Der Stern der Erlösung* (1921), was already dead by 1929; Strauss's book on Spinoza is dedicated to him. Others, such as G. Scholem, the great scholar of medieval mysticism, Y. Baer, the historian of Jewish Spain, and M. Buber, the discoverer of Hasidism, emigrated to Palestine before or after Hitler and made up the small group of founders of the Hebrew University of Jerusalem. Rabbi L. Baeck, who remained in Germany and acted as counsellor and guide, was in a concentration camp during World War II. Others still, like E. Täubler, the historian of antiquity, and L. Strauss ended up in America. Some of these thinkers, above all Franz Rosenzweig, had a marked interest in Hegelianism. K. Löwith, however, has been able to show that Rosenzweig and Heidegger have points in common.[18] Rosenzweig's interest in medieval Jewish thought mostly had to do with the translation and commentary of the poet Judas Levita (1927). The basis for a specific preference for medieval Jewish Aristotelianism had already been set by H. Cohen; it is also strongly present in *Philoso-phie des Judentums* by J. Guttmann (1933), later a professor at the Univer-

17. *What Is Political Philosophy*, p. 45.
18. Now in *Gesammelte Abhandlungen*, Stuttgart, 1960, pp. 68–92. See B. Casper in *Philosoph. Jahrb.* 74 (1967): 310–39. Rosenzweig's influence on E. Levinas is well known.

sity of Jerusalem.[19] But, unless I am mistaken, it was L. Strauss in his book on Maimonides, especially in a chapter containing an important discussion of the interpretation of J. Guttmann, who emphasized that medieval Arab and Jewish philosophy is sui generis because it is based on a law revealed by the prophets that must be comprehended by philosophers. The difference between Maimonides and Plato is that Maimonides does not expect a future philosopher-king; he already has one from the past. In the recent introduction (1962) to the English translation of his 1930 book on Spinoza, Strauss has retraced the history of his agreement with the position of Maimonides as the expression of a theistic rationalism, and he has shown that, with Maimonides as his guide, he was departing from Rosenzweig's more mystical position, which was at the basis of the book he had then written on Spinoza.

Strauss's theism not only explains his antihistoricism in general; it also suggests how one should read his commentary to *Der Begriff des Politischen* by C. Schmitt.[20] It was inevitable that Strauss would sympathize with a thinker who was breaking away from the premises of liberalism. But Strauss ended his study with the sharp and, at the same time, tricky remark that one had to wait and see how Schmitt would have managed to interpret Hobbes over time. In the meantime, Strauss was already working on Hobbes in order to prove that Hobbes's view of human nature marked a complete breach with classical tradition, including Thucydides, to whom Hobbes owed a great deal. While for the classics (according to Strauss) natural law is a rule and an objective measure, independent of human will, which man must obey, for Hobbes natural law represents an ensemble of subjective rights that originate in the human will. The question Strauss was asking Schmitt implied that he was placing Schmitt in a tradition of thought with which Strauss disagreed. K. Löwith, in his famous study of Schmitt, which he published in 1935 under the pseudonym (inevitable under

19. It is, of course, impossible to provide here an introduction to this important movement of thought. The *Year Book* of the Leo Baeck Institute of London, which commenced publication in 1956, includes essays and important bibliography (for example, there are essays on F. Rosenzweig, J. Guttmann, and E. Täubler). N. N. Glatzer, a pupil of F. Rosenzweig and now a professor at Brandeis University, has dedicated to the master a biography followed by an anthology, *F. Rosenzweig: His Life and Thought*, New York, 1961. For many of these figures, see G. Scholem's critique in *Judaica*, Frankfurt am Main, 1963, and elsewhere. An essay by Y. Baer, who worked with Strauss at the Akademie für die Wissenschaft des Judentums, should be compared with Strauss's ideas: *Galut*, English trans., New York, 1947 (written around 1936?). Fundamental for contemporary German culture is now H. Liebeschütz, *Das Judentum im deutschen Geschichtsbild von Hegel bus Max Weber*, Tübingen, 1967.

20. In *Archiv für Sozialwissenschaft und Sozialpolitik* 67 (1932): 732–49.

the circumstances) H. Fiala, had already suggested Strauss's inter-pretation.[21]

In Strauss's more recent books, the theistic and more specifically Jew-ish premises that appear in his early books are less evident. This can be interpreted in many ways. It does not appear to me that Strauss, after his book on Maimonides, has changed his mind about anything; he has only made a greater use of reticence, which he increasingly has come to regard as the characteristic element of classical thought.[22] His theory of natural law is essentially an interpretation of theism as attainable through reason.

Strauss's hermeneutic principle—that there exist a greater number of philosophers than we think who practice reticence when writing—can, of course, also be accepted, or considered worthy of constant veri-fication, by those who do not necessarily relate it to the character of what Strauss calls classical political philosophy. It is also obvious to me that some of Strauss's most important studies—the one on Xenophon, on Thucydides, and, less persuasively, on Aristophanes, to limit our-selves to the ancients—do not depend so much on the principle of reti-cence as on the ability to comprehend and relate understatements, to appreciate the implicit, to become an attentive and perspicacious reader.

21. See K. Löwith, *Ges. Abhandlungen*, pp. 93–127, especially pp. 106 and 108. See also D. Cantimori in *Studi Germanici* (1935): 471–89. Strauss's essay on Schmitt is now trans-lated in the appendix to the English edition of his book on Spinoza (1965). Cantimori, who of course was very familiar with Löwith's study, does not appear to have read Strauss's work, where Schmitt's *Bewunderung der animalischen Kraft* (p. 744) by had been noted as far back as 1932. Strauss's interpretation of Hobbes is critiqued by C. A. Viano in *Rivista Critica di Storia della Filosofia* (1962): 355.

22. As far as I know, the last public statement of Leo Strauss's thought on Judeo-Christian relationships is in "Perspectives on the Good Society: A Jewish-Protestant Col-loquium," an article published in *Criterion*, a journal of the Divinity School of the Univer-sity of Chicago (Summer 1963): 2–9. It is typical of Strauss that in reaffirming his Judaism he should declare: "the most profound truth cannot be written and not even said." He also adds, "a secession from this world might again become necessary for Jews and even for Christians." In the even more recent Frank Cohen Public Lecture, "Jerusalem and Athens," or the City College of New York, 1967, the contrast between reason (Athens) and revelation (Jerusalem) seems extreme; and the implications are not clear to me.

It should be noted that the above bibliography of Strauss's works does not include his early contributions to the review *Der Jude*, edited by M. Buber. These contributions are essential for anyone wishing to reconstruct the genesis of Strauss's thought. We find here a long and important discussion of H. Cohen's interpretation of Spinoza (vol. 8, 1924, pp. 295–314) as well as a penetrating of study the Zionism of M. Nordau (vol. 7, 1923, pp. 657–60). In the same issue (pp. 489–93), a note by J. Guttmann clarifies the initial objectives of the Akademie für die Wissenschaft des Judentums, founded in 1919. Unless I am mistaken, Täubler was the first director.

But with the moral rectitude and dialectic ability of a thinker like Leo Strauss, one should not suggest distinctions—and here I cannot help remembering my memorable meetings with this fragile, proud man on the campus of the University of Chicago. Strauss has been able to uphold certain principles of Arab and Jewish medieval philosophy in the contemporary debate between historicism and sociology; he has developed (under the influence of traditional methods of Talmudic exegesis) an original hermeneutics of texts; finally, he has proceeded from medieval thought to classical thought, not with the intention of rediscovering the modernity of the classics but of drawing inspiration from their example in order to fight the moderns. "Modernity has progressed to the point where it has visibly become a problem."[23] It could almost be said that Strauss's problem was Maimonides' problem.

## In Memoriam: Leo Strauss (February 1977)

Leo Strauss died on October 18, 1973 at the age of seventy-four at St. John's College of Annapolis. He had been Distinguished Scholar-in-Residence there since 1969 and his influence as a scholar and teacher had long been preeminent; he also contributed to making this institution one of the most vital centers of American humanism. During the last years of his life, he had continued to interpret texts by Plato and Xenophon in order to understand the origins of classical political thought in the context of what he considered to be the central problem in human life: the relationship between wisdom and faith. *Xenophon's Socratic Discourse* (1970), *Xenophon's Socrates* (1972), and the posthumous *The Argument and the Action of Plato's Laws* (1973) are Strauss's main contributions from this period. We also must be add the collection of essays from 1968, *Liberalism: Ancient and Modern,* and the 1965 reprint of *Preface to Spinoza's Critique of Religion* (1962), which is increasingly considered a unique combination of autobiography, self-criticism, and philosophical testament. Here, more so than in the enigmatic text *Jerusalem and Athens* (1967), two equally legitimate stances are compared: the acceptance of the commandment of God, which in Judaism is expressed through obedience to the Torah, and the "Wisdom of the Greeks," whose principle is not the fear of God but wonder. Hence, "tertium non datur"? Logically speaking, "tertium non datur." Yet the

23. *What Is Political Philosophy,* 172. (See G. P. Grant in *Social Research* 31 [1964]: 45–72. Among the most recent writings of L. Strauss's "Notes on Maimonides' Book of Knowledge," in *Studies in Mysticism and Religion Presented to G. G. Scholem,* Jerusalem, 1967, pp. 269–83.)

secret position of the philosopher within Judaism (as the example of Maimonides demonstrates) is that of speaking of reason in the world of faith, of defending reason in the name of those who respect and understand faith but do not share it. In essence, this is the secret role that Leo Strauss, a disciple of Maimonides, had assigned himself. Born into an Orthodox family, Strauss had gradually ceased to frequent the synagogue. Nevertheless, he spoke as a Jewish philosopher and was well aware—in fact because he was well aware—of the fact that one is Jewish not out of a philosophical conviction but out of a humble acceptance of divine law. Although he was very familiar with Thomas Aquinas and with Christian and Muslin medieval philosophy in general, and thus could have discussed arguments related not only to Judaism but to Christianity and Islam as well, he refrained from doing so, in part out of a natural respect for the difference of other traditions of life and thought, but more so out of a primitive need to understand clearly the tradition of the fathers and the sense of their secular sacrifice. Few men have loved the faith of the fathers with so much austere love as Leo Strauss, who understood it but did not share it, the German Jew who was inspired by Max Weber, Heidegger, and Carl Schmitt, not to mention Kant and Hegel. Those who have known Leo Strauss can appreciate the truth to the Jewish formula for the dead: "his memory is a blessing."[24]

24. Following Strauss's death, a quantity of articles and memoirs have been published, some of which are mentioned by Emma Brossard in *The Academic Reviewer* (Fall–Winter 1974): 1–5. Particularly interesting is Ralph Lerner's article in *American Jewish Year Book* (1976): 91–97. But much remains to be said.

# 18

# Gershom Scholem's Autobiography

In September 1923 two young German Jews embarked together at Trieste on their way to settle in Palestine. One, Gerhard (Gershom) Scholem, born in 1897, was soon to become the greatest Jewish historian of our century. The other, Fritz (Shlomo Dov) Goitein, born in 1900, was perhaps slower in developing, from a conventional Arabist into a student of the Jewish-Arabic symbiosis of the Middle Ages and beyond. Yet the volumes of *A Mediterranean Society,* which Goitein started to publish in 1967, amount to a revolutionary picture founded upon new sources (mainly from the repository of documents of the old synagogue of Cairo) that bears comparison with Scholem's achievements.

Such was the beginning of the second science of Judaism, no longer in Germany, where the first *Wissenschaft des Judentums* had developed a century before, but in the land of the Fathers—yet still through the agency of Jews born and educated in Germany. The new *Wissenschaft,* like the old one, is characterized by the exploration of recondite texts with all the resources of a rigorous philological method. It has, however, disclosed aspects of Judaism overlooked by the old *Wissenschaft.* Scholem has recovered the gnostic and Kabbalistic trends of thought and action never absent from Judaism since the Hellenistic age. Goitein has changed our knowledge of the intricate economic and social relations between Arabs and Jews.

The comparison between Scholem and Goitein could be continued at length, for both similarities and differences. Scholem came from an assimilated Berlin family where Hebrew had been forgotten: he started as a mathematician and acquired either on his own or with the help of traditional Jewish scholars the mastery of languages and techniques of

Originally published in English in *The New York Review of Books,* 27, 20, 18 December 1980, pp. 37–39. Reprinted by permission of Giulio Einaudi editore s.p.a.

analysis that were necessary for his success. Goitein, the scion of a rabbinical family, apparently learned Hebrew in his Bavarian home and Arabic at the University of Frankfurt. Scholem has not overlooked Islam (how could he, as the biographer of a Messiah converted to Islam?), nor has Goitein overlooked Christianity. But Scholem remains the historian of the European Jews living within the boundaries of Christendom, while Goitein's special attention is reserved for the Yemenite Jews and for the contacts between Jews and Arabs through the ages, which gave the title to the most popular of his books (1955).

While we can only hope that Goitein will develop the short autobiographical sketch published as an introduction to *A Bibliography of the Writings of Professor Sh. D. Goitein* by R. Attal (Jerusalem, 1975), we can now actually read Professor Scholem's autobiography for the years from 1897 to 1925. The original German text, *Von Berlin nach Jerusalem*, published by Suhrkamp in 1977, has now been translated into English by Harry Zohn (*From Berlin to Jerusalem: Memories of My Youth*).

There is no nostalgia or forgiveness in this book. Now, as fifty years ago, Scholem is determined to speak out. Now, as then, he is primarily concerned with the Jewish assimilated society with which he broke violently—and he broke, first of all, with his father, a Berlin printer. Secondly, he reiterates, at every step, that there was no place for a Jew, qua Jew, in German society and culture when he decided to leave, though Hitler was still for him nonexistent. Scholem remains Scholem, not a nationalist, not even a religious Jew, but a man who is certain that the beginning of truth for a Jew is to admit his Jewishness, to learn Hebrew, and to draw the consequences—whatever they may be (which is the problem).

Yet in this book he returns from Jerusalem to Berlin, to the parental house and to the maternal language, the tone of which, in its specific Berlin variety, is still unmistakable today in whichever language Scholem chooses to speak. Scholem is a great writer in German. Emigration has saved him from the distortions of German vocabulary and syntax that Hitlerian racism and post-Hitlerian disorientation produced. The book is therefore untranslatable, in the precise sense in which Scholem declared Franz Rosenzweig's *Der Stern der Erlösung* ("The Star of Redemption") to be untranslatable, until the day when the text will require interpretation for those who are able to read the original.[1] It would be ungenerous to find fault with a translation that is competent and helpful, but was doomed to be insensitive. When Scholem says, "Die Tora wurde seit jeher in 53, in Schaltjahren 54 Ab-

1. See his letter in M. Buber, *Briefwechsel* 2:367–68.

schnitte geteilt" (p. 128), he cannot mean, "The Torah has *always* been divided in fifty-three sections—fifty-four in leap years" (p. 98). Professor Scholem can be expected to know that according to academic opinion the division of the Torah into sections does not go back to Moses our Master.

The book ends with Scholem's appointment to a lectureship in Jewish Mysticism at the Hebrew University of Jerusalem on the strength of the recommendation of Immanuel Löw, the author of a five-volume work on the *Flora der Juden,* who had found in Scholem's first book two excellent pages on the bisexuality of the palm tree in Kabbalistic literature. Scholem's concluding remark is pure Wilhelm Busch: "So kam Lenchen auf das Land." The translation substitutes: "Thus began my academic career."

If there is no nostalgia, there are tenderness and gentleness in this book, and a remarkable avoidance of the most acute controversies and crises in which the author was involved. The book is full of friends rather than enemies. Ambivalent feelings are given a positive twist, as in the case of Franz Rosenzweig, who, if he had lived longer, would have been the only scholar capable of challenging Scholem's interpretation of Judaism. Scholem's brief account of his relations with Rosenzweig is a good sample of his writing in this book:

> Every encounter with [Rosenzweig] furnished evidence that he was a man of genius (I regard the abolition of this category, which is popular today, as altogether foolish and the "reasons" adduced for it as valueless) and also that he had equally marked dictatorial inclinations.
>
> Our decisions took us in entirely different directions. He sought to reform (or perhaps I should say revolutionize) German Jewry from within. I, on the other hand, no longer had any hopes for the amalgam known as "Deutschjudentum," i.e., a Jewish community that considered itself German, and expected a renewal of Jewry only from its rebirth in Eretz Yisrael. Certainly we found each other of interest. Never before or since have I seen such an intense Jewish orientation as that displayed by this man, who was midway in age between Buber and me. What I did not know was that he regarded me as a nihilist. My second visit, which involved a long conversation one night about the very German Jewishness that I rejected, was the occasion for a complete break between us. I would never have broached this delicate topic, which stirred such emotions in us both, if I had known that Rosenzweig was then already in the first stages of his fatal disease, a lateral sclerosis. He had had an attack which had not yet been definitely

diagnosed, but I was told that he was on the mend, and the only thing left was a certain difficulty in speaking. Thus I had one of the stormiest and most irreparable arguments of my youth.

Scholem's father and Martin Buber (whose interpretation of Hasidism it was one of the life tasks of Scholem to repudiate) are not spared, but he has no harsh words for them. The book deliberately avoids entering into the details of the story of how Scholem freed himself from military service during World War I. Readers can turn to his interview with Muki Tsur, published some years ago, where he describes how, to avoid military service, "I put on an act without knowing what I was acting."[2]

Scholem also avoids any deeper probing into his relations with Walter Benjamin and his wife Dora. The fact that Scholem had previously written a book and many papers on his friendship with Benjamin would not have made it superfluous to say something more definite in his autobiographical account, if the tone of the book in general had allowed it.

The book as it is can give us some first impressions about the wealth of emotional and intellectual stimuli Scholem collected in Germany before going to Jerusalem for good. It is not, however, an account of his intellectual formation, and therefore it cannot help to define the presuppositions of his work which were to remain constant throughout the next sixty years or so.

There is no question that Scholem left Germany at the age of twenty-six as a mature man with a program, a method, and a system of references that remained fundamental to his future activity. He may not have known that himself when he left Germany. He says that he then intended to devote only a few years to the study of Jewish mysticism; he expected to earn his living by teaching mathematics. But it turned out that the method for the study of Jewish mysticism he had expounded in his first articles on the subject in Buber's journal *Der Jude* in 1920 and 1921[3] and in his dissertation of 1923 (a critical edition of the mysterious gnostic text *Bahir*)[4] would guide all his life work. More precisely, his concern with language in relation to mysticism, with analytical commentary in relation to sacred texts, and with *anomia*, or

2. In *On Jews and Judaism in Crisis*, Schocken, 1976.

3. *Der Jude* 5 (1920): 363–91; 6 (1921): 55–69 (see his letter to Buber in the latter's *Briefwechsel* 2:86–88).

4. In its published form (*Das Buch Bahir*, Leipzig, 1923), the dissertation contains only the German translation of the text and a commentary.

lawlessness, in relation to Torah, developed, in foreseeable directions, from these early studies.

Scholem tells us that he abandoned an earlier project, a dissertation on the linguistic theories of the Kabbalah, because he realized that he first had to bring Kabbalistic writings under philological control through critical texts and commentaries. What he did not do as a research student, however, he accomplished fifty years later in his essay on the name of God and the linguistic theory of the Kabbalah (included in *Judaica* 3 [1975]).

Scholem's book concludes with his appointment to a job in Jerusalem in 1925. He thus says nothing about the explorations he made in European libraries, especially during his momentous travels of 1927 (which was also the last time in which he had weeks of direct conversation with Benjamin; in 1938 it was only a question of days). In 1927 Benjamin was the first to be told about his discoveries in the manuscripts of the British Museum and of the Bodleian at Oxford about the antinomian trends of the theology of Sabbatai Zevi's followers. But he did all this with the tools of interpretation he had brought with him from Germany. Nothing indicates more clearly the continuity of his method and the gradual clarification of the issues than a comparison between his prodigiously precocious article on the Kabbalah in the German *Encyclopaedia Judaica*, vol. 10, written in 1931, and the article on the same subject about forty years later for the new *Encyclopaedia Judaica*, written in English and published in Jerusalem.

I doubt whether there is anyone now writing who can analyze Scholem's debt to German thought except Scholem himself. David Biale's recent *Gershom Scholem, Kabbalah and Counter-History*,[5] meritorious as it is in other respects, only confirms how remote most American Jews now are from nineteenth-century trends of German thought. For someone like myself, who in the late 1920s and early 1930s read German books and talked to German friends in Italy, it is less difficult to overhear in the prose of Scholem and Benjamin the echoes of those German Romantics—Hamann, Humboldt, and von Baader— who were coming back into fashion. We often heard the dictum "Religion is a vowel and History a consonant," which I later discovered to be a silly remark made in a letter by Rahel Varnhagen.

Not by chance, Rahel Varnhagen early caught the attention of Hannah Arendt for her mixture of Jewish guilt feelings and German metaphysical *"Sehnsucht."* Another Jewess, Eva Fiesel (neé Lehmann),

5. Harvard University Press, 1979.

the extraordinarily able Etruscan scholar, summarized such romantic tendencies in her book *Die Sprachphilosophie der deutschen Romantik* in 1927. Esotericism was in the air. Followers of Stefan George were multiplying among the younger generation of German Jews.

I was mildly amused when, in his by now famous review of the book by L. W. Schwartz on *Wolfson of Harvard* in the *TLS* of November 23, 1979, Scholem seemed to be surprised that Wolfson should boast to him of having delivered a little sermon for Harvard Chapel in which it was impossible to discover what, if any, religious belief he held. Was this so unprecedented in the circles in which Scholem moved in his youth? In his later American days, Leo Strauss, another great German Jew of the same generation, interpreted esoteric attitudes and double meanings as integral to the art of writing in an age of persecution. That persecution has something to do with esotericism is obvious; but the case of Leo Strauss himself—an addict of esotericism, if ever there was one, as those who have read the introduction to the English translation of his book on Spinoza (1965) must know—shows that persecution is not the whole of the matter.

Reticence, allusiveness, and ambiguity were characteristic of Walter Benjamin. Scholem for his part has excluded, even hunted down, any ambiguity or esotericism in the practice of scholarship, politics, or daily life. But he has fully endorsed esotericism as central to the ultimate objects of his life work. In "Towards an Understanding of the Messianic Idea" (1959), he wrote: "It is one of those enigmas of Jewish religious history that have not been solved by any of the many attempts at exploration just what the real reason is for this metamorphosis which makes knowledge of the Messianic End, where it oversteps the prophetic framework of the biblical text, into an exoteric form of knowledge." Even more uncompromisingly he wrote, in the "Ten Unhistorical Statements about Kabbalah" (never translated into English?): "The true language cannot be spoken."

Such comments, however, do no more than suggest that "spirit of the age" which an older reader can recognize in Scholem's writings. We are perhaps nearer to a real problem in the following observation. Scholem has always been an open, though respectful, opponent of the established German-Jewish science of Judaism, the influence of which went well beyond German Jews, as is evident in the work of Italian Jewish scholars from S. D. Luzzatto to Umberto Cassuto—the biblical scholar who was for a while a colleague of Scholem's in Jerusalem. What Scholem found wrong with this scientific approach is that it used categories of German romantic thought without realizing that their creators (Herder, Humboldt, Savigny, etc.) were laying the foundation of a German nationalism that was incompatible with any autonomous Jewish culture inside the German nation.

He also reproached the Jewish scholars of the previous generations for being apologists, that is, for expounding only those sides of Jewish life which the non-Jews were expected to like. Not only Kabbalah and Hasidism, but also the less decorous aspects of ghetto life were kept out of sight. Not unnaturally, Scholem has reserved his more negative judgments for the more recent offshoots of the old science: "Anyone who wants to become melancholy about the science of Judaism need only read the last twenty volumes of the *Jewish Quarterly Review*" (1959).

But one wonders whether Scholem's reaction against that science is not itself rooted in other aspects of German romantic thought that emphasized the magical and mystical potentialities of language and myth and indulged in negative dialectics. Nor were the German romantics unaware of the rough and sordid sides of life. The hypothesis that both the old science of Judaism and the new science of Jewish mysticism, which is identified with the very name of Scholem, reflect contrasting trends of German romantic thought—one decisively Protestant, the other nearer to Catholicism—may help to establish the point in Scholem's development where he turned his back on German thought and began to speak on behalf of a new Judaism.

Scholem has said more than once that if he had believed in metempsychosis he would have considered himself a reincarnation of Johannes Reuchlin, the Christian German humanist who in 1517 published *De arte cabalistica*, the main source of which Scholem himself discovered in the library of the Jewish Theological Seminary of New York in 1938. He has also constantly pointed out that his only predecessor in the study of the kabbalah to have lived in nineteenth-century Germany was the Catholic Joseph Franz Molitor. These are not casual remarks.

Yet there is indeed a point beyond which Scholem becomes unclassifiable according to any school or any category of German thought. That point is where his Zionist and his kabbalistic pursuits intersect. For Scholem the primary meaning of Zionism, so far as intellectual life is concerned, is to make it possible for the Jews to recover all their past history and consequently to call into question all the aspects of their heritage. It is this freedom of movement into the past of the Jewish people that characterizes for Scholem the movement into the future called Zionism.

This radical and total reckoning with the past is obviously far more dramatic and painful in relation to recent times than to the Middle

Ages. Scholem becomes correspondingly more drawn to value judgments when he turns his attention from the origins of the Kabbalah to Sabbatai Zevi, the Polish-Jewish adventurer Jacob Frank, and Hasidism, not to speak of his comments about the "German-Jewish dialogue which never took place." A book like *Ursprung und Anfänge der Kabbala* (1962) basically belongs to the history of ideas. Other books by contemporary German scholars—say Aloys Dempf's *Sacrum Imperium* (1927) or H. Grundmann's *Religiöse Bewegungen im Mittelalter* (1935)—can be compared with it in method, though not in depth of analysis. But all the researches leading to his great book on Sabbatai Zevi (published in English translation) are without any precedent in Germany.

There Scholem faces the entire destiny of modern Jews, and more particularly of himself. The sudden mad convergence of Kabbalistic speculations and messianic hopes in Sabbatai Zevi and his prophet Nathan of Gaza attracted vast numbers of educated Jews who were longing for liberation and a new start within the Jewish tradition itself. In what is perhaps one of his greatest essays, "Redemption through Sin" (1937), Scholem went so far as to argue that the movement which led to the collective conversion of Frank's followers to Catholicism in 1759 had its place within Judaism: "One can hardly deny that a great deal that is authentically Jewish was embodied in these paradoxical individuals, too, in their desire to start afresh and in their realization of the fact that negating the exile meant negating its religious and institutional forms as well as returning to the original fountainheads of the Jewish faith."

There are pages of Scholem's writing which give the impression that he recognized something of himself in the destructive and anomic personalities of Sabbatai Zevi and Jacob Frank and drew back from the abyss. As a collective phenomenon, Zionism has therefore become for Scholem the constructive answer to the purely negative conversions to Islam and to Catholicism of Zevi and Frank and many of their followers. Just because Zionism means to Scholem the opening of all the gates of the Jewish past, it is absurd to expect a specific religious message from him. Part of his case against Buber is that Buber misused scholarship in his religious message. The substantial correctness of Scholem's exegesis of Buber is confirmed by Buber's autobiographical fragments,[6] which show that his discovery of the "I-Thou" religion is independent of his interpretation of the Hasidic tradition.

Nor can I see any evolution in Scholem's thought. On the contrary, he seems to me remarkably constant in his intellectual attitudes, as he

6. *Begegnung*, 1960, pp. 36–38.

is in his political reactions to the daily problems of Israel. But it also seems to me that only as long as he tries to understand the Kabbalah is he justified in considering himself a reincarnation of Reuchlin. When the Kabbalists turn into apostates or illuminists or, finally, Zionists—and then gather in the streets to march into a promised land—no model and no tradition can serve Scholem. He is left on his own, the first Jewish historian able to take full cognizance of the new situation. It is indeed possible that his precocious development prevented him in later years from grasping the full implications of what the Nazis have done to the Jews. Who, after all, is sure even now of what these implications are—or will be?

Other limits of his historical thought, easier to define, are suggested by the symbolic departure from Germany in the company of Shlomo Goitein. For it was Goitein, the more traditionally minded Jew, who penetrated the complexities of social relations between Jews and Arabs and entered into the mentality of the Jews of the Islamic world who, as Scholem is the first to acknowledge, were far from the centre of Zionist attention. Even Fritz (Yitzhak) Baer, Scholem's colleague and friend, who has given us so much original research and thought on many fields of Jewish history, never went beyond the Jews of *Christian* Spain during the Middle Ages.

On the other hand, it is difficult to appreciate adequately all the patience that Scholem, who is not famous for patience, has put into understanding his own relation to Christian thought, and especially to modern Germany. This is inseparable from his effort to understand his friend Walter Benjamin, who in his attempt to preserve his links with Germany and German culture finally chose Marxism or what he believed to be Marxism. It is no consolation to anyone to recognize that by carrying on his dialogue with Scholem to the end (and we have just now been given by Scholem their correspondence of the years 1933–40) Walter Benjamin, that sad and noble victim of Nazism, contributed in ways he perhaps never suspected to securing for Israel and for the world one of the most remarkable historians of our century.

# 19

## Walter Benjamin

### I

As expected, the memory of W. Benjamin, the German-Jewish writer who committed suicide on the border between France and Spain on September 27, 1940, has been kept alive by two friends who represent his opposing (or complementary) interests. Since his early youth, Gershom Scholem has carried on a dialogue with Benjamin on Judaism that not even death has interrupted, while Theodor Wiesengrund Adorno has come relatively close to the Marxism Benjamin professed in the years preceding his death. This dichotomy is only approximate. Indeed these men, and more generally the generation of people who came to maturity in the decade after the first World War, possess an extraordinary talent for communication, tolerance, and curiosity, which the young people of today must have a hard time imagining; we have evidence of this in the most recent criticism on Benjamin.

Of the two books on Benjamin, one by Fuld and the other by Schiavoni, Schiavoni's is the best both for its insight and the information it provides. Fuld is familiar only with the German scene in the 1970s. From a personal note (p. 186), Fuld appears to be inclined to consider Benjamin a twin soul of the maladjusted individual from after the student revolt of 1968. But the problems Benjamin had to face were of a different nature. Schiavoni is familiar with Benjamin's Germany and with many other things. But Fuld's book is in partial agreement with Schiavoni's in questioning Scholem as a source of information. Fuld

---

Review of Walter Benjamin, *Moskauer Tagebuch*, with a preface by Gershom Scholem, Frankfurt am Main, 1980, 217 pp.; Walter Benjamin and Gershom Scholem, *Briefwechsel 1933–1940*, ed. G. Scholem, Frankfurt am Main, 1980, 328 pp.; Werner Fuld, *W. Benjamin zwischen den Stühlen. Eine Biographie*, Munich, 1979, 323 pp.; Giulio Schiavoni, *Walter Benjamin. Sopravvivere alla cultura*, Palermo, 1980, 345 pp.

charges Scholem and Adorno with incompleteness and censorship, thus with reticence in the publication of Benjamin's letters, whereas Schiavoni sees Scholem's interpretation of Benjamin as an attempt to eliminate the antinomic, demonic, and antibourgeois attitudes of his friend.

Scholem's publication of the integral text of Benjamin's travel journal to Moscow between December 1926 and February 1927, which the two critics still ignore, as well the publication as of the entire correspondence between Scholem and Benjamin from the fatal years 1933–40 (Scholem's letters to Benjamin had been confiscated by the Gestapo and were made available only in 1977) mitigates the scope of any criticism, which goes back to 1967, regarding previous publications. Those who are experienced in selecting contemporary documents for publication will be reluctant to make easy laments: we should remember what happened with Gramsci's texts.

In any case, the main problem with understanding Benjamin does not stem from the inevitable simplification his correspondent-antagonist friends carry out in the simple act of selecting what for them is most important in their dear friend. The difficulty lies, if I am not mistaken, in Benjamin's very culture, which was indeed a curious one. Both Benjamin's prevailing theology phase, ending more or less with his book on German baroque drama of 1928, and his later Marxist phase are characterized by a lack of access to the primary sources of his thought. Benjamin's knowledge of Judaism, especially of Jewish mysticism, is derived from *Der Stern der Erlösung* by F. Rosenzweig (1921) and from what Scholem would communicate to him through letters and conversations. In 1932 Benjamin had access to Scholem's article "Kabbalah" in the *Encyclopaedia Judaica*, but a later discussion between the two men on the subject of Kafka, now published in the correspondance from 1934–38, reveals the fact that Benjamin's knowledge of Kafka was dependent on Scholem's letters. Benjamin's understanding of Catholic theology appears to be equally vague, and this is particularly evident since Benjamin was aware of Scholem's increasing interest in it. Benjamin's similar inexperience with classical Marxist texts, with the exception of a study of Marx's analysis of the nineteenth-century French predicament, which was essential for Benjamin's study during those years, indicates that his difficulties with these texts were not just linguistic. This second point calls for someone who has greater familiarity than myself with Benjamin's critical methodology; but if we can ascribe to linguistic difficulties Benjamin's lack of curiosity for the thought of Lenin and Trotsky during his brief stay in Russia, there is no indication of his having conducted a serious study of these thinkers in a translation, nor is there any evidence that he read Marx or Engels in the period 1928–38. Benjamin was, of course, familiar with Ernst Bloch and G. Lukács, who, as Scholem realized, did not replace the authentic coin.

Benjamin's limited knowledge of the sources of his judgments is matched by a somewhat limited confidence in their validity. Neither Marxism nor Judaism convinced him entirely. This was the source of Brecht's hesitation toward Benjamin and of Benjamin's inability to collaborate effectively with Adorno, who was much more understanding. The strength of Benjamin's friendship with Scholem was due, in essence, to the fact that Scholem, in the long run, was ready to take from Benjamin what he was able to give without asking for more. Although Scholem considered Benjamin a new "Rashi"—that is, a modern equivalent of the classical medieval Jewish commentator—he also realized that Benjamin would never produce a great commentary. Benjamin himself described Kafka (and thus himself) to Scholem as the commentator of a truth lost and no longer recoverable (letter from Paris dated June 12, 1938): "he has renounced truth in order to stick to what is transmissible, the *haggadic* element." Benjamin embodies the sadness of the critic who no longer has faith in the intellectual tradition upon which he is commenting. A comparison comes quickly to mind between Benjamin and Attilio Momigliano, a much less original critic, but equal to Benjamin in his honesty and subtlety as one who experienced a similar situation. Attilio lived and survived in the name of poetry, because he had not lost his faith in the Italian literary tradition to which he had devoted his life.

## II

Neither baroque drama, which Benjamin considered the expression of a revolt within the Christian tradition (just as more or less in those same years Scholem was describing the messianism of Sabbatai Zevi as a rebellion within the seventeenth-century Jewish tradition), nor Baudelaire's antibourgeois tradition were able to represent a focus for his personality. There remained his experience with esoteric manipulation in the romantic thinkers, which he had explored as a young man together with Scholem. Scholem later developed a systematic study of the function of language in Kabbalistic thought (a study that progressed until around 1970) and was able to establish a relationship with non-German Jewish scholars of the Kabbalah, such as Reuchlin and Molitor. Thus, Scholem had maintained a direct tie with German thought, and this tie was just as clear and resolute—as I have stated elsewhere—as was his rejection of any compromise concerning the position Jews had accepted (or rather, had been subject to) in Germany. Benjamin's reaction, however, was such that he ended up feeling paralyzed by an excess of insight. In *Berliner Kindheit* and *Einbahnstrasse*, he finally was able to express himself, but this did not provide him with a sense of direction. Communism, more so that Marxism, came to represent the only authentic hope (letter to Scholem dated May 6, 1934). But there is no indication that Benjamin knew what communism was or could be, if only in art. It now has become evident that even his essay "The Work of Art in the Age of Mechanical Reproduction" (1936) is a perfect sociological analysis of an unresolved political ambiguity.

Benjamin had originally meant to explore in an independent study of German culture his personal raison d'être as a Jew within Germany. Indeed, because he was Jewish, he quickly came to play the role of the persecuted and the uprooted. He was, of course, aware that he was involved in a catastrophe that was specifically Jewish, and that the surrounding world, although sometimes sympathetic, did not consider this issue its own affair. Benjamin's awareness of this problem is evident from the dedication to his sister Dora of the anthology *Deutsche Menschen*, which he had published under a pseudonym in 1936. It is quoted by Fuld (p. 144): "Diese nach jüdischem Vorbild erbaute Arche für Dora" ("For Dora, an ark built after a Jewish model"). However, like many other emigrants, Benjamin considered his fate as a personal issue, where the foregoing of stability and the preparation for death by suicide guaranteed daily freedom—until the time of death. Like the Messiah in the tradition of rabbinic Judaism, the revolution was something to be awaited and predicted but without any serious expectation that it would materialize. It goes without saying that Scholem, urgently involved in building a university and a Jewish society in Palestine, did not share this point of view. All but hostile in principle to anomic experiences, Scholem feared, however, that his friend would be caught up in a void. But it is especially noteworthy that the friendship between the two men should remain necessary and creative, not only for the implicit millenarian experience of belonging to the persecuted people, but for the explicit common intellectual exploration of which Kafka was both the object and the symbol.

# 20

## Moses Finley on Slavery:
## A Personal Note

### I

In *Aspects of Antiquity* (1968; Pelican reprint 1972) Moses Finley included the essay "Aulos Kapreilios Timotheos, Slave Trader." It is the
least polemical of Finley's essays on slavery: it is almost a soliloquy in
front of a puzzling ghost from the remote past, the ghost of the ex-slave
who had become a proud slave trader. The basic elements of the picture
of ancient slavery given in this paper had already been anticipated or
accompanied by the 1958 paper "Was Greek Civilization Based on Slave
Labour?" now in the collection *Slavery and Classical Antiquity* (1960; 2d
ed. 1968) and by other papers now included in *Economy and Society in
Ancient Greece* (ed. B. D. Shaw and R. P. Saller, 1981) where "Was Greek
Civilization Based on Slave Labour?" is also reprinted. The same elements were later developed and systematized in what is perhaps the
most influential and discussed book by Finley, *Ancient Slavery and Modern Ideology* (1980). What makes the paper on Kapreilios Timotheos so
poignant is Finley's look at the lonely man who at Amphipolis in the
first century A.D. had declared (or had been made to declare by his heir)
on his own tombstone that he was a slave trader. "Nothing like it exists
on any other surviving Greek or Roman tombstone though by now
their number must be a hundred thousand or more" (2d ed., p. 154).
"The peculiar institution," as Moses Finley knew only too well, was not
"peculiar" in antiquity in the sense in which it became so in the United
States at the time when most of the civilized world had abolished it and
did not like it. It was "peculiar" precisely because it was normal, but of
a normality that could seldom be rationally justified wholeheartedly:
indeed in the Roman Empire it was increasingly recognized as contrary
to nature.

Originally published in English in *Classical Slavery*, ed. M. I. Finley, London, Cass,
1987, pp. 1–6. Reprinted by permission of Giulio Einaudi editore s.p.a.

Finley's interest in slavery was always a strong component of his interest in the ancient world: it had been fostered both by his teachers at Columbia and by his collaboration with the Frankfurt School in its New York version of Institute of Social Research. He himself reminds us in *Ancient Slavery*, p. 55, that he reviewed the article "Sklaverei" in *P.-W.* (1935) by his teacher W. L. Westermann in *Zeitschr. f. Sozialforschung* 5 (1936): 441—and it was a dissenting review. But there is perhaps a more personal experience behind this fundamental interest in slavery, and it may help to explain both Finley's intensity of research into the subject and the limitations of the research itself.

Finley, the scion of generations of eminent rabbis (some going back to Italy in the sixteenth century) had himself received a Jewish education sufficient to make his admission to the Jewish Theological Seminary of New York conceivable. He knew of course from his childhood the admonition of Deuteronomy 15:15: "And thou shalt remember that thou wast a bondman in the land of Egypt, and the Lord thy God redeemed thee." He knew of course also the echo of Deuteronomy in the Passover Haggadah, which every Jewish boy learns by heart: "We were Pharaoh's slaves in Egypt, and the Lord our God brought us forth from there." The Passover ritual is basically a ritual of liberation from slavery. It makes any Jew conscious of having known slavery. Yet there is no indication in Finley's adult writing that he reflected on this ancestral experience. More remarkably, unless I missed something in his books, there is no sign that he was prepared to use the vast amount of evidence in the Talmud about the Jewish theory and practice of slavery in Greek and Roman times. Nor did he seem to reflect on the paradoxical destiny that turned the Jews into slave traders in the Middle Ages (and again, to a more limited extent, on the American continent). The elimination of the Jewish side of the story—with a few exceptions for biblical evidence, for instance, in *Economy and Society in Ancient Greece*, pp. 162–63—inevitably brought with it a diminished interest on the Christian side. The question of whether and how Christianity contributed to the elimination (or the preservation) of slavery could not of course, be entirely absent from Finley's horizon. But how the fundamental distinction in Jewish Law between Jewish and non-Jewish slaves contributed (if it contributed) to the shaping of the Christian attitude toward slavery never seems to have been discussed, at least to my knowledge, by Finley. I looked in vain for his interpretation in its precise multiple context of Paul's 1 Corinth. 7:21–23,[1] just as I looked in

---

1. It may not be superfluous to refer to S. Scott Bartchy, *First-Century Slavery and 1 Corinthians 7:21*, Montana, 1973 (diss. Harvard, 1971).

vain for an evaluation of the position of slaves in Christian monasticism.[2] When Moses Finkelstein changed his name into Moses Finley, a whole set of questions was almost entirely removed from the public side of his thinking. There are still some signs of the violence of this decision. It will be enough to remind ourselves of the conclusion of his exceptional and brief excursion into Jewish territory in *Aspects of Antiquity* (ed. 1972), pp. 183–84 (from an essay of 1965): "Collective Jewish wickedness permeates the whole of Western culture. Are we to undertake a great campaign of elimination, beginning, say, with Bach's *Passion according to St John*, the words and music together? The dead past never buries the dead. The world will have to be changed, not the past." Even the anecdotic side of the Jewish slaves—for instance the clear hint in Philo, *Legatio ad Gaium* 23.155, that a Jewish slave, with his dietary and ritual oddities, produced problems for his owner—does not remain within Finley's horizon, careful as he was to pick up significant anecdotes. More generally, this attitude probably explains his scanty interest in the part of the slaves in the intellectual and religious life of classical antiquity altogether.

The passion, the acumen, and the realism of Finley were therefore concentrated on the clarification of the situation of the slaves within the different societies of the classical world. He had been familiar with Marx from his very beginnings—well before the *Grundrisse* gave new food for Marxist thought on slavery. But he was never a Marxist in any ordinary sense. His concentration on precapitalistic societies rather than on capitalism was not simply a question of historical specialization. Finley always felt that ancient history derived its relevance from the possibility of direct confrontation with the modern world (both in its intellectual and in its political problems), not necessarily always to the advantage of the modern world. He did not feel the need of going through the Middle Ages, which is one of the signs of the good Marxist. The evolution of forms of production concerned him less and less. He felt for himself and for his peers a natural affinity with the Greeks and more precisely with the democratic Greeks. The book *Democracy Ancient and Modern* (1973; 2d ed. 1985) speaks clearly enough on this. It is more difficult to say what the Romans, and particularly the post-Augustan Roman Empire, meant to Finley. It seems to me that he vaguely perceived the Roman Empire to be an anticipation of the United States of America. It did not have the techniques of production

2. See some remarks of mine on Macrina's monastery in *Essays in Honor of Chester G. Starr*, New York and London, 1985, pp. 454–55, and E. A. Clark, *The Life of Melania the Younger*, New York and Toronto, 1984, pp. 100–102.

of its modern equivalent, but it had analogous problems in maintaining unity and prosperity, notwithstanding regional differences and class boundaries. Whenever Finley passed from Greece to Rome his interest in politics decreased, and his attention to social and juridical peculiarities correspondingly increased. His very good training in Roman law helped him in the transition.[3] This, I think, is true even of Finley's book *Politics in the Ancient World* (1983), where he tried to compare Republican Rome with democratic Athens, but failed to take into account the confederate structure of the former. Applied to the problem of slavery, this difference between Greece and Rome meant that in Greece Finley examined above all the relations between servile conditions and political life, whereas in the Roman Empire he observed social stratification as such with little curiosity for the politics of the Romans rulers. It is characteristic that he devoted much attention to Roman farming as such and encouraged work on it: *Studies in Roman Property*, which he edited, goes back to 1976.

## II

The climate of opinion of the late 1950s and early 1960s in which Finley began to exercise his influence in Europe was one of conflict between "orthodox" Marxist historians, who wanted to get to the bottom of the forms of exploitation, and their opponents (mainly West German), who tended to play down the importance of slavery in the classical world or alternatively to emphasize the humanitarian and religious elements that mitigated the evils of slavery and ultimately contributed to its dissolution. We were both present at the 1960 International Historical Congress in Stockholm where the conflict erupted. We learned more about modern Europe than about ancient Greece or Rome. After that, Finley's work gained immediate respect and contributed to changing the atmosphere into one of reasoned disagreement. His superior knowledge both of ancient evidence and of modern literature no doubt played its part, but I would not attribute his success to these factors. In fact it seems to me that the extraordinary command of the literature on slavery in *Ancient Slavery and Modern Ideology* is functional only to a small degree, and even when it is functional it does not add much to the argument. In particular the attack on Eduard Meyer's "nonsense" about slavery misses the point that as early as 1898 Meyer had tried to solve the same problem which Finley put to himself in his book

3. Finley's review of F. Schulz, *Principles of Roman Law*, in *Zeitschr. f. Sozialforschung* 6 (1937): 685, is an early indication.

of 1980: why the creation of city-states, with their free peasants and artisans, had the consequence of persuading the employers of labor to turn to chattel slaves for their activities. Meyer obviously had ideas about ancient industry and proletariat that nobody would repeat eighty years later, but the problem stands. As already implied, the two really important disagreements of Finley were those with Karl Marx himself and with the anti-Marxist "humanitarians" of 1960. As far as I can see, there was not much resistance or counterattack by the humanitarians. Their often very valuable collections of evidence were duly used and appreciated by Finley himself and his pupils in various countries. The opposition by orthodox Marxists was and remains much stronger: witness, for instance, in England G. E. M. de Ste. Croix, in Italy V. Di Benedetto and A. Carandini, and in France the whole school of Besançon (though no doubt qualifications should be introduced about the various members of the last group). It is more difficult to know what the Russian Marxists at present think of Finley—the more so because what they write may not coincide with what they think. With older Russian Marxists, such as E. Štaerman, the possibility of dialogue had never ceased (see *Ancient Slavery*, pp. 135–36).

If one looks at the collective enterprises which can be said to have been inspired by Finley, such as the Italian volumes of 1981, *Società romana e produzione schiavistica*, and at the direct discussions of Finley's work published in *Opus* and *Dialogues d'histoire ancienne*, one is led to believe that at least in the near future the debate will continue on the lines indicated by Finley.[4] He seems to have persuaded fellow scholars to examine the function of slavery within given times and places rather than the contradictions that made slavery (or any other form of production) unstable. What most of the researchers are now trying to do is to describe the situation of the slaves within individual societies and to understand how it was possible to separate slaves from free men. This in turn implies understanding degrees and varieties of freedom, not only degrees and varieties of slavery. While I would not claim that research on language—such as that exemplified by M.-M. Mactoux, *Douleia. Esclavage et pratiques discursives dans l'Athènes classique* (1980)—has made a great contribution to the clarification demanded by Finley, it is significant, however, that such a type of analysis, minutely describing verbal characterization of attitudes to slavery, should flourish in a Finley climate. More importantly, Finley has demanded, and has al-

---

4. As early as 1979 this was already the opinion of L. Sichirollo in the introduction to his important collection of essays *Schiavitù antica e moderna*, with a useful bibliography (Naples, Guida).

ready obtained, the reassessment of specific categories of dependents, such as the *coloni*. Here again one may well disagree with the whole argument proposed in *Opus* 1–2 (1982–83) by J. M. Carrié on the colonate (which partly develops the Köln dissertation by D. Eibach, *Untersuchungen zum spätantiken Kolonat*, 1977). But the revision of the colonate has become central to the understanding of late antiquity (and is pursued in the present volume by C. R. Whittaker). It is in this atmosphere that the discussion on the characteristic features of the villa will continue. It can also be easily predicted that what E. Gabba and his collaborators are establishing about "transumanza" and other forms of land exploitation in central and southern Italy will be increasingly taken into consideration by the students of slavery. Gabba's paper in *Ktema* 2 (1977), "Considerazioni sulla decadenza della piccola proprietà contadina nell'Italia centro-meridionale del II sec. a. C.," can now be greeted as seminal for any research on Italian slavery under Roman rule.[5] Outside the limits Finley traced for himself, there is a need for reassessing the position of slaves and slavery in ancient religions, and more generally in ancient intellectual trends.[6]

A more extensive and variegated exploration of societies largely dependent on slaves will inevitably lead to a new demand for explanation of change—either from societies without slavery to societies with some distinctive type of slavery and vice versa, or from societies with distinctive types of slavery to societies with other distinctive types of slavery. Finley, because of his increasing distrust of the Marxist categories, had become reluctant to enter into questions of change: he liked analysis of situations rather than explanation of change. But, as changes do happen, it is desirable that they should be explained. The Marxists have here their real chance, which is to see what, if anything, survives of the Marxist analysis of the modes of production within a post-Finley phenomenology of slavery.

5. A. Giardina's introduction to the reprint of G. Salvioli, *Il Capitalismo antico* (Bari: Laterza, 1985) gives information on the Italian research since E. Ciccotti and Salvioli.

6. Hints in this direction in a review of B. Farrington, M. P. Nilsson, and H. W. Parke (*Delphic Oracle*) in *Zeitschr. f. Sozialforschung* 9 (1941): 502–10 (still signed M. I. Finkelstein) were not developed later, to my knowledge. It is worth mentioning that this periodical also contains reviews by Mary Finkelstein in 8 (1939–40) 250–51. For Moses Finley's latest views on Greek religion, see his foreword to the Cambridge *Greek Religion and Society* of 1985.

# 21

## Gertrud Bing (1892–1964)

"Emeritus Professor" Gertrud Bing, vice-director (c. 1929–55) and later director (1955–59) of the Warburg Institute (which in the early years in Hamburg was known as the Warburg Library), died in London at the age of seventy-two on July 3, 1964. She died, as we had hoped she would die, without having experienced old age. The mysterious illness that killed her in less than five weeks did not leave her the time to suffer. Thus Bing, the lady with the quick, somewhat heavy step, the firm, examining look, the smile expressing a mixture of affection and defiance, which were typical of her to the end, is no longer among us.

The void she has left in our generation will not be filled. Bing was the survivor of that which was jokingly called the second Warburg Trinity (Warburg, Saxl, and Bing; the first trinity is embodied in the seal of the institute: *Mundus-Annus-Homo*). In everyday life she was also an exceptional initiator and animator of new projects, a critic at once generous and formidable of ongoing projects, a friend who would have crossed the seven seas to bring help.

Bing's roots belonged to the Jewish trading bourgeoisie of Hamburg, where she was born. She graduated from the University of Hamburg with a thesis typical of her milieu: "Der Begriff des Notwendigen bei Lessing. Ein Beitrag zum geistesgeschichtlichen Problem Leibniz-Lessing." Only a typewritten excerpt of this thesis is preserved at the institute. It was but a short step from the school of Ernst Cassirer to the Warburg Library, where Bing was hired as assistant librarian in 1922. At that time Warburg was away from the institute due to mental illness, so Bing was appointed assistant librarian by F. Saxl, the man who was already in charge of the library. But in 1924, when Warburg returned to his position a healthy man, Bing became his most direct assistant. She accompanied Warburg on his trip to Italy in 1927 and later on a second trip, which lasted for almost a year from 1928 to 1929 and was followed within a short time by Warburg's death. No one knew Warburg as a man and scholar better than Bing. One of Warburg's oldest friends and pupils has claimed, "Als ich im Frühling 1939 Gertrud Bing zuletzt in London gesprochen habe, war es uns manchmal, als stünde Warburg selbst leibhaft neben uns"[1] (C. G. Heise, *Persönliche Erinnerungen an A. Warburg,* Hamburg, 1959, p. 12). Bing edited Warburg's writings that had already been published in an exemplary edition in 1932.[2] Later events at the institute made it impossible to publish but a small part of the unedited material. But the preparation of a biography of Warburg, on which Bing had been working for years, was based on a very close study of this unedited material. Unfortunately, this biography was never completed: a profile of Warburg, which Bing published in 1958 and which appeared in a new Italian version in *Rivista Storica Italiana* 72 (1960): 100–113, gives us a sample of what the complete work might have been like.

Although Bing was and liked to call herself the guardian of the tradition of the Warburg Institute, her importance in contemporary culture lies mostly in her cooperation with F. Saxl in extending the original scope of the institute's research and making it possible for the institute to be transferred to England and to thrive there. With Saxl, already married and a father, Bing soon became involved for life in a domestic and scientific collaboration that enjoyed the respect of all. With Saxl, Bing explored ever more diversified themes of research in addition to the current themes of the Warburg Institute. Bing's own articles are few: "A. F. Doni, Nugae circa Veritatem," *Journ. Warburg Inst.* 1 (1937): 304–12, and the essay "The Apocalypse Block-Books and Their Manuscript Models," *Journ. Warburg Inst.* 5 (1942): 142–58, which we can appreciate for its considerable technical virtuosity. But Saxl's research cannot be separated from Bing's collaboration. After Saxl's death in 1948, Bing collected and annotated Saxl's research papers; in one case she recomposed the lectures Saxl had left in manuscript form. Saxl's biography, which Bing wrote as an introduction to *F. Saxl Memorial Essays,* does not mention this collaboration but presupposes it in the very penetrating description she gives of Saxl's work.

Warburg, who combined the cosmopolitan tradition of the mercantile aristocracy of Hamburg with the religious inspiration of the enlightened Jew, had decided he would turn his home into an objective

1. [When I last spoke with G. B. in London, in the spring of 1939, at times we had the sensation that W. himself was next to us in flesh and blood.]

2. A selection of writings by A. Warburg, with a new introduction by Bing, will be published in an Italian translation by La Nuova Italia, Florence. Bing prepared the introduction shortly before her death.

research center for the coming together and exchange of pagan (which to him meant primitive) and Judeo-Christian ideas and emotions in the Western world. In his personal explorations, Warburg had become increasingly aware of the growth of anti-Semitism among the passions of Western man, but he had not given up the belief that from paganism to the Renaissance the process had been one of a growing control over the more obscure emotions: "per monstra ad sphaeram" (see E. Panofsky in *Das Johanneum* 3 [1929]: 248–51). On the one hand, Saxl and Bing were less involved in this exorcism of demons, which for Warburg had been a daily reality; on the other, they were less certain that this exorcism was in itself possible. Further, they had a less "primitive" notion of paganism than Warburg, and they soon came to attach a major role to research on Platonism with the institute's research program. Above all, they tended to adopt iconography as a method of research for the history of culture in general. Although something was undoubtedly lost of Warburg's depth of vision, the very great number of books published—as well as the entire journal of the Institute—testify to the fertility and variety of the research implemented by Saxl and Bing.

Warburg died before he was required to make final decisions to salvage the institute from Nazi destruction. Saxl, who was from Vienna where Hitler had grown up, was quick in grasping the consequences of the situation. He got help in order to transfer the institute unexpectedly to England, while Bing not only assumed the responsibility for the material transfer of the institute but also took care to recreate the patrician ethos of Hamburg in the predicament of London life. It was obvious to both Saxl and Bing that in London the institute should operate as a center to aid and organize those—Jews in the great majority—whom Nazis and Fascists had chased away from their homes and their land. Because of the hospitality and relative security they enjoyed in England, Saxl and Bing were able to develop a strong sense of solidarity with other persecuted people. From 1934 onward, the institute began to provide daily public and private charity for the refugees, which constitutes a title of honor for the institute. But Saxl and Bing believed that, in London, the institute should continue to be a center for the manifestation of German Jewish culture. Although it now has become a part of the University of London and of English culture, the Warburg Institute continues to this day to derive its ideas from Germany, Austria, Burckhardt's Switzerland, Warburg, E. Cassirer, and, in a broader sense, Usener, Nietzsche, Freud, and Riegl. There is one major point in which the institute has remained loyal to Warburg's original idea: within the institute, men and women of different religions and nationalities were expected to meet and cooperate, not by eliminating or repressing what is their own as individuals, but by creating a basis to share in a common experience. The liberalism of Saxl and Bing was so spontaneous and fresh as to appear innate.

Saxl's sudden and premature death in 1948, followed shortly thereafter by the tragic death of his friend and successor as head of the institute, the Dutch Jew H. Frankfort (1954), caused Bing to have to face heavy administrative duties. But she continued to review for publication practically everything that the institute was publishing, and she maintained an active interest in the purchase and the classification of books. Her trips to Italy with the librarian O. Kurz to organize an exchange of periodicals with Italian institutes have become famous. Even after her retirement, Bing did not cease her editorial activity; at the time of her death she was editing the new series of the *Oxford-Warburg Studies*.

Bing had become very fond of England and knew how to get around even in the most unsympathetic circles; she succeeded in establishing devoted friendships in English society. Just as Warburg had described himself as "a Jew by birth, an Hamburgian by heart, and a Florentine by soul," a similar trichotomy can be attributed to Bing. It was not difficult for Bing to reestablish contact with German culture after the war, although she did not forgive some of the people there. She had been back to Hamburg several times and had felt very emotional about it. When she was offered a German decoration, she pointed out that it was not in the tradition of the citizens of the free city of Hamburg to accept Prussian decorations. Her love and understanding of Italy were equal to those of Saxl and Warburg: she felt at home in Florence. But she also loved Switzerland, a crossroads of European culture. In the last years of her life she had discovered Spain and Greece. In her trips, which she avidly enjoyed, as well as in her daily work—which, after Saxl's death, was never without sadness—Bing continued to be a scrupulously informed scholar, attentive to details, interested in exploring the nature of European culture with a rational perspective and without prejudice. When she would shake her head disdainfully and say "why not?" a dry leaf of bigotry or vanity would fall to the ground somewhere.[3]

3. See the remembrances of D. Cantimori in *Itinerari* 79–80 (1964): 89–92. [A posthumous article by Bing on A. Warburg in *Journ. Warburg Courtauld Inst.* 28 (1965): 299–313, the "Memory of Fritz Saxl," is now translated in Fritz Saxl, *La storia delle immagini*, Bari, 1965, pp. 177–209.]

# 22

# In Memoriam—Eduard Fraenkel

If there ever was a *yeshiva bocher* among the children of Israel, it was Eduard Fraenkel (1888–1970). He had all the intellectual qualities that characterize the traditional student of the Talmud: exceptional memory, acumen in interpretation, logical rigor, endurance. He was humbly devoted to his masters and proud of what he had learned from them. He referred to them constantly. He never claimed to have gone beyond them and resented any criticism of them. "Bedust thyself with the dust of their feet and drink with thirst their words" was the quotation from the *Pirke Avot* he liked to repeat. It was perhaps the only saying of the Fathers he remembered or had ever known. For his education had not included Jewish studies, and his parents had kept him away from pious relatives. His teachers had been professors at German universities: Leo, Wilamowitz, Wackernagel, W. Schulze. Even when he had become an acknowledged master in his own right he never ceased seeking new teachers for himself. As a full professor he sat at the feet of Schiaparelli in Florence, of Lenel in Freiburg, of Beazley at Oxford, of Campana in Pisa. For students of lesser breed he had contempt. Comprehension of divergent points of view was not his way. He dismissed with a characteristic ancestral gesture what was not orthodox.

Of foreign countries he knew and loved Italy. Like all German Jews he felt a complex relationship of superiority, inferiority, and affinity with the land where simple people carry about themselves so much of their classical past. During his first visit to Rome he decided to abandon the study of law and to become a classical scholar. His first notable paper was an attempt to establish what Roman "*fides*" was. His first—and perhaps his greatest—masterpiece was his study of Plautus. He did not like to be asked whether the Italians are living characters from

Originally published in English in *Encounter* 36, 2 (February 1971): 55–56. Reprinted by permission of Giulio Einaudi editore s.p.a.

Plautus, or whether Plautus's characters were Italian. But without this implicit ambiguity *Plautinisches im Plautus* (1922) would not have been written.

Until the Nazis came to power Fraenkel had been unreservedly committed to German culture and German patriotism, as one would expect from a man of his generation and upbringing. On some occasions he had even been a chauvinist. In June 1915 he published a virulent attack against the Italians in a special number of the *Süddeutsche Monatschefte* (Eduard Meyer was another contributor). In *Gnomon* (1925) he bitterly rebuked the published Teubner for having produced an edition of Catullus by an American and then had to apologize for his attack. It was also a common illogicality of his generation and group that he combined strong patriotism with unbounded admiration for Goethe. Yet, unlike many other German Jews, he did not accept the tenet that a formal abjuration of Judaism was a sign of allegiance to Germany. About 1912 Friedrich Leo—himself a baptized Jew—warned him that without baptism he would never get a chair in Germany. Fraenkel used to say that he had replied with a German equivalent of "out of the question." By taking the *Staatsexamen* he prepared himself for the eventuality of having to teach in a secondary school.

The Weimar Republic made the precaution unnecessary. Jews gained access to university chairs without undue difficulties. In the 1920s Fraenkel undoubtedly felt himself rather secure in German society— perhaps a new sensation. His marriage to Ruth von Velsen, a pupil of W. Schulze and a friend of the Wilamowitzes, must have consolidated these feelings. Ulrich Wilamowitz extended to Eduard the fatherly affection he had for Ruth, who had been close to his son Tycho before he was killed in the war—and of course he appreciated in full Fraenkel's scholarly abilities. Fraenkel for his part declared that his mother and Wilamowitz had been the greatest influences in his life.

Fraenkel's books and papers of the 1920s display an astonishing mastery of difficult crafts. Problems of style, prosody, juridical and religious language were examined from new angles and in quick succession. At the same time he was open to the new currents of Weimar culture. His attempts to understand Roman classicism (Virgil, Horace) show the influence of Werner Jaeger and even more of Friedrich Gundolf—about whom he always spoke with the utmost respect. Though fundamentally he remained what his pre-1914 teachers had made him, he appeared to be in tune with some of the dominant voices of the Weimar Republic.[1]

1. Fraenkel did not reprint any of his humanistic essays in his severely selective *Kleine Beiträge zur klassischen Philologie*, Rome, 1964. The most important are: *Die Stellung des*

With the support of Wilamowitz, Fraenkel's ascent was deservedly quick. He held chairs in Kiel, Göttingen, and Freiburg. His influence was as great in Germany as in Italy (where his friend Giorgio Pasquali, who had been Leo's pupil, worked in close contact with him). What exactly he felt when he was compelled to leave his country in 1934 we can only guess. Fraenkel never spoke about his deeper sorrows. The blow came less unexpectedly to him than to others. He had prepared his inner defenses in advance by starting the great commentary on Aeschylus's *Agamemnon*, which was to keep him busy and alert in England for fifteen years. F. Jacoby turned to Homer and Hesiod to support himself in the last years of the Weimar Republic. Fraenkel chose tragedy, but typically never thought it necessary to explain what he had found for himself in the *Agamemnon*.

In later years he repeatedly said that he had been a lucky man throughout his life—and never more so than when he was elected to the Corpus Christi Chair of Latin one year after his arrival in England. The story of his settlement in Oxford is, however, a complex one. Never an easy and self-assured man, in his first English decade he was prone to fall into a disconcerting alternation of aggressiveness and self-deprecation. Nor was there universal understanding for his situation among his Oxford colleagues.

Recognition and affection grew around him when his seminar became famous and his *Agamemnon* (1950) imposed itself as one of the philological masterpieces of the century. It consequently became easier for him to recognize what he was himself and what he owed to the foreign country in which he was such an honored guest. A journey to Israel in 1963 moved him profoundly. He read Goethe to the children of his Israeli pupils, but also became more disposed to admit what at the bottom of his heart he had always known—that his own vicissitudes belonged in the context of millenarian Jewish history. It was perhaps natural that in these quieter times he should return to his beloved Horace (and to Aristophanes). There was much wishful thinking in his image of Italy under Augustus. But it supported his subtle and patient interpretation (1957) of the poet whom he saw as the aristocratic and classic counterpart of the archaic plebeian Plautus.

Fraenkel appeared happier in his last years than he had ever been since his arrival in England. Perhaps part of his calmer attitude toward life was due to the preparations he had obviously made for a timely

---

*Römertums in der humanistischen Bildung,* Berlin, 1926, which was discussed by O. Regenbogen, *Gnomon* 3 (1927): 226–41; *Gedanken zu einer deutschen Vergilfeier,* Berlin, 1930; "Die klassische Dichtung der Römer," in *Das Problem des Klassischen und die Antike,* Leipzig, 1931, pp. 47–73.

departure from it. Readiness for suicide has been a steadying feature of Jewish life at least in recent periods (but the roots go deep into the centuries). It is not a Stoic feature because it is condemned in theory. Three days before his suicide Fraenkel sent a Latin distich to Vincenzo Di Benedetto to congratulate him on his appointment as a professor in Pisa. On the eve of his death he is said to have made arrangements for his next seminar on Sophocles. The death of his wife was the signal for his own death. He did not want to decline sadly in his old age, like the two persons to whom he had dedicated his *Agamemnon*.

Fraenkel cannot be understood merely in terms of scholarly achievement. His basic need was to transmit what he had received. He wanted to be no more than a link in the chain of the transmitters. He was a great master because he had been a devoted pupil. He studied the classics as his forebears had studied the Torah, not only for knowledge, but for companionship, simple wisdom, and uncompromising truth. There is in Jewish liturgy a variant of the Kaddish to be recited, after study, in memory of the dead. Eduard Fraenkel, who would have understood the meaning of it, now joins the masters for whom this Kaddish is particularly appropriate.[2]

2. See the statement by H. Lloyd-Jones in *Gnomon* 43 (1971): 634, with *Gnomon* 44 (1972): 224.

# 23

## The Absence of the Third Bickerman

The death of Elias J. Bickerman (Bikerman, Bickermann) in Tel Aviv, where he was attending an international conference in August 1981, cannot be ignored. Elias Bickerman was one of the greatest, most original historians of antiquity of our times. A jurist by instinct more than by his background, Bickerman studied with incredible accuracy and originality aspects of Greek, Hellenistic, and Roman public and private law, beginning with his famous 1926 Berlin dissertation on an edict of Caracalla. But Bickerman has left his mark mainly on the study of Judaism within the Hellenistic world, with which he was very well acquainted because of his superb knowledge of Seleucid institutions and their Persian background and because of his sophisticated analysis of Jewish literary texts. Bickerman's knowledge was the result of a close study of the similarities and differences among Judaism, "pagan" cults (especially the imperial cult), and primitive Christianity. Some of his early works are criticisms of the New Testament. All we have been saying thus far is well known and generally acknowledged. But if anyone in the future were to define the personality of this unique historian, he or she will not have an easy task. While the main facts about Bickerman's life are known—he was in Russia at the time of the czar, where he had the opportunity to meet Rostovtzeff; in Berlin after the war, where he became a pupil of U. Wilcken and E. Norden; in Paris, where he became a friend of L. Robert; and in the United States, where he gradually emerged as teacher at Columbia University in New York —events from his political and religious life have been mentioned only vaguely. The writer of this note has known him personally and followed him in his extraordinary life for more than fifty years; my only intention in writing this note is to acknowledge the difficulty with describing Bickerman's life by providing a concrete example.

This concrete example is furnished by two autobiographies, one by his father and the other by his brother, which that brother, Jacob J. Bikerman, has merged into one book. The book, printed in New York (Vantage Press) in 1975, is entitled *Two Bikermans" Autobiographies by Joseph and Jacob J. Bikerman* (209 pp.). These two autobiographies have remained practically unknown because they were not sold and were soon withdrawn from circulation. The father, Joseph Bikerman (1868–1942) has written a partial autobiography, until 1922, in Russian during his second exile in France in the 1930s. The English translation belongs to his son Jacob (1898–1978?), who was writing in 1973 but carried his autobiography only through 1945. I have learned from private sources that Jacob Bikerman had invited his brother Elias, older by a year, to complete the family triptych with his own autobiography. As the title of the book reveals, the third Bikerman (who had already manifested a certain independence by changing the spelling of his name) refused to join the other two.

And yet the three men—the father and his two sons—had lived as a real family; they had been united in decisive moments of their lives and had shared long-term political and religious beliefs.

The father, Joseph ben Menasce (I am reporting the spelling that appears in the autobiography), was born in Podolia into a poor family of Russian Jews. Always on the fringe of poverty and hunger, they sold vodka by governmental privilege and produced dairy products in unfriendly towns. Their intellectual life typically consisted in a total ignorance of literary Russian, the use of the Yiddish language, and the aspiration to the study of Hebrew and the Talmud to the extent that this was compatible with daily poverty. The family went out of its way so that Joseph, gifted as he was, could become a rabbi. But the study of the Talmud was only a first step, and Joseph soon began to explore the surrounding culture; he studied Kant, learned Russian grammar and mathematics, and through private tutoring was able to support himself, his old parents, and his own family. At the age of thirty, already married and the father of Elias, he obtained a baccalaureate and managed to be included in the quota of Jews admitted to the University of Odessa. In 1901, while still a student, he began his career in journalism, which became his profession for life—if we can speak of a profession, given that he was compelled to emigrate to Germany in 1922 and to France in 1936.

However, the beginning of his career was clamorous. He acquired a certain reputation with an article opposing Zionism, which became one of the major pivots of his political orientation; the second point was the struggle for the acknowledgment of the right of Jews to obtain full citizenship in Russia. Those who are familiar with the history of parties in Russia in the years 1905–17 will be able to interpret the meaning of Joseph Bikerman's wavering between newspapers and groups of the D(emocratic) C(onstitutional) party and the S(ocial) R(evolutionary) party. Bikerman was also charged with writing a book on the area of Jewish settlement (1911) and on the role of Jews in the trade of grains and fish (1912). The Revolution turned him into a counterrevolutionary. The ensuing verdict is found on page 36: "Milyukov-Kerenski-Lenin, these are the stages of the Russian disaster." For a short while, during the Kerenski stage, his sons were emotionally separated from their father (p. 51), but family unity was quickly reestablished. Despite the increasing murkiness of the story, it was clear that the major concern of the three was to flee Russia. It appears that in those years Elias was a cadet in a school for military officers. It was possible to escape in 1921, when the treaty between Poland and Russia acknowledged the right for Polish residents in Russia to return to Poland. With the help of false documents, the Russian Bikerman became the Polish Berman, and favored by the fact that no one expected Polish Jews to be speaking Polish, they succeeded in entering Poland and from there in reaching Berlin in March 1922. Thus, 1918, the date the Israeli *Encyclopaedia Judaica* provides for Elias Bickerman's emigration to Germany, should be adjusted accordingly. At this point the autobiography of the father comes to an end, but that of his son Jacob continues up to 1945, providing a rather interesting supplement to the story. An eminent chemist by profession and a dilettante of Russian poetry, Jacob began working in Germany. Beginning in 1936, he was in England for ten years, then finally in the United States, associated with such important institutions as MIT.

Both the father and his two sons were active in czarist circles in Berlin after 1922. The father was a supporter of the propaganda for the restauration of monarchy in Russia (the article devoted to him in 1929 by the German *Encyclopaedia Judaica* is revealing) But as in Russia, where Joseph had been one of the so-called privileged Jews, with permission to reside in St. Petersburg and to send his children to the university, his field of operation appears to have remained limited to Jewish circles. In 1924, when these facts were beginning to matter less in Berlin (although not in Paris), Joseph became the founder of the Patriotic Union of Russian Jews Abroad. This was not a very successful movement, as can be inferred from the well-known book *Russian Jewry 1917–1967* by G. Aronson, J. Frumkin, and others (1969), and even more by the fact that it is not mentioned in *The Russian Jews under Tsars and Soviets* by S. Baron (1964). Joseph Bickerman had the time to finish a work on Don Quixote and Faust, which he had begun in Russia and which I know from a Spanish translation (Barcelona, 1932; see the review of the German text by A. Castro in *Rev. Fil. Esp.* 17 [1930]: 292). Another work on freedom and equality was composed directly in German. Joseph Bickerman's only writing from exile on a Jewish subject that is available to me is the long essay "Rossija i russkoe evrejstvo" in the collection *Rossija i Evrej*, which was published in Berlin and was supposed to serve as an introduction to the ideas of the newly founded Patriotic Union. Here (pp. 9–96) Bikerman is clearly concerned with three obvious elements: the Jews' reputation for having introduced Bolshevism in Russia and elsewhere; the difficulty with reconciling a program for the restauration of the czar (however remote the possibility was at the time) with the anti-Semitic trend of the previous czarist regime; and finally, and perhaps above all, the definition of Judaism within the framework of a renewed Russian civilization. The same concerns are discussed in the other essays in this book. These concerns are understandable in a situation in which Jewish exiles were hoping that in a different Russia loyalty to the past czar would be rewarded by a future czar by granting the rights of full citizenship to the Jews. It would not make sense to discuss these concerns today. But Joseph Bikerman does not appear to realize what the pogroms of 1903 and 1905 meant to Russian Jews, not only in terms of suffering but in terms of intellectual reflection as well. This is evident from his long analysis of what constitutes a pogrom in his book and in his later autobiography. Here, honestly speaking, Bikerman's Russian prose takes us back to the Jewish poetry of Bialik, to that poem "In the City of the Massacre," which sets up a dividing line in the history of the Jewish communities in Russia for their twofold relationship with God and with the czar (police included).

As late as 1973 (judging from his autobiography), the chemist son Jacob appears to have remained faithful to many of his father's principles. Thus, he was able to write from some part of the United States that "there was more freedom in the Russia of my times (that is, czarist Russia) than there is in many Western democracies today" (p. 106). His example was that a Russian Jew could acquire the rights of a citizen through an easy conversion to a different religion while a white American was compelled to send his children to school with blacks. Yet Jacob claimed he had been the first in the family, when still in Russia, to return to traditional religious practices, such as fasting on Yom Kippur, which his father had obliterated.

The silence of the son Elias in this family dialogue deserves respect. The great historian of Hellenistic Judaism, who died in Israel where he had established strong ties after teaching at Columbia and at the Jewish Theological Seminary in New York, had a more complex view of life. He had written in his dissertation, "Ich bin jüdischer Abstammung und bekenne mich zum mosaischen Glauben" ("I am of Jewish origin and I profess the Mosaic faith").

# Appendixes

# Appendix 1

# A Review of Cecil Roth's *Gli Ebrei in Venezia*

The book *Gli Ebrei in Venezia* by Cecil Roth, which is so interesting, so filled with rare erudition, reveals nonetheless a basic error, or, to speak more accurately, a basic lack of historical perspective. Many details of Jewish life in Venice are recounted; little-known and unknown episodes and figures are conjured up until finally, a detail among details, an episode among episodes, we read of the passion and commitment with which the Jews of Venice cooperated in the defense of the Republic in 1848. But this cannot be viewed as a simple episode, one among many in the history of the Jews of Venice; indeed, it is the very conclusion of the entire history of the Jews of Venice, and thus constitutes the leitmotiv that enables us to understand this history. The history of the Jews of Venice, like the history of the Jews of any other Italian city, is essentially the history of the development of their Italian national conscience. This development (and we should bear this in mind) does not ensue from a preexisting Italian national conscience so that Jews had to assimilate a preexisting Italian national conscience. The development of an Italian national conscience for Jews is parallel to the formation of a national conscience by the Piedmontese, the Neopolitans, or the Sicilians; it is part of the same process and characterizes the process itself. Just as from the beginning of the seventeenth century to the nineteenth century, regardless of previous events, the Piedmontese and the Neopolitans have become Italian, Jews living in Italy have at the same time become Italian. Obviously, this has not prevented Jews from retaining, to a greater or lesser extent, Jewish peculiarities, just as the fact of becoming Italian has not stopped the Piedmontese or the Neopolitans from retaining regional characteristics. When the gates of the ghettos were opened, this process was, generally speaking, already accomplished. Jews were already feeling a part of the Italian nation; on the other hand, the major political figures of the Italian Risorgimento proved with facts that they understood that the emancipation of Jews vis-à-vis other Italian citizens was a major step for the creation of the Italian state. This slow but ultimately resolute acquisition of an Italian conscience, for which there is plenty of evidence, explains that throughout the Italian Risorgimento Jews were in the forefront: in 1848, in Venice, the head of the temporary government, Daniele Manin, came from a Jewish family (his paternal grandparents were converted Jews); two of his major collaborators, Leone Pincherle, the minister of agriculture, and Isacco Maurogonato, the finance minister, were Jewish; among the many Jews in the national assembly, there were two rabbis, while many Jews served in the national guard both as soldiers and officers and others contributed greatly with their money to the defense of the Republic.

In order to prevent our history of the Jews of Venice from being treated as a series of superficial representations, or from limiting the story to the usual, generic episodes that characterize every Jewish community and differ only in minor details depending on the individual cases, we must pay attention above all to the spiritual orientation of the Venetian community and focus the narration of events on this spiritual orientation. This means that we should narrate the history of the penetration and exchange with the surrounding culture that took place within the ghetto, the conflicts and compromises to which it had to adjust until the time of the effective cooperation for the making of the new Italy. It goes without saying that the writer of this note considers this solution as absolutely definite, and not only for the Jews of Venice. Anyone reminding an Italian Jew of his Jewish background as opposed to his Italian one deserves the answer that, as history shows, the Hebrew tradition (if one does not limit it to the times of Noah or Abraham but considers it in its concrete, historical development of our times) is, indeed, what has made him Italian.

Roth's book has a lot of material to offer for the writing of a history of Venetian Jews as we have described it; hence, this book should be one of ready reference, despite the limits inherent in the fact that it lacks notes and a complete bibliography (for example, it does not mention Solmi's book on Leone da Modena or Laterza's edition of the *Dialoghi d'Amore*.) But I do not wish to appear ungrateful to this learned foreigner who has examined Italian archives with competence and fervor for years and had devoted a remarkable book to a chapter of Florentine history. I do not wish to appear ungrateful in claiming that his book contains far too many anecdotes—interesting though they may be and of the kind only a researcher of his caliber can provide—and not enough history. For example, the figure of Leone da Modena, to whom

Roth has devoted many pages in chapter 6 of *Figures and Types*, drawing from his curious life in order to brighten up, as one used to say, the erudition of his book, deserves more serious consideration. Leone's torment and unrest express a complex dissatisfaction with Judaism as well as with pagan culture, and this is among the most important pieces of evidence of the changes that were taking place in Judaism in the seventeenth century.

Finally, there is another less important but far from negligible aspect of the history of Venetian Jews that should have been dealt with more clearly: the role of Jews in the making and destruction of the economic fortunes of Venice. I must confess that, despite the many facts that are reported, I have not managed to get a sense of the economic role played by Venetian Jews.

But we should not forget that Roth has been the first to write an comprehensive history of the Jews of Venice. When one pioneers a work, errors of perspective can come easily; it is already enough that Roth has offered us the opportunity to rethink this history, and that he has provided us with many precious elements in order to evaluate it more closely. The translation, which is due to the competence of Dante Lattes, is excellent as usual.

# Appendix 2

# Judaism and Anti-Semitism

A. GRAMSCI

In reviewing a book by Cecil Roth (*Nuova Italia*, 20 April 1933),[1] Arnaldo Momigliano makes some good observations on the subject of Judaism in Italy:

> The history of the Jews of Venice, like the history of the Jews of any other Italian city, is essentially the history of the development of their Italian national conscience. This development (and we should bear this in mind) does not ensue from a preexisting Italian national conscience so that Jews had to assimilate a preexisting Italian national conscience. The development of an Italian national conscience for Jews is parallel to the formation of a national conscience by the Piedmontese, the Neopolitans, or the Sicilians; it is a part of the same process and characterizes the process itself. Just as from the beginning of the seventeenth century to the nineteenth century, regardless of previous events, the Piedmontese and the Neopolitans have become Italian, Jews living in Italy have at the same time become Italian. Obviously, this has not prevented Jews from retaining, to a greater or lesser extent, Jewish peculiarities, just as the fact of becoming Italian has not stopped the Piedmontese or the Neopolitans from retaining regional characteristics.

Momigliano's thesis, accurate in its essence, should be compared with that of another Jew, Giacomo Lumbroso, in *I moti popolari contro i Francesi alla fine del secolo XVIII (1796–1800).*[2] While the facts narrated by

1. *Gli Ebrei in Venezia*, trans. Dante Lattes, Rome, 1933.
2. Florence, 1932, 8 vols. See *Critica*, 20 March 1933, p. 140ff.

A. Gramsci, *Il Risorgimento*, Turin, 1949, pp. 166–68.

228

Lumbroso deserve to be examined and interpreted, we find no evidence of a nationalistic spirit in the popular insurrection he describes. Indeed, this insurrection was "popular" only to the extent that it represented the misoneism (the hatred of new things) and the passivity of backward and uncivilized peasant masses. The insurrection became significant because of the enlightened forces that instigated it and guided it more or less openly; these forces were clearly reactionary and antinational or anational. Only recently, Jesuits have begun to assert the Italianism of the Sanfedisti, who "only wanted to unify Italy their way."

Another important observation appears in Momigiano's review: that the torment and unrest of Leone the Hebrew expresses a complex dissatisfaction with Judaism as well as with pagan culture, and that this feeling is "among the most important pieces of evidence of the changes that were taking place in Judaism in the seventeenth century."

There is no anti-Semitism in Italy for the very reasons Momigliano mentions—that a national conscience developed and established itself after having overcome two cultural forms: municipal particularism on the one hand, Catholic cosmopolitanism on the other. These forms were closely related and accounted for the most typical evidence of the persistance of medieval and feudal forces. It goes without saying that the overcoming of Catholic cosmopolitanism and the ensuing formation of a lay spirit, not only independent of but at odds with Catholicism, caused Jews to develop a national conscience and to abandon Judaism. This is why Momigliano is probably right in claiming that the development of the Jews' Italian national conscience characterizes the entire process of the development of an Italian national conscience, in the sense of a dissolution of both religious cosmopolitanism and particularism. For Jews, religious cosmopolitanism becomes particularism at the level of the national states.

# General Index

Abarbanel, Isaac, 93
Adorno, Theodor Wiesengrund, 199, 201
Aemilius Sura, 7; *De Annis populi romani*,
    30
*Against Apion* (Josephus), xii, 18, 69
Ahimaaz of Oria, 134
Akiba, 96
Aleichem, Shalom, 172
Alexander, Paul (ed.), *The Oracle of
    Baalbek*, 104
Alexander Polyhistor, 15
Alexander the Great, 30–31, 33; Jerusalem
    visit, 79–87
Alfonsi, Petrus (a.k.a. Moses Sephardi),
    112
*Alien Wisdom* (Momigliano), xiv
Alroy, David, 93
Anania, 39
*Ancient Judaism* (Weber), 173
*Ancient Slavery and Modern Ideology*
    (Finley), 203–4
Ancona, Alessandro d', 128
*Annulus sive Dialogus inter Christianum et
    Judaeum* (Rupert of Deutz), 111–12
*Anti-Judaism in Christian Theology* (Klein),
    137
Antiochus III, 80
Antiochus IV, 19–20, 35; and Temple at
    Jerusalem, 36, 38, 40–41, 43
Antiochus V, 41
Antiochus Epiphanes, 31
Anti-Semitism: fascism and anti-
    Semitism, 135–38; in Italy, xv, xvi n. 15,
    xix; Jewish stories and memoirs, 135–43

Antonius Iulianus, 165
Apocalypse: in Hebrew tradition, 88–100;
    historiography and prophecy, 101–8
Apocalyptics, triumph of good over evil,
    viii, xii–xiii, 22, 24
Aquilas, 14
Aramaic and Hebrew languages in 2d
    century B.C., 13–14
Aratus, 19
*Archaelogia Judaica* (Josephus), 60
Archaeology: in research of biblical and
    classical studies, 4; interpreting Judeo-
    Hellenistic symbols, 48–57, 51 n. 5
Archevolti, Samuel, 122
Arendt, Hannah, 142, 194; Judaism as
    pariah religion, 171–72
*Argument and the Action of Plato's Laws*
    (Strauss), 188
Arias, Gino, 132
Arieti, Silvano, *Parnas*, 139–40
Aristobulus, 84
Aristophanes, 179, 183, 187
Aristotle, 179; on Jewish origins, 17
Armillus and messianic hope, 92–93
Arrigoni, Giampiera, xxvii
Artapanus, biography of Moses, 18
Artom, Emanuele, 133
Artom, Isacco, 126–27
Ascoli, Graziadio, 128
Ascoli, Max, *Le Vie dalla Croce*, 132
Assyria, and imperial succession, 29–31,
    33
*Atheismus im Christentum* (Bloch), 88
Attal, R., 191

231

# Index

233

# Index

Roman Empire, vii; "Religion der Vernunft," xxiv; World War II refuge in England, xv–xvi
Momigliano, Attilio, x, xxvi, 130–31, 201
Momigliano, Donato, ix, xxv
Momigliano, Eucardio, 137
Momigliano, Felice, viii, x, xxvi, 130, 137, 144–47; *Il Messaggio di Mazzini*, 146
Momigliano, Marco, ix, xxv, 122, 144
Momigliano, Riccardo, 137
Momigliano, Salomone Riccardo, xxv–xxvi
Mommsen, Theodor, xvii, xix, 140, 157–58, 161, 164; *Römische Geschichte*, 158
Mondolfo, Rodolfo, 130
Monro, D. B., 156
Montefiore, Claude, 130, 144
Montefiore, Hugh, 165
Montmélian, Lionel de, 124
*Monumenta Germaniae Historica* (Niemeyer), 109–11
Moore, G. F., *Judaism*, 48, 64
Morais, Sabato, 127
Moravia, Alberto, 131
Morpurgo, Anna, 127
Morpurgo, Rachele, 127
Mortara, Lodovico, 128
Mortara, Mantua Marco, 128
Moses as philosopher-leader, 18
Motzo, Bacchisio, *Studi di storia e letteratura, giudeo-ellenistica*, 86
Müller, Max, 151, 155–56, 160
Munz, Peter, *The Shape of Time*, 5
Mussafia, Adolfo, 128
Mussafia, Benjamin ben Immanuel, 128
*Mussolini and the Jews* (Michaelis), 136

Nahon, Umberto, 124
Nathan, Ernesto, 130
"Natural Right and History" (Strauss), xx
Nebuchadnezzar, Daniel interpreting dream and imperial succession, 31, 34
Nehemiah and social order, 12, 21, 23
Nettleship, Henry, 156
*New Literary History* (White), 5
Newman, John, 148–50
Newman, W. L., 156
Nicholas of Damascus, 31
Nicolet, Claude, "La Nouvelle Clio," 69
Niebuhr, B. G., 148–49, 153

Niemeyer, Gerlinde, *Monumenta Germaniae Historica*, 109–11
Niese, B., 41
Nietzsche, F., 160, 162–63
Nock, Arthur Darby, xiv, 107
Norden, Eduard, xvi–xvii, 169, 217
"Nouvelle Clio" (Nicolet), 69
Numenius of Apamea, 16

Olivetti, Gino, 132
Olivetti company, 126
Omodeo, Adolfo, xvi
Onia, 39
*On the Sublime* (Longinus), 16
*Opusculum de conversione sua* (Hermannus quondam Judaeus), 109, 111, 113, 116
*Oracle of Baalbek*, 104
Origen, 27
Orpheus, 19
Ottolenghi, Giuseppe, 129

Pacifici, Alfonso, 133
Panzini, Alfredo, 147
*Parnas* (Arieti), 139–40
Pasquali, Giorgio, 215
Passover Seder, utopian view of apocalypse, 98 n. 5
Pattison, Mark, 148–51, 156, 163; *Memoirs*, 149, 151; *Scaliger*, 150–51, 156, 160–62, 169
Pentateuch, translation of, 14, 19
*Persecution and the Art of Writing* (Strauss), xxi, 180
Persia and imperial succession, 29
Pertz, K., 158
Pharisaism: immortality of soul, resurrection of dead, 23–24; in Judaism, 63
*Pharisees* (Herford), 64
Philo, 14–15, 19, 26–27, 90; *Hypothetica*, 64–65; and Judeo-Hellenistic symbols, 48–50, 53, 55–57
*Philosophie des Judentums* (Guttmann), 185–86
Phocylides, 19
*Phokion und seine neueren Beurtheiler* (Bernays), 167
Piety, and development of religion, 12
Pincherle, Leone, 226
Pirandello, L., 146

237

Wasserstein, Bernard, *Britain and the Jews of Europe, 1939–1944,* 136–38
Weber, Max, 189; *Ancient Judaism,* 173; defining Judaism as pariah religion, 171–77; *Economics and Society,* 173–74
Weil, Heinrich, 162
Welcker, F. G., 153
Wellhausen, J., xiii, xvii, 169
White, Hayden: *History and Theory,* 5; *Metahistory,* 5–6; *New Literary History,* 5; *Topics of Discourse,* 5
Whittaker, C. R., 208
Wickert, L., 159
Wilamowitz, Ulrich, xvii, 160–61, 169–70, 214–15
Wilcken, U., 217
Wilpert, P., *Judentum im Mittelalter,* 109
Wisdom of Solomon, 19, 42

Wiseman, D. J. *See* Sachs, A. J., and D. J. Wiseman
Wolf, F. A., 156
Wolfson, H. A., 53

Xenophon, 179, 182, 187–88; *Hyeron,* 182
*Xenophon's Socrates* (Strauss), 188
*Xenophon's Socratic Discourse* (Strauss), 188

Zerubbabel, Book of, 92–93
Zionism: and Hasidism, 142–43; and Italian Jews, 133; as rebirth of Judaism, xxiii
*Zohar,* ix, xxv, 133, 141; *Zur Religion des Exodus und des Reichs* (Bloch), 88
Zohn, Harry, 191
Zoller, Israel, 123

# Index to Biblical and Talmudic References